Excavating Our Past

Perspectives on the History of the
Archaeological Institute of America

Edited by
SUSAN HEUCK ALLEN

ARCHAEOLOGICAL INSTITUTE OF AMERICA
BOSTON, MASSACHUSETTS

Colloquia and Conference Papers 5

© 2002 by the Archaeological Institute of America

All rights reserved. This book may not be reproduced, stored in a retrieval system, or transmitted, in whole or in part, including illustrations, in any form or by any means (beyond that copying permitted by Sections 107 and 108 of the U.S. Copyright Law and except by reviewers for the public press), without written permission from the publisher.

Cover illustration: Francis Henry Bacon surveying the stylobate of the Temple of Athena at Assos. Photo by John Henry Haynes. (From J.T. Clarke, Francis Henry Bacon, and Robert Koldewey, Investigations at Assos II [1921/1922] 163, Fig. 1). Courtesy of the John Hay Rare Books Library of Brown University.

∞ The paper in this book meets the guidelines for permanence and durability of the Committee on Production Guidelines for Book Longevity of the Council on Library Resources.

Cover and text designed by Peter Holm, Sterling Hill Productions
Printed in the United States of America by Sheridan Books

05 04 03 02   5 4 3 2 1

Library of Congress Cataloging-in-Publication Data

Excavating our past : perspectives on the history of the Archaeological Institute of America / edited by Susan Heuck Allen.
p. cm. — (Colloquia and conference papers ; no. 5)
ISBN 0-9609042-8-X (alk. paper)
1. Archaeology—United States—History. 2. Archaeological Institute of America—History.
I. Allen, Susan Heuck, 1952– II. Archaeological Institute of America. III. Series.
CC 101.U6 E97 2002
930.1'06'073—dc21   2002018503

CONTENTS

List of Illustrations
ix

List of Essay Contributors
xi

Acknowledgments
xiii

Archaeological Institute of America Timeline, 1879–2001
*Phoebe A. Sheftel**
xv

The Archaeology of the AIA: An Introduction
*Susan Heuck Allen**
1

CHAPTER 1
Spirit of the Times: 19th-Century European Intellectualism
*Nancy Thomson de Grummond**
29

CHAPTER 2
Charles Eliot Norton and the Archaeological Institute of America
*Elizabeth Lyding Will**
49

CHAPTER 3
"Americans in the East": Francis Henry Bacon,
Joseph Thacher Clarke, and the AIA at Assos
*Susan Heuck Allen**
63

CHAPTER 4
The American School of Classical Studies at Athens:
Scholarship and High Culture in the Gilded Age
Caroline Winterer
93

CHAPTER 5
"Sending Out of Expeditions": The Contest for Delphi
*Phoebe A. Sheftel**
105

CHAPTER 6
Between Athens and Babylon: The AIA and the Politics
of American Near Eastern Archaeology, 1884–1997
*Neil Asher Silberman**
115

CHAPTER 7
The "Western Idea": Local Societies and American Archaeology
James E. Snead
123

CHAPTER 8
The Dream that Failed: The AIA's Department of Canada (1908–1915)
*James Russell**
141

CHAPTER 9
The Archaeological Institute of America between the Wars
*Stephen L. Dyson**
157

CHAPTER 10
The Great Divides: The AIA and Professional
Responsibility in Archaeology
Clemency Coggins
169

CHAPTER 11
Computer Technology and the Archaeological Institute of America
Harrison Eiteljorg II
189

APPENDIX 1
Past Presidents of the Archaeological Institute of America and
Editors-in-Chief of the *American Journal of Archaeology* (1879–2002)
Susan Heuck Allen* and Kim M. Hebert
205

APPENDIX 2
Award and Fellowship Winners of the
Archaeological Institute of America (1965–1999)
Susan Heuck Allen* and Kim M. Hebert
207

APPENDIX 3
PART 1. Current Local Societies of the Archaeological Institute
of America in Order of Their Charters of Foundation
Susan Heuck Allen* and Kim M. Hebert

PART 2. Inclusive List of AIA Local Societies with Name
Changes and Dates of Foundation and Dissolution
Wendy O'Brien
217

APPENDIX 4
Charles Eliot Norton Lecturers
Priscilla Murray
227

* These individuals participated in the original colloquium, which also included Phyllis Pollak Katz.

Excavating Our Past

SEAL OF THE ARCHAEOLOGICAL INSTITVTE OF AMERICA MDCCCLXXVIIII

VI
RVM

MON
V
MEN
TA
PRIO
RVM

ILLUSTRATIONS

1.1. View of the Tower of the Winds
1.2. Robert Wood and James Dawkins Enter into Palmyra, 1774
1.3. Ground plan of tomb excavated at Volterra, ca. 1728
1.4. Photograph of Eduard Gerhard
1.5. Casa Tarpeia on the Capitoline Hill, Rome, original seat of the Instituto di Corrispondenza Archeologica
1.6. Frontispiece, engraving from Abel Blouet et al., *Expédition scientifique de Morée* (1831–1838)
1.7. Portrait of Carlo Fea
1.8. The Temporary Elgin Room in the British Museum, 1819
1.9. The Theseum (Hephaisteion), Athens, engraving from Abel Blouet et al., *Expédition scientifique de Morée* (1831–1838)
2.1. Charles Eliot Norton in later life
2.2. Norton's summer home in Ashfield, "The Locusts," as it looks today
2.3. Norton and George William Curtis ca. 1880
2.4. Norton's home, "Shady Hill," in Cambridge
2.5. The Norton family plot in Mount Auburn Cemetery, on the edge of Cambridge
3.1. Francis Henry Bacon and Joseph Thacher Clarke aboard the Dorian in Constantinople harbor, 1879
3.2. a. Francis Henry Bacon's plan of Assos
3.2. b. Francis Henry Bacon's plan of the acropolis at Assos
3.3. Francis Henry Bacon's drawing of a vaulted tomb in the Street of the Tombs
3.4. The Agora at Assos restored, by Francis Henry Bacon
3.5. Francis Henry Bacon and a marble sima fragment from the Temple of Athena Ilion
8.1. Francis W. Kelsey, president of the Archaeological Institute of America, 1907–1912
8.2. Prospectus announcing the formation of the Ottawa society of the Archaeological Institute of America and the inaugural lecture, 3 December 1908

ESSAY CONTRIBUTORS

SUSAN HEUCK ALLEN
Smith College, Brown University,
and Chair, AIA Archives Committee

CLEMENCY COGGINS
Boston University, recipient of the AIA Gold Medal Award

NANCY THOMSON DE GRUMMOND
Florida State University

STEPHEN L. DYSON
State University of New York at Buffalo,
Chair, European Committee, and Past President of the AIA

HARRISON EITELJORG II
Center for the Study of Architecture

JAMES RUSSELL
University of British Columbia, Past President of the AIA

PHOEBE A. SHEFTEL
Center for the Study of Architecture

NEIL ASHER SILBERMAN
Ename Center for Public Archaeology

JAMES E. SNEAD
George Mason University

ELIZABETH LYDING WILL
University of Massachusetts, Amherst

CAROLINE WINTERER
San Jose State University

ACKNOWLEDGMENTS

I would like to acknowledge the help and advice of Jane Scott, former chair of the Archives Committee of the Archaeological Institute of America, who suggested that I organize and chair the colloquium that resulted in this volume. Jane also recommended me as editor of the volume, a task that has taken me down many interesting paths that I otherwise might not have trod. I would also like to thank Priscilla Murray, who originally organized and catalogued the archives, and Edward Bader, who helped move them to their current location at the AIA headquarters, located at Boston University, 656 Beacon Street, Boston, Massachusetts 02215. To Mark Meister, former AIA Executive Director; Wendy O'Brien, former Assistant Director; Crista Livecchi, former Executive Assistant; Christine Moynihan, former Administrative Coordinator; and Kim M. Hebert, Director of Membership and Operations, I owe a debt of gratitude for their assistance with the preparation of this volume as well as for permission to cite the letters and documents housed in the AIA's archives. Most of all, I would like to acknowledge the participants in the original colloquium and those not present on that occasion, who graciously offered their exemplary additions to this volume.

Archaeological Institute of America Timeline, 1879–2001

Compiled by
Phoebe A. Sheftel

1879 • The Archaeological Institute of America (AIA) is founded in May, with the stated goals of "promoting and directing archaeological investigation and research, . . . sending out of expeditions for special investigation, . . . aiding the efforts of independent explorers, . . . and publication of reports of the results of the expeditions which the Institute may undertake or promote" (AIA 1880, 6; de Grummond, this volume). Charles Eliot Norton (1827–1908) assumes the presidency after historian Francis Parkman (1823–1893) declines the position (Will, this volume).

1880 • Adolph Bandelier (1849–1914) is supported by the AIA for five years in his exploration of pueblos in Pecos and other prehistoric sites in the Southwest and Mexico (Snead, this volume).

1881 • The Institute starts excavations at Assos led by Joseph Thacher Clark (1856–1920) and Francis Henry Bacon (1856–1940) (Allen, ch. 3, this volume).

1882 • The American School of Classical Studies at Athens opens (Winterer, this volume).

1883 • Excavations at Assos conclude (Allen, ch. 3, this volume).

1884 • The first local society of the AIA is established in Boston.
 • The AIA supports the Wolfe Expedition to Mesopotamia, which begins work at Nippur (Silberman, this volume).

1885 • The *American Journal of Archaeology and the History of the Fine Arts* is founded and edited by Arthur Lincoln Frothingham, Jr. with Charles Eliot Norton as Advisory Editor.

1887 • The AIA and the Baltimore Society sponsor excavations soon aborted at the temple of Hera Licinia at Croton under the direction of Joseph Thacher Clarke and Alfred Emerson (1859–1943) (Allen, ch. 3, this volume).

1888 • The AIA begins seriously pursuing a permit for excavating Delphi (Sheftel, this volume).

1889 • By the end of its first decade, the AIA has four local societies in Boston, New York, Baltimore, and Philadelphia (Allen and Hebert, app. 3, this volume).

1890 • Seth Low (1850–1916) assumes the presidency of the AIA. Norton remains as president of the Boston Society and vice president of the Institute.

1891 • The quest for the permit for Delphi comes to an unsuccessful conclusion; the French secure the site (Sheftel, this volume).

1892 • The Institute funds a three-year exploration of Argos led by Charles Waldstein (1856–1927).

1894 • The Institute discusses establishing an American school in Rome with the Congress of Philosophical Societies.
• The Institute supports a two-year survey of Crete by Federico Halbherr (1857–1930).

1895 • The American School of Classical Studies is founded in Rome (Winterer, this volume).
• The Institute sets up a Lecture Fund to send scholars to local societies to give professional lectures.

1896 • The American School of Classical Studies at Athens begins excavations at Corinth.

1897 • The *American Journal of Archaeology* is designated the official publication for work carried out under the auspices of the AIA.
• Sarah Wyman Whitman, president of the Boston Society, designs the Institute's seal (Allen, Introduction, this volume).

1898 • Charles Eliot Norton opens the first Annual Meeting of the AIA, held in New Haven, Connecticut.

1899 • The American School for Oriental Study and Research is founded in Jerusalem (Silberman, this volume).

1901 • The Institute undertakes a reproduction of the Venetian Codex Marcianus Graecus 474 (7 plays of Aristophanes) in collaboration with the British Society for the Promotion of Hellenic Studies.

1902 • Harriet A. Boyd (1871–1945) becomes the first woman chosen to be a traveling lecturer for the Institute (Allen, Introduction, this volume).

1904 • At the time of its 25th anniversary, the Institute membership stands at 1,200, with 13 local societies: Boston, New York, Baltimore, Philadelphia, Chicago, Detroit, Wisconsin, Cleveland, New Haven, Washington, Iowa, Pittsburgh, and Colorado.

1906 • The Institute is incorporated in Washington, D.C., by an act of Congress.

1907 • The School of American Archaeology is established in Santa Fe; it is later renamed the School of American Research (Snead, this volume).

1908 • Richard Norton (1872–1918) begins excavations at Cyrene under the auspices of the Institute (Silberman, this volume).

1909 • James Loeb (1867–1933) endows the Norton Lectureship with a gift of $20,000; a preference for European scholars is stipulated.

1910 • The St. Louis society provides funds for the excavation of the Mayan site at Quirigua.

1911 • Herbert Fletcher De Cou (1868–1911), assistant director of the Cyrene excavations, is murdered at the site. The Institute appeals unsuccessfully to the United States State Department and President William Howard Taft to intervene in punishing the Italian government, which was suspected of instigating the murder in retaliation for the Americans having gained control over an area coveted by the Italians for its supposed sulphur and potash deposits.

• The central office of the Institute moves to Washington, D.C., and shares space with the American Institute of Architects in a building known as the Octagon.

1912 • Charles L. Freer (1850–1919) and Eugene Meyer (1875–1959) donate $10,000 toward a study on establishing an American School in China (possibly Peking). Langdon Warner (1851–1955) of the Museum of Fine Arts, Boston, chairs the study and is sent to do an archaeological survey of China.

• The Council votes to turn the *Bulletin* into an illustrated popular magazine called *Art and Archaeology*.

1913 • The American School of Classical Studies in Rome merges with the American Academy in Rome.

1914 • The first issue of *Art and Archaeology* is published after $4,000 is raised through guaranteed subscriptions (the *Bulletin* is retained as a separate publication) (Dyson, this volume).

1915 • An economic depression brought on by World War I leads to closing the School in Jerusalem, putting on hold plans for schools in Peking and Mesopotamia, and withholding payment from many society lecturers.

• The Council of the AIA establishes the Committee on Colonial and National Art in North America to study the history and monuments of American art.

1916 • The Institute begins supervising the publication of *Mythology of All Races*.

1918 • The Council discovers that 30% of the funds for life memberships, which were supposed to have been invested, have been used for current expenses.

1920 • The Washington Society assumes control of the publication of *Art and Archaeology*.

1921 • The Institute joins with the American Anthropological Association to found the American School of Prehistoric Research. The School undertakes excavation and publication, but does not establish itself at a fixed location (Snead, this volume).

• The American School for Oriental Study and Research (with branches in both Jerusalem and Baghdad) is independently incorporated as the American Schools of Oriental Research (Silberman, this volume).

• The publication of the Assos excavations is finally completed (Allen, ch. 3, this volume).

1922 • The possibility of starting a school in Istanbul is discussed.

1927 • The members of the Committee on Colonial and National Art in North America dissolve the group, believing that the work would be done more appropriately by other organizations interested in American art.

1929 • The AIA President appoints a Board of Trustees to safeguard the Institute's endowment. Their first concern is to retire a $5,000 debt that the Institute had incurred by borrowing against endowment funds, a move later declared illegal by auditors and the AIA's legal counsel.

1931 • Mary Hamilton Swindler becomes the first female editor of the *American Journal of Archaeology* (Allen and Hebert, app. 1, this volume).

1933 • William B. Dinsmoor (1886–1973) suggests that the Institute discontinue *Art and Archaeology* because it deals more with art than archaeology (Dyson, this volume).
• The endowment funds lose 13% of their value in one year.

1934 • The AIA ceases publication of *Art and Archaeology* and the Washington Society withdraws its required "contribution" to the Institute in protest (Dyson, this volume).
• Hetty Goldman (1881–1972) receives AIA funding for a three-year excavation of Tarsus in Cilicia, Turkey

1940 • The Council votes to look into starting a school in South America.

1942 • The Annual Meeting is canceled through 1944 because of wartime gas rationing.

1944 • Publication of the *Corpus Vasorum Antiquorum* is transferred from the American Council of Learned Societies to the Institute.

1945 • Membership reaches a low of 1,121, following a 15-year decline from a high of 3,460 members in 1930.

1946 • Jotham Johnson (1905–1967) begins an informal newsletter, reporting to the membership on the excavations and activities of the Institute and its schools.

1947 • AIA President Sterling Dow (1886–1972) reports, as a "happy innovation," the election of the first female trustee (Ethel C. Freeman), noting that "archaeology is a subject in which feminine abilities have found increasing scope and success" (AIA *Bulletin* 38 [1947–1948] 28).

1948 • The Institute and the College Art Association begin publishing a series of monographs on archaeology and the fine arts. Thirteen are published before the Institute withdraws in 1972.
• *Archaeology* appears as a popular magazine and is immediately credited with promoting membership gains (Dyson, this volume).
• The Washington Society returns as a contributing member of the Institute.

1950 • The American School of Prehistoric Research merges with the Peabody Museum at Harvard University.

1951 • The American Research Center in Egypt is established with William Stevenson Smith (1907–1969) as its first director.

1956 • The newsletter, begun by Jotham Johnson, is discontinued.

1961 • The Institute assumes administration of the Olivia James Trust from the Carnegie Foundation for the Advancement of Teaching.

1962 • William B. Dinsmoor, Jr. (1923–1988) receives the AIA's first Olivia James traveling fellowship (Allen and Hebert, app. 2, this volume).

1964 • The Executive Committee approves $2,500 for a charter membership in the American Research Institute in Turkey; the Trustees initially oppose the funding.

1965 • The Institute, with the support of Leon and Harriet Pomerance (1907–1988 and 1915–1972), establishes a Gold Medal Award of Merit to honor significant and innovative contributors to special fields of archaeology. Carl W. Blegen (1887–1971) is the first recipient (Allen and Hebert, app. 2, this volume).

1967 • Margaret Thompson becomes the AIA's first female president (Allen and Hebert, app. 1, this volume).

• The Institute starts a program of archaeological tours with trips to several sites in Africa.

• The Institute becomes a charter member of the American Institute on Iranian Studies in Tehran.

1968 • The Institute investigates the possibility of returning to excavate at Assos, but the Turkish government refuses permission.

1970 • The Institute receives its largest single gift to date: $78,000 for the von Bothmer Publication fund (Coggins, this volume).

1971 • A fellowship to support work in Aegean Bronze Age archaeology is established in memory of Harriet Pomerance. Robert Bridges receives the first award in 1973 (Allen and Hebert, app. 2, this volume).

1975 • The Institute inaugurates a regional symposium fund with a program on "What is Etruscan?" organized by the Tallahassee society.

• The Archaeological Conservation Act is passed. It requires that Federal funds allocated for construction or reclamation must include funding for archaeological assessment work at registered sites (Coggins, this volume).

1976 • The Committee on American Archaeology is reconstituted.

1977 • The Council discusses terminating the agreement to hold the

Annual Meeting in New Orleans in 1980, based on the fact that Louisiana had not ratified the Equal Rights Amendment. Legal counsel later decides that it would be more prudent to honor existing contracts than to face substantial legal liability.
- The Committee on European Archaeology holds preliminary organizational meetings.

1978
- The year ends with a financial loss, starting a series of deficit years, which does not end until 1987.

1979
- *Archaeology* adds features, such as film reviews and columns on travel and science, to appeal specifically to the increasing number of lay subscribers.
- Work is started on drafting on an AIA code of ethics (Coggins, this volume).
- 1980 Seed funds are provided for a newsletter on South and East Asian archaeology.
- The first Pomerance Award for Scientific Contributions to Archaeology is awarded to Marie Farnsworth (Allen and Hebert, app. 2, this volume).
- Reflecting the increasing difficulties young scholars face in finding a job in the field, a program is added to the Annual Meeting on unemployment issues.

1981
- The tour program is revived with a trip to Crete.
- The monograph series, defunct since 1972, is revived.

1982
- Membership briefly goes above 10,000, spurred by a proposed increase in dues.
- The January edition of the *American Journal of Archaeology* is the first produced on a computer.

1983
- The Institute receives a challenge grant for $575,000 from the National Endowment for the Humanities; it is required to raise $1,725,000 in matching funds.
- Boston University offers the Institute rent-free office space for 10 years.
- The deficit accumulated since 1978 has reached $829,584; the financial crisis leads to a spending freeze.

1984
- The Board of Trustees and the Executive Committee are combined into a Governing Board with 12–18 General Trustees, nine Academic Trustees, and three Society Trustees.

- The financial crisis spurs a realization that the growing number of *Archaeology* subscribers (now at 70,000) are potential AIA members and donors. As a result, ads began appearing in the magazine soliciting donations to the Institute.

1985
- The *American Journal of Archaeology* celebrates its centennial with a special edition in January 1985, supported by a grant from the Getty Foundation.
- Poster sessions are initiated at the Annual Meeting.
- The tour program is (again) revived with a trip led by Machteld J. Mellink to the "Mounds and Monuments of Anatolia." It continues to the present with several interruptions caused by terrorist activities and the Gulf War.

1986
- The National Endowment for the Humanities Challenge Grant Campaign is successfully completed with $2,300,000 raised.
- Budget cuts result in reducing to two the number of lecturers sent to the local societies.
- Three new lectureships are added in honor of Anna Marguerite McCann and Robert D. Taggart; George M.A. Hanfmann (1911–1986); and Homer A. and Dorothy B. Thompson.
- Work on drafting a code of ethics is revived.
- The Governing Board examines the feasibility of a television series.
- A report prepared by Malcolm Weiner details the critical financial state of the Institute. The deficit stands at $1,000,000, against an endowment of only $1,300,000. The Board has abandoned prudent investment policies, borrowing close to 15% annually from its endowment to pay expenses. Two investment managers are hired, and the use of income funds is set at the accepted standard of 5% of the 3-year rolling average.

1987
- The Institute achieves its first budget surplus in 10 years.
- The Governance Committee presents to the Governing Board draft #29 of their proposed revisions to the Regulations (by-laws). Adoption is suspended after rancorous discussions about the Board's need for more financial expertise, coupled with concerns that the professional members will lose standing in the direction of the organization.

1988
- Subscriptions to *Archaeology* surpass 100,000 with the January/February issue.

1989 • The AIA holds the first Joint Archaeological Congress with the American Schools of Oriental Research and the Society for Historical Archaeology.
- The James R. Wiseman Book Award is first given to Anna Marguerite McCann for *The Roman Port and Fishery of Cosa: A Center of Ancient Trade* (Princeton, 1987) (Allen and Hebert, app. 2, this volume).
- The viability of the Norton Lectureship is questioned because the endowment produces only $8,000, which is expected to cover the lecturer's expenses and compensation for a two-month, 20-lecture tour. Stephen Dyson remarks, "the whole system has a great deal of the nineteenth century, steamer trunk way of doing archaeology about it. Very few scholars can leave their institutions overseas for two months to face penury in the United States" (AIA *Bulletin* 1988–1989, 15).
- Central office support for a third lecture (eliminated in 1986) is restored to the society programs.
- Consideration of a television series is put on hold because of lack of funding and other priorities.
- A motion is made at Council to provide childcare at each year's Annual Meeting.
- The first Award for Distinguished Service is presented to James H. Ottaway, Jr., a former Trustee and Treasurer, and Leon Pomerance (posthumously) (Allen and Hebert, app. 2, this volume).
- The Executive Committee votes to ban smoking at all sessions of the Annual Meeting.
- A new committee of five Trustees is established in another attempt at revising the by-laws.

1990 • *Archaeology* assumes responsibility for developing a television series.
- The Kershaw Fund is established to endow the publication of a newsletter for the membership.
- The Society for the *American Journal of Archaeology* is started to support the *Journal*.
- The President's Lecture Fund is started with an anonymous donation of $150,000. With increased support for society lectures, the Norton Lecture program is reduced to a more manageable 10 lectures.

- While an effort had been made to restore the funds borrowed from the endowment during the deficit years (1978–1986), the Board decides to write off the $700,000 still outstanding.
- The Council adopts a code of ethics (work on this had first started in 1979) (Coggins, this volume).
- 1992 Boston University extends its donation of rent-free space to the Institute in perpetuity, with a review every 10 years.
- Council finally approves new Regulations (by-laws). They provide for a First Vice President and Vice Presidents for Professional Responsibilities, Publications, and Societies.
- AIA membership surpasses 11,000, but immediately starts to decline.
- *Archaeology* subscriptions surpass 150,000.
- The New World Archaeology Committee is revived and funds are donated to establish a New World Lecture Series.
- 1993 James Russell of Canada becomes the first AIA president from outside the United States.
- A new monograph series publishes its first volume, *The Entrance to the Athenian Acropolis Before Mnesicles,* by Harrison Eiteljorg, II.
- A Committee on Old World Archaeology in Higher Education is established to respond to threatened staff and department cuts in several colleges and universities.
- The President's Lectures are renamed the Martha Sharp Joukowsky Lectures.

1994
- A Committee on Near Eastern Archaeology and a Subcommittee on Women in Archaeology are established (Silberman; Allen, Introduction, this volume).
- The *Institut Archeologique d'Amerique* incorporates in Canada to allow for tax-deductible donations by Canadian citizens.
- The Council adopts the code of Professional Standards (Coggins, this volume).

1995
- The Institute increases efforts to develop interest in archaeology among youth by publishing an annotated guide to curriculum materials for primary and secondary school children, and considering publication of a children's magazine.

1996
- Several activities support a strong focus on education: the establishment of a traveling fellowship for dissertation research in Italy

and the western Mediterranean, the creation of an undergraduate teaching award, and planning for a summer institute for secondary school teachers.

1997
- Academic members of the Institute raise discouraging reports on the health of Old World archaeology departments and teaching at the graduate and undergraduate level.
- Breaking a long-standing and much-debated tradition, the Governing Board approves a change of the Annual Meeting from December to January, starting in 2001.

1999
- The first issue of *Dig, Archaeology*'s magazine for children, is published in April.

2000
- The Institute enters the new century with over 11,500 members in the United States and 440 members in Canada.
- *Archaeology's Dig* wins multiple awards.
- The *AJA* goes online.

2001
- *Archaeology's Dig* is sold as financial troubles return to the AIA.
- Membership declines to below 9,500.
- The Charles Eliot Norton Legacy Society is founded.

REFERENCES

Archaeological Institute of America. 1880. *First Annual Report of the Executive Committee of the Archaeological Institute of America, 1879–1880.* Cambridge, Mass.
———. 1908– . *Bulletin of the Archaeological Institute of America,* vols. 1– . Boston.

The Archaeology of the AIA: An Introduction

◈

Susan Heuck Allen

E*xcavating Our Past* grew out of a Presidential Colloquium of the same name at the Annual Meeting of the Archaeological Institute of America (AIA) in Chicago on 28 December 1997. The colloquium, organized and chaired by the editor, was suggested as a way of stimulating scholars to dig into the organization's own rich and varied stratigraphy through its recently catalogued archives (Scott 1997). Most papers delivered at that session are included here as well as several additional essays from individuals who have worked extensively with the archives (for abstracts of this and other papers in the Colloquium, see *AJA* 102 [1998] 364–6). These essays highlight the history and development of the AIA, an organization of professional archaeologists and informed lay members devoted to the interpretation of material culture and the social fabric of the ancient world. Subjects include the founders, institutions, practitioners, and the times that shaped them. Whereas a certain distance is often advantageous when writing history, many of these authors have played a vital role in the AIA, and their unique perspectives, both internal and external, enrich and privilege the discourse on the Institute and its involvement in the discipline of archaeology in the United States.

Intellectual historian Peter Novick has described several approaches to the writing of history. The "internalist" approach concentrates on what goes on in the Institute itself, "slighting or ignoring its relationship with the surrounding environment" while the "externalist" focuses "on one or another aspect of that external relationship" (1988, 9–14), the AIA's interface with elements and events outside the Institute. A number of papers stress the social, cultural, political, ideological, and economic conditions that influenced the course of the Institute and its work. The goals of this volume are not only to document and celebrate the Institute's history, but also to provide a self-reflective history about the nature of the AIA for the membership and greater understanding of the Institute and its impact for those outside of it. The authors critically examine various aspects of the AIA in order to analyze the way in which individual members of the AIA and the Institute itself have influenced, and felt the influence of, the discipline of archaeology as practiced in the Mediterranean, Mesopotamia, and the Americas.

To commemorate the centennial of the founding of the AIA, Phoebe Sheftel (1979), Homer Thompson (1980), and Sterling Dow (1979; 1980), addressed aspects of its history in several articles. Past president of the Institute, Stephen Dyson, characterized these as "antiquarian in nature and somewhat self-congratulatory in tone" and criticized practitioners of classical archaeology for their lack of introspection in contrast to those engaged in anthropological archaeology (1985, 459). Since then, a number of relevant histories of European archaeological institutes and foreign schools, and a few broader studies of the intellectual genealogies of classical archaeology have been published, such as Morris (1994), Marchand (1996), and Shanks (1996). In 1996 Nancy de Grummond published a useful two volume *Encyclopedia of the History of Classical Archaeology* with short articles on key individuals, sites, and institutions. With the exception of the articles, however, none of the above sources pays particular attention to the AIA and its role. Lamenting the limited published commemorations for "important anniversaries like the centenaries of the Archaeological Institute of America and the *American Journal of Archaeology*," Dyson published *Ancient Marbles to American Shores: Classical Archaeology in the United States* in 1998, a year after this colloquium took place.

The present volume, like Dyson's, is designed to address that need, by commemorating the centennial of the AIA Annual Meeting in December 1998. Whereas Dyson's somewhat polemical but illuminating historical synthesis focuses on the discipline of classical archaeology, *Excavating Our Past* includes an examination of all spheres in which the AIA has been active. Thus, it is the first book specifically focused on the broader history of the Archaeological Institute of America.

The first seven contributions in this volume cover largely 19th-century initiatives. Nancy de Grummond addresses the intellectual currents, particularly in the 18th and early 19th centuries, which sparked the creation in Europe of those learned societies meant to communicate new findings and to fund and publish the results of expeditions devoted to classical archaeology which preceded and inspired the AIA. Contextualizing AIA founder Charles Eliot Norton, Elizabeth Will relates his impact on a number of fields and traditions beyond the Institute from Dante and Donne to the preservation of Niagara Falls. Will cites Norton's consummate prestige as critical to the founding of the AIA. My own contribution examines the Institute's earliest Mediterranean excavations at Assos from 1881 to 1883 and the difficulties experienced by early excavators as they tried to forge careers in the new profession. Caroline Winterer offers a study of Norton's founding vision for post-graduate studies in Greece, realized in the establishment of the American School of Classical Studies at Athens (ASCSA), which harmonized the divergent objectives of broad exposure, cultivated erudition, and narrow specialization. Within the changing intellectual atmosphere of the latter half of the 19th century, this humanistic goal of cultivated erudition gave way to professionalized scientific training. Phoebe Sheftel eschews the Whig interpretation of history where principles of past progress are emphasized in order to ratify and glorify the present. She offers a glimpse of what might have been and expands her 1979 treatment of the AIA's ambitious, but tortured and unsuccessful, bid for American control of the hotly contested site of Delphi (which ultimately was awarded to the French). Neil Silberman uncovers the nationalistic and religious agendas and biases that shaped early AIA involvement in southwest Asia and North Africa and anticipates the AIA's role in preservation ethics and outreach with modern inhabitants of ancient lands as well as traditional audiences.

Bridging the 19th and 20th centuries, James Snead's essay examines the AIA's fickle treatment of American archaeology. Snead, Russell, and Dyson each highlight the AIA's repeated efforts toward outreach, and several contributors single out the seminal role of Francis Kelsey in this regard. Snead shows how the AIA grew through the creation of local affiliated societies, specifically in the southwest, and how these in turn communicated to the national office the lay public's interest in American antiquities. He also underscores the tensions between the Hellenist agenda of the east coast and the conflicting interests of societies located in the midwestern and western parts of the country. James Russell follows Kelsey's impulse into Canada and documents his creation of the AIA-Department of Canada in 1908. Power plays between the U.S.-based general secretary and his Canadian equivalent contributed to the collapse of this short-lived venture, to which World War I dealt the *coup de grace*. Russell's essay represents a significant expansion, contextualization, and clarification of the brief account of the history of classical archaeology in Canada in general from between the wars to the present by Alexander McKay (1994, lxi–lxiii). Building on ideas expressed in his aforementioned 1998 ethnography of classical archaeology in America, Stephen Dyson treats the interwar period with its threats of Bolshevism and International Modernism as a return to the secure roots of western civilization, a concept which, according to Turner (1999, 384), was conceived by Charles Eliot Norton. Dyson highlights the financially disastrous struggle between individuals intent on restricting AIA membership to academic professionals working in the Mediterranean and others who attempted to popularize archaeology by reaching out to a lay audience in order to save the AIA, whose membership plummeted from 3,460 in 1930 to 1,121 in 1945 (1998, 221). Dyson also reviews the battles between those who preferred that the AIA focus its funds on the academic *American Journal of Archaeology (AJA)* and those who fought for *Art and Archaeology*, the popular publication that was the forerunner of *Archaeology* magazine. Thus, the two flagship publications of the AIA in the 20th century reflect the dual and sometimes dueling nature of the organization's membership, of which only about one-quarter of the total are professionals. Clemency Coggins delineates the consciousness-raising struggle within the organization concerning issues of cultural property as academics struggle to balance scholarship, ethics, and the AIA's reliance on the patronage of collectors and museums. This, too, constitutes a form of outreach as the AIA attempts to inform the public about archaeological sites and objects as finite resources deserving legal protection. Finally, Harrison Eiteljorg's contribution details the challenge and opportunities represented by computer technology and demonstrates how the AIA-List, support of virtual reality projects, and electronic publishing are helping the Institute reach out to the mushrooming audience in cyberspace.

Several important themes in the history of the Institute touched upon in these essays receive fuller treatment below while other issues, not the subject of discrete essays, but important to the larger picture of the history of the Institute, are also treated here. Critical for an understanding of the climate in which the AIA was founded are the political and cultural agendas of Hellenism, the 18th-century sociopolitical concept that idealized ancient Greece as the cradle of European culture, and its 19th-century legacy in Romanticism, where one sought to escape the realities of industrialization by contemplating the aesthetic perfection of a timeless classical Greece (Clarke 1989; Trigger 1989; Morris 1994, 11; Shanks 1996; Dyson 1998, xi; and Winterer, this volume). From the time of Johann Joachim Winckelmann (1717–1768) European intellectuals viewed Greece as the childhood of Europe and, by extension, that of the United States as well, and saw classical antiquity as their cultural pedigree. In particular, the writings of German Protestant philosophers, classicists, and art historians privileged Hellenism partly as a reaction to the French Catholic lock on Rome (Trigger 1989, 66). The Greek War of Independence (1821–1830) further galvanized the bond between Europe and Greece, especially in Germany, where great importance was already imparted to the classical world as evidenced by the 10 university chairs of archaeology established by 1848 whereas in France, England, and the United States, there were none at that time (Shanks 1996, 95).

James Turner's recent biography of Charles Eliot Norton (1827–1908) records details in Norton's life that shed light on his role and that of the AIA in 19th-century intellectual discourse. Norton the institution builder was uniquely situated socially, financially, and intellectually to found such an organization (Will, this volume). Well-educated both at home and at Harvard (although he never took an advanced degree), Norton had intimate and often personal knowledge of early archaeological initiatives and pioneering excavators. After meeting Ephraim Squier (1821–1888), who had explored and excavated remains of the Moundbuilders in Ohio in 1847 and had coauthored *Ancient Monuments of the Mississippi Valley* (1848), Norton wrote an account of "Ancient Monuments of America" for the *North American Review* 68 (1849, 466–96). He joined the broadly based American Oriental Society, founded in 1842, which opened a classical section in 1849 for "the cultivation of classical learning, so far as auxiliary to oriental research." He read Austen Henry Layard's (1817–1894) account of his discoveries at Nineveh. On a business trip at age 22 Norton crossed the subcontinent of India and visited many of its monuments, both ancient and modern. As he made his way home in 1850 he met pioneering geologist Charles Lyell (1797–1875) and Darwin's evolutionist colleague Herbert Spencer (1820–1903) in London. Cuneiform decipherer Henry Rawlinson

(1810–1895) escorted him through the galleries of the British Museum where they viewed Layard's bulls and other glorious antiquities such as the Elgin marbles. After touring Rome, Veii, Tivoli, and Sicily, an inspired Norton wrote an article on the catacombs of Rome (Turner 1999, 64, 91, 133, 140–2, 150–1). These experiences distracted him from his work as an East India trader, but contributed decisively to his lifelong interest in archaeology. The sum of this wealth of experience was a uniquely prepared and fertile mind, open to a broad range of archaeological interests.

In America Congregationalists gravitated toward biblical studies while Unitarians were drawn to the classical world (Patterson 1995, 26). Although he benefited from his privileged exposure to the archaeological remains of the New World (in his acquaintance with Squier) and the Old World through his travels and meetings with scholars, as the son of a staunch Unitarian, Norton was drawn to Hellenism and grew to appreciate its cultural capital while still retaining an appreciation of American antiquities. Like most members of the Boston intelligentsia, Norton was enamored of European cultural tradition and respected German erudition in the field of classical scholarship. His familiarity with European learned societies and museums through his extended travel and residence abroad heightened his awareness of their absence in America, barely a century old and still recovering from a bitter civil war.

Charles Eliot Norton and the other founders of the AIA believed in the social role of archaeological research in providing a material background of Greece and Rome useful for fostering high culture in the growing American middle class of their times (Will; Winterer, this volume). Norton and other intellectuals felt that the burgeoning American middle class in the last quarter of the 19th century was culturally impoverished, and they viewed classical archaeology as one means of combating the gross materialism of post-Civil War industrialism. He himself asserted that "of all civilized nations," the United States was "the most deficient in the higher culture of the mind, and not in the culture only but also in the conditions on which this culture mainly depends" (1889, 36). The fruits of archaeology would provide models for the moral and aesthetic improvement of American society. Thus, the early members of the AIA Executive Committee (most of whom were Cambridge academics or Boston elite) were preoccupied with fostering on American shores an appreciation for what they perceived as the superior cultural values of a static ancient Athens in order to uplift American aesthetic awareness. Such were the cultural politics of classical archaeology in America during the second half of the 19th century.

Following the semi-centennial of the German Archaeological Institute, in April 1879 Norton circulated a timely proposal to create a learned society that would promote a broad-minded agenda of "archaeological and artistic investigation and research" signed by 11 Bostonians and Harvard faculty members. Embracing the contemporary European humanistic rhetoric of professionalization distinguishing scientific archaeology from gentlemanly antiquarianism, he stressed "the increasing interest in archaeological science…the importance of historical and artistic results of properly conducted explorations, . . . in the New World as well as in the Old . . . in order to encourage and aid the efforts of individual explorers, and to send out special expeditions such as no individual could readily undertake," adding that America "has had little share in the splendid work of rediscovery of the early civilizations of the Old World." In anticipating the benefits accruing "not only to the science of archaeology, but to Classical and Biblical studies, and to the fine arts, by quickening the interest in antiquity" (AIA Archives, box 1.3),[1] Norton placed himself firmly within the text-based humanistic tradition of archaeology as handmaid to philology.

On 17 May 1879 the AIA was formed in Boston, the "Athens of America," and Norton was elected its first president. Although there was clearly a Bostonian and east coast bias to the new organization as was common for the time, Norton had a grander vision and solicited members or "associates from all parts of the country." He wrote that "the name 'Archaeological Institute of America' had been adopted because our agents would then be considered as representing a national and not merely a local society; and also because similar . . . societies abroad had similar titles." In so doing he validated the recently strengthened post-Civil War national consciousness in America, conformed to established European tradition, and allowed for future growth across the nation (AIA Archives, box 1.3).

Excavations

The impetus for this new organization was clearly national pride as much as concern for establishing cultural foundations. Norton was very much aware of recent German archaeological activities. In the decade following the unification of Germany in 1870, the Germans, intent on *Kulturpolitik*, had secured prize sites where they practiced "big archaeology": Troy, Olympia, and Pergamon (Emerson 1889, 48–56; Marchand 1996). In 1879 Heinrich Schliemann (1822–1890) had just begun his sixth season at Hisarlik (Troy); Ernst Curtius (1814–1896) had been excavating Olympia since 1875, and by 1878 the Germans had established a presence at Pergamon. The French had been excavating Delos and were looking for other ancient sites on which to stake their claim, and Ferdinand Fouqué had just published the French explorations on Thera (*Santorin et ses Eruptions*). Norton and other elite Bostonians did not wish the United States to be left out of the nationalistic intellectual scramble for access to the ancient world and its patrimony.

From its founding in the 18th century, European classical archaeology was dominated by the search for original works of art for museums and private collections (de Grummond, this volume), hence the focus on major sanctuaries and public spaces of city-states where such treasures were displayed in antiquity. By recovering and exhibiting Greek statues, vases, and other antiquities, European countries showed "their commitment to Hellenism, their civilized status, and also their imperialist might" (Shanks 1996, 82). The AIA founders felt keenly the competition with France and England, and especially Germany, for archaeological sites as well as for original works of art for museums. Since German unification, the pace had quickened and the recent acquisition by the Germans of literally tons of ancient sculpture from the site of Pergamon for a new museum in Berlin (Emerson 1889, 48–56; Marchand 1996) posed a formidable challenge, prompting concern on Norton's part that America had "taken small part in work of this sort, and has reaped but small benefit from it" (April 1879, AIA Archives, box 1.3).

The Executive Committee of the fledgling AIA was not merely concerned with its "influence on the progress of Greek studies, but also . . . [with] the contributions it may make to the resources of our museums and universities." Norton solicited institutional support and pledged to "increase the collections of the Boston Museum of Fine Arts or the select collection for the purposes of instruction in Harvard College" and "the Art Gallery of New Haven" if the Institute secured financial support from them (AIA 1880, 24). Thus was set in motion the plan to exploit sites within the weakened Ottoman empire, which had lenient antiquities laws that allowed ancient works to be exported. Since the Ottomans were conveniently perceived by imperialist Europeans as the "other" and thus easily taken advantage of, European and AIA archaeologists simply "saved"; that is, exploited, archaeological sites and cultural patrimony within the empire and related their finds to classical or ancient near eastern civilizations (Gates, 1996). Nevertheless, the goal of acquiring antiquities as an end in itself was problematic to Executive Committee member Francis Parkman (1823–1893), anthropologist and author of the famous *Oregon Trail*. At the second Annual Meeting he asserted that the purpose of the AIA was "the acquisition of Knowledge and not the acquisition of objects or works of art" (Minutes, 15 May 1880, AIA Archives, box 1.1), an idea less than consonant with founders who had also recently established the Museum of Fine Arts, Boston.

The Mediterranean-based agenda of Norton and others conflicted with the vision of some founding members of the AIA who felt that the Institute should be more involved with fieldwork within its own shores. It was initially unclear whether the AIA would locate archaeology within the humanities (philology) or the natural sciences with its emphasis on human origins and variety of cultures. As archaeology struggled to define itself in America there was a power play between those aesthetes who valued classical archaeology for its potential to raise the cultural standard of the population and those who preferred the intellectual puzzles of the new field of prehistoric archaeology with which New World archaeology was identified (Lubbock 1865; Stocking 1987). Norton, who was interested in both (although he was ultimately more concerned with ancient Greece), and three of the attendees of the first meeting of the new AIA on 14 April 1879, formally expressed an interest in the archaeology of the Americas (Snead, this volume). At the time Americanists were concerned about the destruction of sites in the west that was occurring with rampant development and took a Darwinian interest in prehistoric humanity, which they believed could be explored in America itself. The debate that emerged within the Institute could be characterized as the childhood of Europe versus "the childhood of all humanity" (Trigger 1989, 68).

When Norton chose John Wesley Powell (1834–1902), one of the chief contributors to American archaeology and director of the Bureau of American Ethnology (founded like the AIA in 1879), to address the subject of American archaeology at the second Annual Meeting of the Institute, the classical constituency almost revolted at the thought that the inferior American aborigines would be the focus of their high-brow efforts (Minutes, May 15, 1880, AIA Archives, 1.1). Even Norton, the mediator and initiator of Powell's invitation, betrayed his own bias: "While the archaeology of America offers many instructive analogies with the prehistoric archaeology of the Old World, it affords nothing to compare with the historic archaeology of civilized man in Africa, Asia, and Europe" (AIA 1880, 20–1). This stance later prompted Powell to lament that "our archaeologic [sic] institutes, our universities, and our scholars are threshing again the straw of the Orient for the stray grains that may be beaten out, while the sheaves of anthropology are stacked all over this continent; and they have no care for the grain which wastes while they journey beyond the seas" (1890, 562).

Despite the classical agenda of the founder and the majority of his committee, the first AIA-sponsored archaeological expedition actually took place in the American southwest under Adolph F. Bandelier (1840–1914) from 1880 to 1885 and was published in 1892. Moreover, the celebration of the 10th anniversary of the Institute included presentations on recent progress in both classical and American archaeology (Emerson 1889; Haynes 1889). But Bandelier was aware of prejudice within the Institute which in 1882 received donations of $5,620 for classical work and $200 for American and spent, respectively, $10,266.64 on Assos and $2,456.90 in America (Bandelier to Mrs. Lewis Henry Morgan, 18 July 1883, in Lange and Riley 1966, 49, n. 31). After that early effort, however, the AIA only expended a modicum of energy on the New World (Snead, this volume), and in spite of a reaffirmation of interest in "promising archaeological studies by investigation and research in the U.S. and foreign countries" expressed in the Act of Incorporation of the AIA in 1906, American Eurocentrism took precedence by the late 1880s and has remained paramount ever since. After World War I virtually all subsequent AIA operations occurred in the Old World, a focus that has continued to this day (Hinsley 1986).

The AIA burst onto the international archaeological stage with excavations at the classical site of Assos in Turkey between 1881 and 1883 (Allen, ch. 3, this volume). Although challenged by the exigencies of an inhospitable isolated site and the director's youthful inexperience, in the eyes of a contemporary archaeologist this excavation "remains the most noteworthy instance of the capacities of the American people for encouraging and carrying to successful conclusion an enterprise of discovery on classical soil. It certainly served the purpose, at the very outset, of justifying in the distrustful eye of European criticism the existence of the Archaeological Institute of America" (Emerson 1889, 61). During the first decades of its existence the AIA indeed suffered many false starts in sponsoring fieldwork in the competitive world of Mediterranean archaeology, including aborted or stillborn excavations at sites such as Knossos, Croton, Cyrene (Allen, ch. 3, this volume), and Delphi, (Sheftel, this volume). By contrast, its expedition to Assos achieved a number of the Institute's goals, although the tardy publication of excavation results, foreshadowing a chronic problem that persists in the discipline to this day, lessened the impact and may have had negative consequences for future excavations, notably with respect to fundraising. Although its sponsorship of excavations at Gortyn in 1894–1895 was successful, the Institute eventually left excavation to its subsidiary organizations, such as the ASCSA and other foreign schools, museums, local societies, and universities, partly as a result of the difficulties involved with securing sufficient funds to undertake such endeavors.

Funding

Large-scale archaeology presented an enormous challenge for the ambitious AIA because major excavations in the United States could not count on the government support that was enjoyed by archaeologists of the great colonial and imperial western European powers. This was emblematic of the emphasis in the United States on private enterprise initiatives and a failure of the federal government to sponsor cultural and artistic endeavors. So, initially, the Institute relied on private subscriptions exacted from its Boston members to support the Assos excavations (AIA Archives, box 1.3), but this inefficient method could not compete with the lavish public funding of large comprehensive projects sponsored by European countries. Lack of adequate financial support was cited by John Sterrett (1851–1914), a pioneering American classical archaeologist, as a major cause for the initial failure of Americans to compete with Europe: "The work done hitherto by America in archaeological research has always been unsatisfactory, has always been incomplete, and with few exceptions it will have to be done over again by more scientific, more systematic expeditions working with larger resources; for the research done by Americans has always been crippled by slender and inadequate means." Then he contrasted it with the "really scientific, systematic, exhaustive work pursued to a finish" characteristic of digs sponsored by "France, Austria, and Germany whose governments, understanding the value and importance of real idealism in molding national character, supply their scholars with ample means wherewith to carry on research" (1911, 12). Foundering from a lack of adequate support, the AIA expanded its financial base by broadening its constituency, enhanced in 1884 by the creation of local societies in New York and Baltimore (Allen and Hebert, app. 3, this volume). This had the effect of creating new channels for patronage by local societies and individual sponsors who collected funds for work in particular geographical regions or supported specific expeditions, such as Catherine Lorillard Wolfe (1828–1887).

In the 20th century important private donors, such as James Loeb (1867–1933), Allison Armour (1863–1941), William Semple (1881–1962) and Louise Taft Semple (d. 1961), John D. Rockefeller, Jr. (1874–1960), and others stepped into the breach and bankrolled classical excavations. Private foundations and the National Geographic Society also raised funds for excavations. Whereas Americanist archaeology began to receive federal funding with the creation of the National Research Council's Division of Anthropology and Psychology in 1919 and large-scale federal support for archaeology in 1933 (Patterson 1986, 133; 1995, 73), classical archaeology's dependence on private patronage only began to change with the advent of the Social Sciences division of the National Science Foundation (NSF) in 1954 and, more importantly for the AIA, the archaeology research section of the National Endowment of Humanities (NEH) from the mid 1970s to 1995, though funding levels fluctuated (Patterson 1986, 16; 1995, 116–7; Dyson 1998, 228, 283). In general, NEH funding for archaeology favored big projects and so continued the tradition of architectural archaeology begun at Assos (Allen, ch. 3, this volume) and represented today by excavations at the Athenian Agora that began in 1931 (Patterson 1995). In the 1970s NSF-sponsored anthropological archaeology and NEH-sponsored classical archaeology increasingly went their separate ways as a close affiliation with philology and art history tended to increase the isolationist position of classical archaeologists within the larger discipline of archaeology, which elsewhere had undergone a paradigm shift both in its discourse and agenda after 1960 (Patterson 1995, 116–7). This separation culminated in the AIA's acute financial crisis in the 1980s (Sheftel, timeline, this volume). Following a short period of severely reduced funding from the NEH beginning around 1995, when once again private philanthropy was key to the support of American excavations, government funding began rising again in the late 1990s. Revenues from *Archaeology* magazine hit an all-time high in the 1990s and helped to bolster the finances of the Institute, but these began to drop in 2000, ushering in another era of fiscal crisis.

Foreign Schools

Competition with European powers also involved the establishment of semi-autonomous American overseas research centers and schools around the Mediterranean to stimulate scholarship and facilitate fieldwork. Mindful of the French (1846) and German (1874) research centers already established in Athens, Norton noted that a similar American school might "enter into honorable rivalry with those already established" and pushed for the establishment in 1881 of the American School of Classical Studies (AIA 1880, 25), the first of its kind (Winterer, this volume). Various scholars weighed in with their visions for the School. Pioneer American archaeologist, Joseph Thacher Clarke (1856–1920) expressed concern over the discipline's prevailing tendency to place archaeology as an adjunct to philology and called for "a revolution in the presentation of the classics" that would bring about "a rejuvenation of philological studies by that living knowledge of antiquity gained by practical archaeology." Comparing philologists to the Cyclops for their blindness to material remains, he hoped that the School in Athens would be something more than a "philological seminary" and urged that a "material discipline of the science of antiquity" be created (1889, 90–1, 101). Yet Allan Marquand (1853–1924) of Princeton wrote Norton that he "was particularly pleased to find the School from the start dealing with practical archaeological questions and not expending all its energy on language" (31 March 1883, AIA Archives, box 4). Although philological competence has always been a requirement for admission, excavation has been an important component of the school's agenda from its inception, when it served as a vehicle for AIA fieldwork, and has remained critical throughout its history with numerous early excavations of short duration around Greece and major long-term excavations at Corinth and the Athenian Agora now when it is functionally independent from the AIA.

East versus West

Although Norton's elite vision dominated the 19th century and was well suited to the times, a very different approach was required for the 20th century, during which outreach has been a critical and recurrent theme. In the 1880s and 1890s two factions emerged: the eastern establishment dominated by large corporations and bankers from Boston to Washington and what Thomas

Patterson has called the core culture, from the south, midwest, and west (1995, 44–5). The tension between Hellenist and Americanist constituencies that was present from the Institute's infancy in Boston soon was aggravated as the AIA expanded to the west and eventually resulted in friction between east coast Hellenists and midwest and western societies more interested in local native American remains (Snead, this volume). Patterson maintains that the split between the eastern establishment and the populist core culture occurred after 1890, although class alliances dominated by elite factions of each still existed (1986, 20; 1995, 44–5). As certain presidents reached out to create an audience for the AIA, differing interests of these two factions often reflected the conflicting agendas of professional elites and enthusiastic lay members. Partly as a result of these tensions, AIA membership had declined around the turn of the century, and new strategies were needed to create a broader base, a larger audience. The individual chiefly responsible for implementing such an outreach was Francis Willey Kelsey (1858–1907), AIA president from 1907 to 1912 and professor at the University of Michigan. A man of unlimited energy, daring, and popular appeal, Kelsey ignited enthusiasm, recruited new members, and extended the AIA's base to the midwest, western states, and Canada (Snead, Russell, and Dyson, this volume).

Professionalization and Employment

Other problems plagued the AIA in its early years. As the Institute ambitiously undertook the sponsorship of excavations, its practitioners in the field looked for related employment at home, but the transition from amateur to professional was difficult for these AIA pioneers (Allen, ch. 3, this volume). Opportunities for excavating existed, but the newness of the field meant few permanent jobs. As late as 1889, no chair of archaeology had been created in an American college or university. Since American museum collections fell far short of those in Europe (Emerson 1889), they required few specialized curators. Although higher education was a "minor growth industry" in the United States between 1870 and 1890, and the number of institutions rose from 582 to 1,082 (Patterson 1995, 47) for the rare academic positions for which experienced excavators might apply, college administrators increasingly demanded advanced training in an attempt, as they did for other fields, to codify academic requirements, standardize methods, and disseminate information (Ross 1994, 292).

One victim of this situation was Joseph Thacher Clarke, Norton's protégé in the AIA's first generation of practical archaeologists (Allen, ch. 3, this volume). Between 1881 and 1887 he directed or was slated to direct almost every AIA initiative in the Mediterranean and looked to the future optimistically. He observed that "it has first become possible to the younger generation to-day to enter into full possession of the milk and honey of Greek perfection. And this possibility is almost wholly due to the investigations of practical workers upon classic soil, and to those archaeological scholars who have taught the world the true value of the materials thus obtained" (1889, 103). Lacking philological training and an advanced degree, however, Clarke failed to find employment in the profession, dropped from view, and later left archaeology altogether. Against his will, he abandoned the profession while others wandered from one academic position to another, joined museum staffs, or purchased antiquities for collectors. Those archaeologists who succeeded in academia were those with advanced degrees who were able to combine archaeology with philology, such as Alfred Emerson (1859–1943) and John Sterrett, both professors of Greek.

The situation gradually improved in the 20th century with archaeology being taught at a number of colleges in departments of Classics, fine arts, and anthropology. After World War II the G.I. Bill extended higher education to hundreds of thousands of veterans. By the 1960s colleges and universities were likely the main source of employment for archaeologists with Ph.D.s, and the vast majority of archaeologists who were hired in the 1960s and early 1970s were men who then taught the Baby Boom generation. As the number of archaeologists increased, so did the membership of the AIA, from 955 in 1944 to 2,271 by 1950 to 6,753 in 1970 (Patterson 1995, 80–1). But in the early 1970s the expansion in academia ground to a halt. In 1980 the Annual Meeting included a panel on unemployment, which examined the constriction in prospects for AIA archaeologists and complacency and crisis in classical archaeology in general (Dyson 1989a). In 1995 the AIA surveyed its members and estimated that a quarter to a third of its membership was in some way active professionally; that is, holding an advanced degree, publishing, giving papers at conferences, receiving grants, participating in fieldwork, or devoting a significant amount of their time to archaeology. Of those, over a third live in the northeast. Of the 58% who hold Ph.D.s and 26% who hold M.A.s, 41% hold degrees in an area of archaeology with the others in classics, art history, anthropology, ancient history, etc. (Cullen 1999, 6–7).

Employment figures are not yet available, but the recent "Expedient and Expendable: Part-Time and Adjunct Faculty in Classics and Archaeology" session at the Centennial of the Annual Meeting in 1998 examined the trend toward exploitation of a highly qualified but underemployed work force, which services both the AIA and the discipline of archaeology as a whole.

Women in Archaeology

The topics of women in the AIA and gendered archaeology are, unfortunately, neither the subject of any essay in this volume nor singled out in the AIA histories so far cited. Curtis Hinsley has charged that between 1850 and 1900 archaeology was "almost exclusively a male exercise" where women were "to observe, appreciate, and admire. To the extent that women participated in archaeology it was as audience, helpmates, or preservators: curatorial roles" (1989, 94). In this way Fannie Bandelier (d. 1936) and other wives excavated with their husbands beginning in the 19th century. From its inception, the AIA included women among its members. A number became involved as patrons of expeditions, co-founders of local societies, or as society presidents. Tobacco heiress Catherine Lorillard Wolfe of New York, a substantial donor to the ASCSA, funded the first American archaeological expedition to Mesopotamia for the AIA led by William H. Ward (1835–1916) in 1884 (Fox 1971). President of the Boston Society of the AIA and a prominent book artist, Sarah Wyman Whitman (1842–1904) designed the seal that was used on the title page of the new series of the *AJA* inaugurated in 1896 (see frontispiece), a modified version of which can be seen on the cover of the *AJA* today. Sarah Yorke Stevenson (1847–1921) first broke with what Hinsley calls the tradition of "the male presentation to metropolitan females" (1989, 88). Predisposed to an interest in archaeology from living in Mexico before her married life in Philadelphia, she corresponded with Frederic Ward Putnam (1839–1915), curator of Harvard's Peabody Museum and a founding member of the AIA. Stevenson became an amateur Egyptologist who helped found the Department of Archaeology at the University of Pennsylvania, became curator of antiquities and president of the Free Museum of Science and Art at Penn, later known as the University Museum, co-founder of the Mediterranean Section of the American Exploration Society, president of the Pennsylvania Society of the AIA, and a member of the AIA Council. In 1893 she served as vice president of the jury for ethnology at the famed Columbian Exposition in Chicago and later was sent to Rome and Egypt on special archaeological missions for the American Exploration Society. Elected a fellow of the American Association for the Advancement of Science, and a member of the American Philosophical Society and the American Oriental Society, Stevenson received an honorary degree of Doctor of Science from the University of Pennsylvania (*National Cyclopaedia of American Biography* 13, 83–4).

As women's colleges opened their doors to a new generation of students, they also provided professional status for those receiving advanced education. Smith College was singled out in a review of "Recent Progress in Classical Archaeology" for its "choice selection of casts of the most instructive Greek and Roman sculptures, in historic sequence." (Emerson 1899, 93). Annie Smith Peck (1850–1935), who later taught at Smith, was the first woman to enroll as a regular student at the ASCSA in 1885. Because women were initially only tolerated as second-class members at the School and treated accordingly, in 1898 a fellowship in the name of Agnes Hoppin was provided by the Hoppin family because "the activity of the School for women students was limited to a certain degree" (Lord 1947, 94).[2] Smith College graduate May Louise Nichols, the first woman to win a fellowship in archaeology at the School, was also the first appointee to the Hoppin Fellowship. (Lord 1947, 82). Fellow Smith alumna Harriet Boyd (1871–1945) was the first woman to receive an AIA Fellowship in its first 16 years of existence and later succeeded Nichols as Hoppin Fellow (Ibid.). When denied the opportunity to excavate with the School because of her gender (Allsebrook 1992, 228), Boyd used her fellowship funds to initiate her own fieldwork at Kavousi on Crete.[3] After publishing the Kavousi results in the *AJA*, she earned her M.A. from Smith in 1901. At the AIA's 1900 Annual Meeting, Boyd presented the findings of her first season and, as a result of this lecture, she secured the sponsorship of Stevenson's American Exploration Society in 1901 for her new excavations at Gournia. She also became the first woman to speak nationally as traveling lecturer to local AIA societies on Gournia in 1902. Seeking to foster a "network of female interaction" in the Gournia excavation and publication (Picazo 1998, 211), Boyd involved Smith alumnae, including Blanche Wheeler (1870–1936) and Edith Hall (1877–1943).[4] Only four years after the close of her excavations, she published the first archaeological monograph on a Minoan site in 1908. Before she abandoned fieldwork for family responsibilities, Harriet Boyd

(Hawes) taught Greek archaeology, epigraphy, and modern Greek at Smith from 1901 to 1906. She received the college's first honorary degree of Doctor of Humanities in 1910 and lectured at Wellesley from 1920 to 1936, thereby creating a powerful role model for her students.[5] Edith Hall (Dohan) earned her Ph.D., and, despite having children, managed a career in museum curatorial work and served as Book Review Editor for the *AJA* (Thompson 1971, 497). Both were honored in the centennial celebration of American excavations on Crete and at the AIA's Annual Meeting in 2001.

For the rest, progress was slow and less dramatic. Where statistics exist, although there was a general decline in percentages of women enrolled in colleges from 1920 (47.1%) to 1940 (40.1%) and 1958 (35.2%), the percentage of women who were AIA members in the same period rose from 37.4% in 1935 to 40.1% in 1957 to 40.2% in 1964 (Patterson 1995, 81, 83). Yet the percentage of women presenting papers at the AIA Annual Meeting remained well below that of the female membership itself: 21.6% in 1923, roughly 20% in the 1930s and 1940s, 26.5% in 1953–1954, declining sharply to 15% from 1957 to 1962 and then rising again to 22% from 1963 to 1968 (Patterson 1995, 82). Still, women's participation exceeded that of their sisters at the Society for American Archaeology (SAA) where they constituted only 9–13.6% of the membership from 1936 to 1956, 12.5% in 1960, and 14.7% in 1969, yet gave 13.8% of the papers at their annual meeting between 1935 and 1941, 3.9% from 1946 to 1955, 10.2% from 1956 to 1960, and 7.5% from 1965 to 1968 (Patterson 1995, 82–3). "Survivorship" remains a problem as women professionals drop out for a variety of reasons: slower progress through academic ranks, greater percentage of part-time employment, fewer and smaller grants, family responsibilities (Boyd Hawes), with those successful professional women more likely to remain unmarried or have higher divorce rates (Kelley 1992, 85–6).

In 1994 Shelby Brown and Tracey Cullen helped to found the AIA Subcommittee on Women in Archaeology, following the 1970s lead of colleagues at the American Anthropological Association. Among its mandates are the monitoring of women's status in the field and the encouragement of archaeological research involving the concept of gender. In 1996 the subcommittee conducted the first census by the AIA of its professional members. The preliminary analyses of these and other data show that roughly one quarter to three tenths of the total membership is professional or active in the field. Of those, 45% are female (Cullen and Keller 1999, 6). They comprise just slightly less than half of the total professionally active membership of the Institute, but they publish significantly fewer books, articles, and reviews than their male counterparts and are thus less visible in the profession and receive less recognition. Although women have recently contributed half or more than half of the papers presented at the Annual Meeting, for the AIA invited lecture series, including society lectures and the prestigious endowed lecture tours only 26% of the invitees were women, a number which rose to 29% in 1996 and 1997 (Cullen and Keller 1999, 7). In sum, women have been in the field in large numbers for fewer years, have fewer tenured positions, and have more adjunct or temporary positions. Fewer women marry and still fewer have children (Cullen 1999, 7). Those who do, because of family responsibilities, tend to conduct fieldwork less frequently than their male peers (Cullen and Keller 1999, 7).

Recent statistics show a kind of gender bias in the discipline whereby men often do the fieldwork and women, the "archaeological housework"; that is, the classification, study, and analysis (Gero 1985, 344). This is borne out by a consideration of ASCSA field projects in Greece from 1900 to 1980, where 12% of the 49 projects were directed by women (five from 1900 to 1940 and two from 1940 to 1980). Figures from 1982 to 1994 show an increase to 27% (Cullen 1996, 413). Looking toward the future, there is progress in the increasing number of female Ph.D. recipients who find work and publish in the field. But gender equity is another matter with a "rarity of women in disciplinary histories, and in the higher ranks of academia, museums, and contract firms. . . . The disadvantaged status of women is made resoundingly clear . . . perpetuated by the structured values of archaeology itself" (Cullen 1995, 1045). Certainly in his centennial memoir Dow (1979, 10) chose to focus on "the important accomplishments of Archaeology . . . [and] the great men," treating women as an afterthought at best, an oversight in part corrected here.

Within the ranks of the Institute, out of 28 AIA presidents, only four (one-seventh) have been women, the first being elected in 1965. An even worse situation can be seen at the *AJA* where only two out of 17 editors-in-chief have been women (Allen and Hebert, app. 1, this volume).[6] Fewer than one-ninth of the prestigious Norton lecturers have been women (Murray, this volume). The Institute's record with respect to prestigious awards given to women is slightly better. The Gold Medal Award for Distinguished Archaeological Achievement, recognizing career contributions, was awarded to women only four times during the first 19 years of its existence (1965–1983), but since then women have received 11 out of 20 medals awarded, including 5 of the last 10 conferred. The situation of the Pomerance Award for Scientific Contributions to Archaeology, however, is less encouraging. Only 3 of 29 awards have gone to women since the prize was first awarded in 1980 (Allen and Hebert, app. 2, this volume),[7] although this may be attributable to the fact that there are fewer women engaged in the sciences in general and archaeometry in particular. There is parity in the receipt of the Wiseman Book Award. Finally, women exceed men as recipients of AIA research fellowships (Allen and Hebert, app. 2, this volume).

Theoretical Orientations and the "Great Divide"

Recent recognition of women in the AIA has not necessarily aided the subcommittee's mandate to encourage research on gender in archaeology. Already in 1993 scholars questioned why there has been such resistance and apathy regarding a feminist agenda in the organization, noting that the AIA has been sluggish in its support of feminist scholarship in classical archaeology. Brown reviewed works concerning archaeology and gender, a subfield inaugurated by anthropological archaeologists Margaret Conkey and Janet Spector (1984) who, in their discussion of the past as a dynamic construct, document androcentric bias in the interpretation of the archaeological record. Brown concluded that "feminist analyses of ancient art undertaken in the past decade have appeared in volumes edited by classicists, anthropologists, and art historians rather than by classical archaeologists," yet she discerned a growing interest within the AIA in the "social and symbolic significance of art and architecture," which could create a feminist-friendly environment for the analysis of gendered behavior in the archaeological record (1993, 245, 259). Thus, the subcommittee has supported colloquia on relevant topics at most of the recent Annual Meetings.

The long-standing general reluctance of the AIA to consider gendered interpretations of archaeological remains and past societies is related to the larger problem of its relationship to archaeology as a broader discipline. Situating the AIA within the practices of the discipline of archaeology in the United States as a whole from 1879 to 2001 is a complex subject only briefly touched upon here. Renfrew (1980), Snodgrass (1985), Dyson (1981; 1989b; 1998), and others have all addressed this issue far more extensively with regard to classical archaeology versus the rest of the discipline of archaeology. Patterson (1995, 37, 51) has charged that the creation of the AIA marked a change in view of archaeology from the study of ancient societies to ancient remains. Dyson maintains that the turn away from the *altertumswissenschaft* of German classical archaeology towards a privileged position for philology over archaeology, the primacy of the big dig, and fine art connoisseurship from 1920 to 1950 contributed to the decline in the vigor of the discipline in the United States (1998, 218). Yet, from the time of Boyd's work at Gournia, a limited contingent of AIA members has been excavating and publishing prehistoric sites in innovative, interdisciplinary ways. Among these are three AIA gold medal recipients: Robert Braidwood, who explored paleoenvironmental issues beginning in the 1940s in Iraq; William McDonald, who conducted surveys of southwestern Greece from the 1950s onward; and George Bass, who pioneered new methods and technology for underwater archaeology from the 1960s to the 1980s. As they dealt with economic and demographic problems through settlement patterns, raw materials access, new technologies, and quantitative analysis, some prehistoric Aegean archaeologists tended to ally themselves more and more with anthropology while most classical archaeologists clung to textual and traditional approaches at urban sites where excavations continued for decades. Thus, much of the AIA's agenda remained unchanged from the concerns of the late 19th and early 20th centuries.

With the "New [Processual] Archaeology" of the 1960s and 1970s Americanist and classical archaeologists grew increasingly estranged. American scholars in anthropological archaeology and some Europeans took the lead in theoretical issues, interdisciplinary approaches, and high-technology applications of science to the field. These were not easily incorporated by text- and event-based archaeologists in the AIA as evidenced by Colin Renfrew's plenary address, "The Great Tradition versus the Great Divide," at the 1979 Annual Meeting celebrating the Institute's centennial (Renfrew 1980). The AIA's traditional architectural and object-oriented archaeology, closely affiliated with art history, focused on the empirical rather than the theoretical, the historical event rather than the processes and systems behind it.

Traditional classical archaeology became "cut off from the mainstream of that kind of intellectual advance which can manifest itself in several disciplines at the same time" (Snodgrass 1985, 37, 33). Dyson wryly observed that "a 1985 AIA program was not materially different from one in 1935 both in format and in topics covered by the papers" (Dyson 1989b, 133). The *AJA*'s New World Book Review Editor was dropped in 1973, and although the *AJA* was committed to representing a "wide range of points of view and methods . . . [as] a showcase for the diversity of scholarship," the excellent series of reviews of Americanist archaeological literature was discontinued as falling outside its geographical and chronological boundaries (Kleiner 1986,1). Dyson complained that the *AJA* "showed no interest in either theory, method, or innovative approaches to archaeology as survey and environmental analysis" (1985; 1989b, 133).

The effects of the paradigm shift in the outlook of the AIA that began in the area of prehistoric and Bronze Age Aegean archaeology can be seen in the AIA abstracts of innovative papers, posters, workshops, and colloquia presented at the annual meetings of the last 15 years. Innovations crept in, such as the first *AJA* fascicle in 1995 on "Science in Archaeology," and book review editors covering more books on archaeological method and theory, gender research, virtual archaeology, paleoenvironment, demography, and landscape archaeology than ever before. Current *AJA* editorial policy solicits "new interpretations, theories, methods of inquiry, the announcement of important discoveries, synthesis of recent research in a particular field, and critical discussions of significant questions and problems, specifically inviting contributions from the sciences and social sciences relating to the art and archaeology of the ancient world" (Hitchner 1999, 1). A perusal of the 1999 *AJA* shows articles not only on major excavations as before, but also on experimental archaeology, social organization, gendered interpretations, and intellectual history. The present book review editors "present the new methodologies and techniques that related areas and disciplines introduce," seeking "a balance . . . that reflects both established and new archaeologies." (Rehak and Younger 1999, 699).

Morris (1994) and Shanks (1996) have outlined ways in which the discipline of classical archaeology has moved and must continue to move toward the tradition of anthropological archaeology to keep in pace with the field of archaeology as a whole. Much has been done to bridge the "divide" as AIA classical archaeology is incorporated into the theoretical and methodological practices of postprocessual archaeology, which seeks to marshal the tremendous body of data closely associated with texts for interdisciplinary approaches to classical archaeology (Snodgrass 1985, 37).

New Challenges and Initiatives

The AIA has been encouraging new initiatives in archaeology in a number of ways. In his 1979 plenary address Colin Renfrew exhorted the AIA to help promote and fund publications, and the new monograph series, of which this volume is a part, began in 1993. It has also expanded the range of awards it confers annually to recognize excellence (Allen and Hebert, app. 2). The Centennial award honored the most important single contribution to archaeology in the AIA's first 100 years, the development of ^{14}C dating by Willard F. Libby. The James R. Wiseman Book award recognizes excellence in publication. The Undergraduate Teaching award celebrates the ability to communicate effectively to students. The Kershaw award honors outstanding local societies of the AIA while the Martha and Artemis Joukowsky Distinguished Service award and Public Service award commend critical stewardship and volunteer efforts in the field. Finally, the Conservation and Heritage Management award honors those stewards who are protecting cultural patrimony and archaeological sites for future generations. These awards and the increased AIA research fellowships: Olivia James, Harriet and Leon Pomerance, Helen Woodruff, Anna C. and Oliver Colburn, Kenan Erim, and the Woodruff Traveling Fellowships reflect the Institute's concerns with sustained achievement, innovative scientific methods and technologies, responsible publication, and enhancement of outreach through teaching and local programs (Allen and Hebert, app. 2, this volume). In addition, *Archaeology* magazine launched a television series in the 1990s and a children's magazine, *Dig*, in 1995.[8]

Already in 1979 Sheftel noted that "conservation and preservation have become watch-words for a modern society increasingly aware of its devastating effect on the fragile remains of history. The Institute has moved to become an effective force working to safeguard both the known as well as the yet undiscovered monuments of man's past. To this end it has proposed strong measures to deter individuals and institutions from the acquisition of stolen artifacts, has worked with other organizations in determining professional criteria for selecting archaeologists to participate in federally funded projects, and has supported measures to insure the preservation of archaeological sites for the future" (1979, 17). From its early interest in acquiring classical objects for American museums the Institute increasingly has taken a strong stance on cultural property issues, beginning with nascent attempts to preserve monuments of early native Americans in 1899 to its present role as ever-alert watchdog and strong advocate against the sale of antiquities from clandestine excavations on the art market (Coggins, this volume).

Increasingly, AIA archaeologists must bridge the divide between academia and the public and participate in the critical cultural debates so as to remain visible and viable and make its positions known in the field of archaeological ethics in the 21st century. Leaving the ivory tower of academia in 1999, officers of the AIA engaged publicly with collectors and journalists to address issues of cultural property at the Columbia University conference on that topic and tackled the White House concerning a questionable appointment to the federal government's Cultural Property Advisory Committee (Coggins, this volume). The presidential panel on the "Politics of Archaeology in the Global Context," a topic explored at the 1999 Annual Meeting, documents AIA commitment to responsible ethics on a global scale. Two workshops at the 2001 meeting stressed archaeology education for the public and the need for excavators to present their sites to the public effectively. And most recently, the AIA's president protested the destruction of cultural patrimony in Afghanistan.

In piecing together the agendas behind the founding and shaping of the AIA in its first century and beyond, we achieve a better understanding of its position and role in the wider context of global archaeology. A relevant and proactive AIA is key in the 21st century, and outreach is critical. The identity politics and culture wars of the late 20th century among minority and marginalized groups in the United States brought demands of recognition and rights based on those identities as well as the beginnings of ethnic studies programs (Patterson 1995, 130, 134). In archaeology this has led to the juggling of competing viewpoints (whether of dominant or submissive cultures) of the archaeologist as well as claims for restitution of patrimony to countries exploited by past imperialist practices, including the United States itself. "The deconstruction of American heritage has led to the recognition and acknowledgment of a multiplicity of cultural pedigrees" (Patterson 1995, 134) not just that which was privileged by Norton and the founders of the AIA. With growing awareness of cultural complexity and global responsibility, the AIA and its archaeologists must continue to speak out in public *fora* to inform the widespread interest in the field nurtured by the National Geographic Society and popular media. At the cusp of the millennium the Institute flourished with more than 100 local societies, 11,500 members, and over 200,000 subscribers to *Archaeology* magazine (Katz 1998, 366). Although the number of societies has since risen to 104, the membership now stands at fewer than 9,500. As the founders tried to negotiate their way between an archaeology celebrating civilization (Greece, Rome, and the Bible) and that exploring humans as part of the natural world (the Americas), we are challenged to unite our "multiple dispersed almost hermetically sealed centers of gravity with disparate or even divergent interests" (Patterson 1995, 138) through communication and cooperation. The Institute's task in the 21st century is to unite text- and monument-based archaeology with the methods and theoretical bases of its anthropological cousin and reach out to an interested public.

REFERENCES

Allsebrook, M. 1992. *Born to Rebel: The Life of Harriet Boyd Hawes.* Oxford.

Archaeological Institute of America (AIA). 1880. *First Annual Report of the Executive Committee, with Accompanying Papers, 1879–1880.* Cambridge, Mass.

Bolger, D. 1994. "Ladies of the Expedition: Harriet Boyd Hawes and Edith Hall at Work in Mediterranean Archaeology." In *Women in Archaeology*, edited by Cheryl Claasen, 41–50. Philadelphia.

Brown, S. 1996. "Feminist Research in Archaeology: What Does It Mean? Why Is It Taking So Long?" In *Feminist Theory and the Classics*, edited by N.S. Rabinowitz and A. Richlin, 257–8. New York.

Clarke, G.W., ed. 1989. *Rediscovering Hellenism: The Hellenic Inheritance and the English Imagination.* Cambridge.

Clarke, J.T. 1889. "A Plea for Archaeological Instruction." In *Methods of Teaching History*, edited by G. Stanley Hall, 89–103. Boston.

Conkey, M.W., and J.D. Spector. 1984. "Archaeology and the Study of Gender." *Advances in Archaeology* 7:1–38.

Cullen, T. 1995. "Women in Archaeology: Perils and Progress." *Antiquity* 69:1042–5.

———. 1996. "Contributions to Feminism in Archaeology." *AJA* 100:409–14.

Cullen, T., and D. Keller. 1999. "Productivity in Archaeology: Report on the AIA Survey." *AIA Newsletter* 15 (1):6–7, 10.

Dow, S. 1979. *A Century of Humane Archaeology.* Privately printed.

———. 1980. "A Century of Humane Archaeology." *Archaeology* 33:42–51.

Dyson, S. 1981. "A Classical Archaeologist's Response to the New Archaeology." *Bulletin of the American Schools of Oriental Research* 242:7–13.

———. 1985. "Two Paths to the Past: A Comparative Study of the Last Fifty Years of *American Antiquity* and the *American Journal of Archaeology*." *American Antiquity* 50:452–63.

———. 1989a. "Complacency and Crisis in Late Twentieth Century Classical Archaeology." In *Classics: A Discipline and Profession in Crisis?*, edited by P. Culham and L. Edmunds, 211–20. New York.

———. 1989b. "The Role of Ideology and Institutions in Shaping Classical Archaeology in the Nineteenth and Twentieth Centuries." In *Tracing Archaeology's Past*, edited by A.L. Christenson, 127–35. Carbondale, Ill.

———. 1998. *Ancient Marbles to American Shores: Classical Archaeology in the United States.* Philadelphia.

Emerson, A. 1889. "Recent Progress in Classical Archaeology." *Tenth Annual Report of the Executive Committee of the Archaeological Institute of America, with Accompanying Papers*, appendix 1, 47–94.Cambridge, Mass.

Fox, D. 1971. "Wolfe, Catherine Lorillard." In *Notable American Women 1607–1950: A Biographical Dictionary*, vol. 3, edited by E.T. James, J.W. James, and P.S. Boyer, 641–2. Cambridge, Mass.

Gates, C. 1996. "American Archaeologists in Turkey." *Journal of American Studies in Turkey* 4:47–68.

Gero, J. 1985. "Socio-politics and the Woman-at-Home Ideology." *American Antiquity* 50:342–81.

Haynes, H.W. 1889. "Recent Progress in American Archaeology." *Tenth Annual Report of the Executive Committee of the Archaeological Institute of America, with Accompanying Papers*, appendix 2, 95 ff. Cambridge, Mass.

Hinsley, C.M., jr. 1986. "Edgar Lee Hewett and the School of American Research in Santa Fe, 1906–1912." In *American Archaeology Past and Future*, edited by D. Meltzer, D. Fowler, and J. Sabloff, 217–33. Washington, D.C.

———. 1989. "Revising and Revisioning the History of Archaeology: Reflections on Region and Context." In *Tracing Archaeology's Past*, edited by A.L. Christenson, 79–96. Carbondale, Ill.

Hitchner, R. Bruce. 1999. "A Letter from the Editor-in-Chief." *AJA* 103:1.

Katz, P.P. 1998. "The Archaeological Institute of America and Outreach: Fifty Years of *Archaeology* Magazine." *AJA* 102:366.

Kelley, J.H. 1992. "Being and Becoming." In *Rediscovering Our Past: Essays on the History of American Archaeology*, edited by J. Reyman, 81–90. Aldershot, England.

Lange, C.H., and C.L. Riley. 1966. *The Southwestern Journals of Adolph F. Bandelier*. Santa Fe.

Lord, L. 1947. *The American School of Classical Studies at Athens*. Cambridge, Mass.

Lubbock, J. 1865. *Prehistoric Times*. London.

McKay, A.G. 1994. "Classical Scholarship in Canada." In *Biographical Dictionary of North American Classicists*, edited by W.W. Briggs, Jr., xl–lxiv. Westport, Conn.

Marchand, S. 1996. *Down from Olympus: Archaeology and Philhellenism in Germany, 1750–1970*. Princeton.

Morris, I., ed. 1994. "Archaeologies of Greece." In *Classical Greece,* edited by I. Morris, 8–47. Cambridge.

Nelson, S.M. 1997. *Gender in Archaeology: Analyzing Power and Prestige*. Walnut Creek, Calif.

Norton, C.E. 1889. "A Definition of Fine Arts." *Forum* 7:36.

Novick, P. 1988. *That Noble Dream: The "Objectivity Question" and the American Historical Profession.* Cambridge.

Patterson, T.C. 1986. "The Last Sixty Years: Toward a Social History of Americanist Archaeology in the United States." *American Anthropologist* 88:7–26.

———. 1995. *Toward a Social History of Archaeology in the United States.* Fort Worth, Tex.

Picazo, M. 1998. "Fieldwork is Not the Proper Preserve of a Lady: The First Women Archaeologists in Crete." In *Excavating Women: A History of Women in European Archaeology,* edited by M. Diaz-Andreu and M.L. Sorensen, 198–213. New York.

Rehak, P., and J. Younger. 1999. "Editorial Statement." *AJA* 103:699.

Renfrew, C. 1980. "The Great Tradition versus the Great Divide: Archaeology as Anthropology?" *AJA* 84:287–98.

Ross, D., ed. 1994. *Modernist Impulses in the Human Sciences 1870–1930.* Baltimore.

Scott, J.A. 1997. "AIA Archives: Ready for Use and Awaiting Additions." *AIA Newsletter* 12:1, 3.

Shanks, M. 1996. *Classical Archaeology of Greece: Experiences of the Discipline.* London.

Sheftel, P.S. 1979. "The Archaeological Institute of America, 1879–1979: A Centennial Review." *AJA* 83:3–17.

Snodgrass, A. 1985. "The New Archaeology and the Classical Archaeologist." *AJA* 89:31–7.

Sterrett, J.R.S. 1911. *A Plea for Research in Asia Minor and Syria Authorized by Men Whose High Achievements and Representative Character Make the Project a Call of Humanity at Large for Light in Regard to the Life of Man in the Cradle of Western Civilization.* Ithaca.

Stocking, G.W. 1987. *Victorian Anthropology.* New York.

Thompson, D.B. 1971. "Dohan, Edith Hayward Hall." In *Notable American Women 1607–1950: A Biographical Dictionary,* vol. 1, edited by E.T. James, J.W. James, and P.S. Boyer, 496–7. Cambridge, Mass.

Thompson, H.A. 1980. "In Pursuit of the Past: The American Role 1879–1979." *AJA* 84:263–70.

Trigger, B. 1989. *A History of Archaeological Thought.* Cambridge.

Turner, J. 1999. *The Liberal Education of Charles Eliot Norton.* Baltimore.

Vogeikoff-Brogan, N. 2000. "Life at the School B.L.H. ('Before Loring Hall')." *ASCSA Newsletter,* Summer.

Waterhouse, Helen. 1986. *The British School at Athens: The First Hundred Years.* London.

NOTES

[1] The AIA archives are housed in the Institute's headquarters in Boston, Massachusetts. All citations throughout the volume refer to box and file. They are cited with permission of the former AIA Executive Director, Mark Meister.

[2] With the brief exception of 1922–1923 women were not allowed to live at the School before 1929 and had to find their own accommodations (Vogeikoff-Brogan 2000). Richardson, ASCSA director, actively excluded women from his excavations in Sparta and a portion of the School trip to the Peloponnese. Similarly, the British School at Athens

admitted women in the 1890s, but denied them access to studentships or fellowships until 1910, and residence in the hostel as well as participation on digs until after World War I (Waterhouse 1986, 132).

[3] Boyd submitted her excavation report to the ASCSA director, who ignored it and only mentioned his own in his annual report for 1899–1900, although her dig was under the auspices of the School (Lord 1947, 298).

[4] Hall won the last Hoppin Fellowship and later excavated her own site on Crete.

[5] Both Boyd and Hall attended private secondary schools and Smith College, and both later taught Classics, an acceptable field for women (Bolger 1994, 49). Among Boyd Hawes's Wellesley students is my own professor, Phyllis Williams Lehmann, who has had a distinguished academic career at Smith, participated in American-sponsored excavations at Samothrace, authored a volume and edited final reports on those excavations, and co-founded the Western Massachusetts society of the AIA.

[6] The AIA compares favorably with its younger counterpart, the SAA, which elected its first woman president in 1986 and appointed a woman the first editor of its journal, *American Antiquity*, in 1981.

[7] The curious numbers are attributable to the multiple recipients of the award in 1993 and 1994.

[8] The children's magazine won several prestigious prizes before being sold in 2001.

— I —

Spirit of the Times: 19th-Century European Intellectualism

Nancy Thomson de Grummond

The century of the founding of the Archaeological Institute of America was a time during which archaeology itself became a well-organized discipline with a systematic methodology. Formal expeditions were mounted, corpora of antiquities were initiated, great museums were opened, antiquities services were created, institutions were formed. As a means to understanding the intellectual atmosphere at the time of the founding of the AIA, I review these trends and concentrate on these developments as they relate to archaeological research in the classical lands, especially Greece and Italy, focusing particularly on group activities rather than individual achievements, to delineate the forerunners and parallels for the AIA.[1]

In the 18th century, archaeology was a popular pastime with many individual scholars and dilettantes, but serious research was conducted at an irregular pace, and with little formal support for those who practiced it. Nevertheless in this century several developments were to be of considerable significance for the history of archeology and would set the stage for the flowering in the 19th century. In 1733 the Society of Dilettanti was founded in England (Cust 1898; Kopff 1996b), which originated as a club for discussing and enjoying the arts along with the consumption of appropriate beverages. Soon it sponsored a formal, organized expedition to Greece by two of its members, James Stuart (1713–1788) and Nicholas Revett (1720–1804), both trained painters and architects (Lawrence 1938–1939; Rowe 1996a,

Fig. 1.1. View of the Tower of the Winds, from James Stuart and Nicholas Revett, *The Antiquities of Athens* I 1762.

1996b). Their well-known mission to Athens to draw and record its monuments (1751–1755) resulted in the handsome corpus of *The Antiquities of Athens*, with the first volume appearing in 1762, and the subsequent four being issued sporadically until the final volume in 1830 (fig. 1.1). Similar projects sponsored by the Dilettanti were the expedition to the Greek cities of Asia Minor by Richard Chandler (1738–1810) (Eliot 1996) along with Revett and William Pars (1742–1782) (Chandler 1971; de Grummond 1996t)—published in four volumes as *Ionian Antiquities* (1769–1881), and the explorations by Robert Wood (1717–1771) (de Grummond 1996w) of *The Ruins of Palmyra* (published 1753) and *The Ruins of Balbec* (published 1757). Wood and his comrade James Dawkins were depicted in a romantic entry into Palmyra by Gavin Hamilton, with the two gentlemen garbed in classical-style drapery (fig. 1.2). The spirit and atmosphere of the Dilettanti was captured equally well in the first formal portrait of the Society, created by Sir Joshua Reynolds in 1777 at the time of the election of Sir William Hamilton (Ramage 1990, 469–80 and 1992, 653–61; Cook 1996b).[2]

Paralleling the work in Greece and Turkey were the excavations pursued more or less continuously at Herculaneum (from 1738) and Pompeii (from

Fig. 1.2. Robert Wood and James Dawkins Enter into Palmyra, engraving, 1774, after a painting by G. Hamilton. (Courtesy of The Warburg Institute, University of London)

1748) (Richardson 1996d and 1996f). It is customary to vilify the work carried out under the aegis of the Bourbon monarchy, since scathing criticisms of the excavations at Pompeii were made by Johann Joachim Winckelmann (1717–1768) (Etienne 1992, 146–9), and since it is clear that a principal goal was to find works of art for display in the royal collections. But Winckelmann, having been snubbed by the court, certainly had motivation for his bitter attack and may not have given a truly objective account. And while it is true that treasures were extracted without sufficient regard for context, nevertheless fine architectural plans and drawings were produced by the Swiss engineer Karl Weber (1712–1764) (Parslow 1995), which stand fair comparison with those of Stuart and Revett. In addition, an interesting innovation was made in regard to publication by the scholarly committee known as the Academia Herculanensis (formed 1755; de Grummond 1996c): this group met every two weeks with the express purpose of discussing the finds

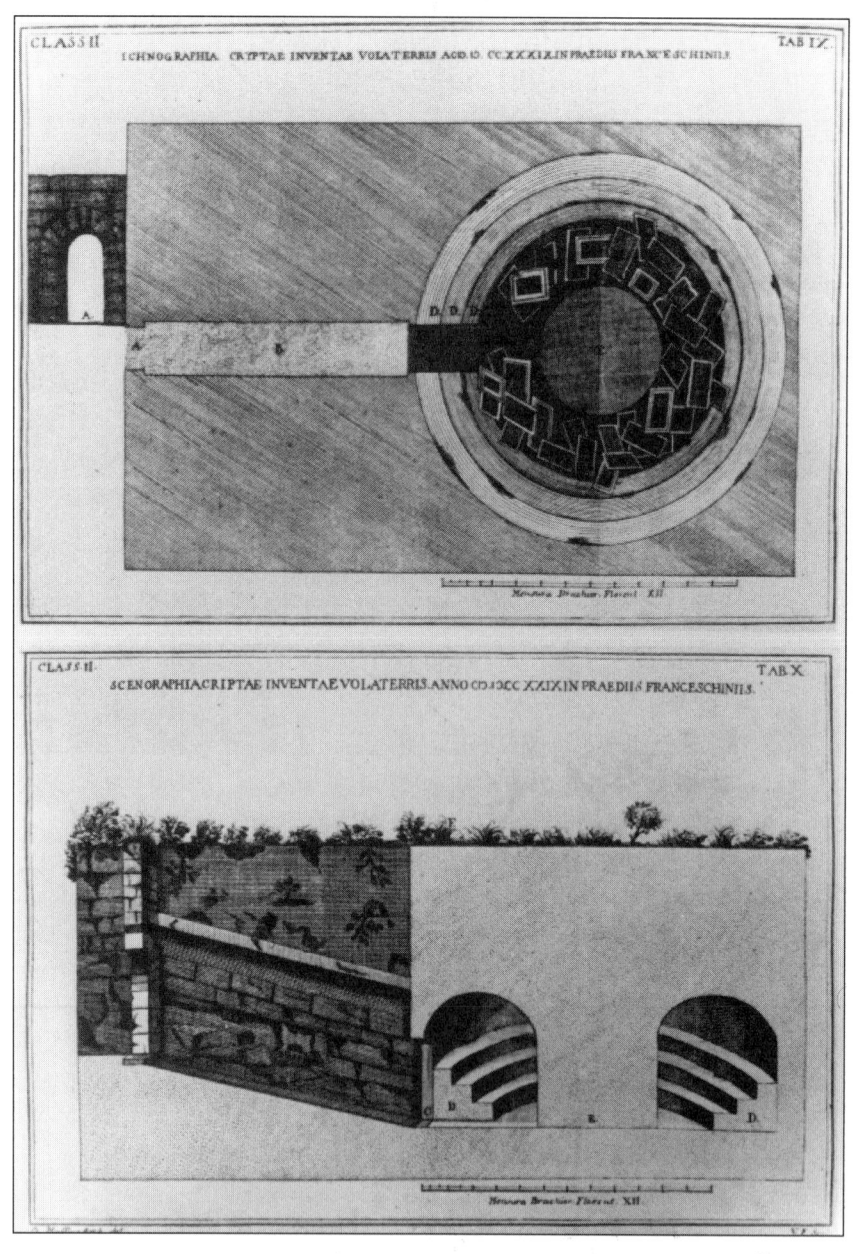

Fig. 1.3. Ground plan of tomb excavated at Volterra, ca. 1728, engraving by Francesco Gori.

Fig. 1.4. Photograph of Eduard Gerhard. (Courtesy of the Deutsches Archäologisches Institut, Berlin)

Fig. 1.5. Casa Tarpeia on the Capitoline Hill, Rome, original seat of the Instituto di Corrispondenza Archeologica, engraving from *Monumenti inediti* 2, 1834–1838. (Courtesy of the Deutches Archäologisches Institut, Rome. Inst. neg. 38.575)

from Herculaneum and publishing them in *Le antichità di Ercolano*, a handsome corpus of eight volumes (Naples, 1757–1792).

The Accademia Etrusca (de Grummond 1996b), founded in 1727 at Cortona, held regular meetings, too, with occasions for reports on new finds and papers on antiquities. The truly scientific seriousness of this body is manifest in the reports on the meetings, published as *Notti Coritane* ("Cortona Nights") in 13 volumes. Among the members was the Florentine Anton Francesco Gori (1691–1757) (Cristofani 1983; de Grummond 1996j), who published comprehensive corpora of Etruscan antiquities *(Museum florentinum*, 10 volumes, 1731–1762, and *Museum etruscum*, 3 volumes, 1736–1743) and who showed a sophisticated approach to excavation in his work on tombs at Volterra (1728 and following), in which he recorded in great and objective detail the finds of ash urns and pottery and made elevations and plans, including a top-view map showing the findspots of the urns (fig. 1.3).

But the pace of archaeological organizing quickened perceptibly in the early 19th century. Perhaps most important of all, archaeology became an internationally shared activity. A group of northern Europeans who joined forces in Rome in 1823, calling themselves the Hyperboreans (de Grummond 1996l), held regular meetings to read classical texts together and to seek archaeological adventure in the Italian countryside. Eduard Gerhard (1795–1867) (fig. 1.4), Theodor Panofka (1800–1858), August Kestner (1777–1853), and Otto Magnus von Stackelberg (1787–1837) (Elliott 1996; de Grummond 1996s; 1996u) formed the core of an organization that would add members from several other countries, and would take the name of the Instituto di Corrispondenza Archeologica (Michaelis 1879; Richardson 1996e). Their colleagues then included the Italian Carlo Fea (1753–1836) (Ridley 1996b), the French Duc de Luynes (1802–1867) (de Grummond 1996n), the Danish Bertel Thorvaldsen (1770–1844) (Mejer 1996), and the German Christian Karl Julius Bunsen (1791–1860). The official date of founding was 21 April—Rome's birthday—1829. Under the leadership of Gerhard and Wilhelm Henzen, with headquarters on the Capitoline Hill (fig. 1.5), the Instituto would eventually evolve into the Deutsches Archäologisches Institut (Wickert 1979; Bittel 1979; Richardson 1996c), officially so designated in 1871.[3] At the same time, a central national office was established in Berlin, and it supervised the activities of the Rome bureau and of another new branch set up in Athens in 1874. The French answered by founding their own archaeological school in Rome, the École française de Rome (Richardson 1996b) in 1873. In Greece the earliest national school to be founded was the French, in 1846, under the sponsorship of the Académie des inscriptions et belles lettres (Picard 1948; de Grummond 1996f), followed by the German in 1874 (Jantzen 1986; de Grummond 1996i).

Gerhard and his friends had early noted the need for corpora of antiquities in order to put archaeological research on a firm foundation. Gerhard himself prepared one volume of a catalogue of the important body of sculptures in the Naples museum, *Neapels antike Bildwerke* (1828); one volume of a corpus of ancient sculptures in Berlin, *Berlins antike Bildwerke* (1836); four volumes on vase paintings, *Auserlesene griechische Vasenbilder*, (1839–1858); and four volumes on Etruscan mirrors, *Etruskische Spiegel* (1840–1867). Theodor Mommsen (1817–1903) (Wickert 1959–1980; Gordon 1996) initiated the *Corpus Inscriptionum Latinarum* in 1862, while Otto Jahn (1813–1869) (Calder 1996c and 1996e), a colleague of Mommsen, started the corpus of Roman sarcophagi, the first volume of which appeared in 1869, with the work continued by his student Carl Robert (1850–1922). The *Corpus Inscriptionum Graecarum* had been begun by August Böckh (1787–1867) (Calder 1996a) in 1828, with four volumes completed by 1859. Heinrich von Brunn

(1822–1894) (Calder 1996b) was a great compiler, whose *Geschichte der griechischen Kunstler* appeared in two volumes in 1853 and 1859. Two of the most useful corpora were generated by Johannes Overbeck (1826-1895) (de Grummond 1996q), who published his collection of literary sources on Greek art in 1868, *Die Antiken Schriftquellen zur Geschichte der bildenden Kunste bei den Griechen*, and his corpus of Greek mythology in art issued in five parts, beginning in 1871 and finishing in 1889.

Formal expeditions and excavations became more and more frequent. The impetuous rush to newly discovered Etruscan tombs at Tarquinia by the Hyperboreans in the 1820s and 1830s culminated in the drawings by Stackelberg and an even more valuable corpus of copies of Etruscan paintings by Carlo Ruspi (1786–1863) (De Puma 1996). Earlier, Stackelberg had been in Greece with Carl Christoph Haller von Hallerstein (1774–1817) (de Grummond 1996k) and Charles Robert Cockerell (1788–1863) (Vickers 1996), excavating at Aigina in 1811 (Morris 1996) and at Bassai in 1811–1812 (de Grummond 1996d). Cockerell's results were finally published in 1860 as *The Temples of Jupiter Panhellenius at Aegina and of Apollo near Phigaleia in Arcadia*. Stackelberg issued a report on the latter site at Rome in 1826. During these years the best planned and best prepared investigation was the multidisciplinary expedition of the French to the Morea or Peloponnese, entitled the *Expédition scientifique de Morée* (fig. 1.6). From 1829 to 1831, a French team under the naturalist Jean-Baptiste Bory de Saint-Vincent (1788–1846) took on the mission to explore and describe the landscape, history, and monuments of the Peloponnese, the Cyclades, and Attica. As Susan Petrakis has described it, "Bory and his brigades of topographers, geologists, botanists, zoologists, entomologists, antiquarians, artists, draftsmen and epigraphers conducted an exhaustive survey . . . collecting specimens, mapping, drawing and recording" (Petrakis 1996, 421). The archaeological section, overseen by Guillaume Abel Blouet (1795–1853) (de Grummond 1996e), was published in 3 volumes between 1831 and 1838.

At the same time, the Greeks themselves began to demonstrate a passionate devotion to their antiquities, in the atmosphere created by the liberation of the nation from the Turks. The government's Greek Archaeological Service was founded in 1833 and was complemented by the Archaeological Society in Athens, under charter from King Otho in 1837 (Coulson 1996a, 1996b; Petrakos 1987). The latter immediately played an active role in excavations, for example in Athens at the Theater of Dionysos, the Akropolis, the

Fig. 1.6. Frontispiece, engraving from Abel Blouet et al., *Expédition scientifique de Morée* (1831–1838). (Courtesy of the Deutsches Archäologisches Institut, Rome. Inst. neg. 68.5323)

Tower of the Winds, and the Agora, and then later at the Kerameikos cemetery. Of the greatest importance was a law restricting the export of antiquities from Greece, passed in 1834. This soon necessitated the provision of a museum for the housing of the antiquities thus retained in the country.

The parallel developments in Italy during these years may be traced in Rome and at the Vatican, where Carlo Fea (fig. 1.7) served in the all-important role of Commissario delle antichità (Ridley 1996a) for the Pope from 1800 until his death in 1836. He worked relentlessly to establish state ownership of the cultural patrimony and formulated key edicts to protect antiquities and inhibit their export. But oddly enough, one of the most important chapters in the history of excavation in Rome pertains to the activities of a foreign power. As Ronald Ridley has shown in his book, *The Eagle and the Spade: The Archaeology of Rome during the Napoleonic Era, 1809–1814* (1992), the French carried out a systematic program in Rome long before the French School itself was established. Under a well-organized Commission of Monuments, Italian and French archaeologists and architects cleared or restored virtually every major classical monument of the city.

Later in the century, nationalism played a major role in archaeology in Italy just as it had in Greece. With the unification of Italy in the 1860s came a series of actions that affected the excavation of sites and the housing of antiquities. At Pompeii, Giuseppe Fiorelli (1823–1896) (Fiorelli 1939; Richardson 1996a) was appointed as inspector of antiquities and undertook a complete reorganization of the way the work was carried out, instituting, for example, the recording of the site with reference to *regio* and *insula*; in 1863 he became director of the new Museo Nazionale (de Grummond 1996p) and there, too, achieved a fresh, systematic organization of the collections. In Rome, the national administration would divide up the previously excavated antiquities so that the Museo Nazionale Romano (de Grummond 1996v) would hold all of the antiquities excavated in the city of Rome and others of the Greco-Roman tradition, while the Museo Nazionale di Villa Giulia (Ridgway 1996) would be the repository of Italic and Etruscan material (process completed in 1889). And in Florence, a completely new archaeological museum was decreed in 1870 by King Victor Emmanuel II (1820–1878), to contain Etruscan antiquities, particularly from the long-existing collections of the Medici (de Grummond 1996g).

The movement to create great public museums with a major archaeological component was a European phenomenon of the second half of the 18th

Fig. 1.7. Portrait of Carlo Fea. (Courtesy of the Deutsches Archäologisches Institut, Rome. Inst. neg. 76.1820)

Fig. 1.8. The Temporary Elgin Room in the British Museum, 1819, with Sir Benjamin West in the foreground on the left; painting by Archibald Archer, London, British Museum. (Courtesy of The Warburg Institute, University of London)

and the 19th century. Again, the British were at the forefront, with the founding of the British Museum in 1753 (Cook 1996a). Spectacular additions to the museum from classical lands were made with the acquisition of the Greek vases of Sir William Hamilton (1730–1803) in 1772, the Parthenon marbles in 1816 (fig. 1.8), and the friezes from the Mausoleum of Halicarnassus in 1846, to name only a few. The Louvre, with its previously existing royal collections, opened in 1793, but did not show many antiquities until 1803, when wagonloads of antiquities plundered by Napoleon in Italy were placed on display (Ridley 1996c; de Grummond 1996m). Most of these were returned to Italy after the fall of Napoleon, but soon government-sponsored missions such as the *Expédition scientifique de Morée* enriched the collection. The French presence in Greece and the Aegean secured masterpieces such as the Venus de Milo (1820) and the Winged Victory of Samothrace (1863); both were obtained through the intervention of French ambassadors, the Hera of Cheramyes from Samos (1875) and the Rampin Horseman from the Athenian Acropolis (discovered in 1877). In Berlin, a public museum was opened in 1830, containing some

Fig. 1.9. The Theseum (Hephaisteion), Athens, engraving from Abel Blouet et al., *Expédition scientifique de Morée* (1831–1838). (Courtesy of the Deutsches Archäologisches Institut, Rome. Inst. neg. 1937.1168)

classical antiquities; the collection would grow to much greater importance late in the century (Teviotdale 1996a). In Munich, the Glyptothek (Teviotdale 1996b) of Ludwig I of Bavaria (1786–1868) opened its displays of the Greek sculptures from the temple at Aigina in 1830, and the vase collection of Ludwig was placed on public display in 1841 in the Alte Pinakothek (Schweiger 1996). In Madrid, the national archaeological museum was founded in 1867 by Queen Isabella II (1830–1904) to consolidate national archaeological treasures (Eaverley 1996), while the Prado, which opened its doors in 1819, developed a major display of antiquities from the royal collection in 1839 (Harris Frankfort 1996). And to circle back to Greece, the Royal decree of 1834 founded the National Archaeological Museum (Kokkou 1977; Lyons 1996), proclaiming the site of the Theseum (or rather Hephaisteion) as the first location for the museum (fig. 1.9) (Camp 1996). Soon the Theseum became so congested that it was necessary to utilize the Library of Hadrian and the Tower of the Winds as well. Finally, in 1866, a new building was erected specifically for all the antiquities that had been and continued to be amassed.

Doubtless many other examples could be added of such activities. But enough background has been given to permit the present focus on the decade of the 1870s and the emergence of an American presence in this previously European phenomenon. It is especially interesting that the international movement to create archaeological museums struck on the east coast of the U.S. in 1870, the year in which the Metropolitan Museum of Art received its charter (de Grummond 1996o) and the Massachusetts state legislature decreed the founding of a Museum of Fine Arts in Boston (Whitehill 1970; Wasano 1996). Both museums would open officially in 1872, and both would attract great attention from the public by showing newly excavated antiquities from Cyprus, collected by Luigi Palma di Cesnola (1832–1904) (McFadden 1971; Traill 1996) during the time he was consul to Cyprus, beginning in 1865. There is considerable irony in the fact that these museums gloried in showing antiquities that had been ruthlessly ripped from their archaeological context in vast, unjustifiable numbers (Coggins, this volume). It was also the decade when Heinrich Schliemann (1822–1890) claimed to discover what he called the Treasure of Priam at Troy,[4] as well as the period when he excavated at Mycenae (1874–1876). Excavations for the royal Prussian state at Olympia began in 1875 (Jantzen 1986; de Grummond 1996r), and on another front, the Berlin museum sponsored the transport of the Great Altar of Pergamon to Berlin in 1878–1879 (Gunter 1996b). The cultured public was in fact quite mad for archaeology during this period, and the colorful books of Cesnola (*Cyprus: Its Ancient Cities, Tombs and Temples*, American edition, 1878) and Schliemann (*Troy and its Remains*, 1875; *Mycenae*, 1878) fanned the flames of this passion. And although this article on the AIA is concerned with archaeology in the classical lands, it is worth mentioning that exotic discoveries like those at Troy and Mycenae and on Cyprus were paralleled by sensational discoveries in Egypt and the Near East, especially by the English and the French (Stiebing 1993, 55–118). Intriguing results at European prehistoric sites had also received considerable attention (Stiebing 1993, 44–51). In Europe, archaeology was no longer focused exclusively on the classical tradition, and this broader outlook had appeared in America as well, where exciting discoveries had been made in Central and South America in the 19th century. Americans were also intrigued by finds within the United States, in the Native American cultures in the southwest and in the Ohio River Valley (Stiebing 1993, 175–97).

The founding of the Archaeological Institute of America in 1879 (Sheftel 1979, 1996) can thus be inserted neatly into the history of archaeology in the 19th century. Charles Eliot Norton (1827–1908) (Vanderbilt 1959; Calder 1996d; and Will, this volume) had in mind three major goals for the institute, which reflect very well the contemporary trends in the discipline. He wanted to establish research bases in Greece and Italy, and thus the AIA opened the American School of Classical Studies at Athens in 1882 (Lord 1947; Meritt 1984; Hoff 1996; and Winterer, this volume), and later, in 1895, there was established a school for classical studies in Rome that would soon be embraced in the American Academy in Rome (Valentine and Valentine 1973; Yegül 1991; Kopff 1996a). The Americans were not the first to found schools in Greece and Italy, but they were not the last either. The situation makes an interesting comparison with the founding of some of the other foreign schools. The German Archaeological Institute arose gradually *sua sponte* in Rome, and this led to the creation of the "parent" organization as well as another branch in Greece. The oldest of the foreign missions in the classical lands, the French School in Athens, was founded by a scientific and academic organization similar to the AIA, and yet the Académie des inscriptions obviously had a far broader sphere of intellectual interests than the Institute.

The American School of Classical Studies would soon begin its well-known excavation at Corinth in 1896 (de Grummond 1996f), and this dig was thus concurrent with the Great Excavation of the French at Delphi (*Redécouverte de Delphes* 1992), which had begun in 1892. If Norton had had his way, the Americans and specifically the AIA, would have gained the glory of excavating Delphi. The story is a messy one, but it is told with clarity by Phoebe Sheftel (Sheftel 1979 and this volume; *Redécouverte de Delphes* 1992).

But all of this touches on a second goal of the founders of the AIA, and that is the initiative to sponsor excavations in the classical lands. The excavations at Assos in Asia Minor (1881–1883) under Joseph Thacher Clarke (1856–1920) and Francis Henry Bacon (1856–1940) (Allen, ch. 3, this volume) and the resulting delivery of antiquities to America, specifically to the Boston Museum of Fine Arts, exemplify the success of Norton's drive to have Americans digging for the AIA (Gunter 1996a; Wasano 1996).

A third and final goal was the publication of results of excavations and other archaeological topics, and to this end Norton supported the founding in 1885 of the now well-known journal, the *American Journal of Archaeology*.

The first of the Assos reports appeared in 1898 (Allen, ch. 3, this volume), and the AIA would support many other publications. But now I am moving into the 20th century, and these matters are discussed in much detail by others in this volume.

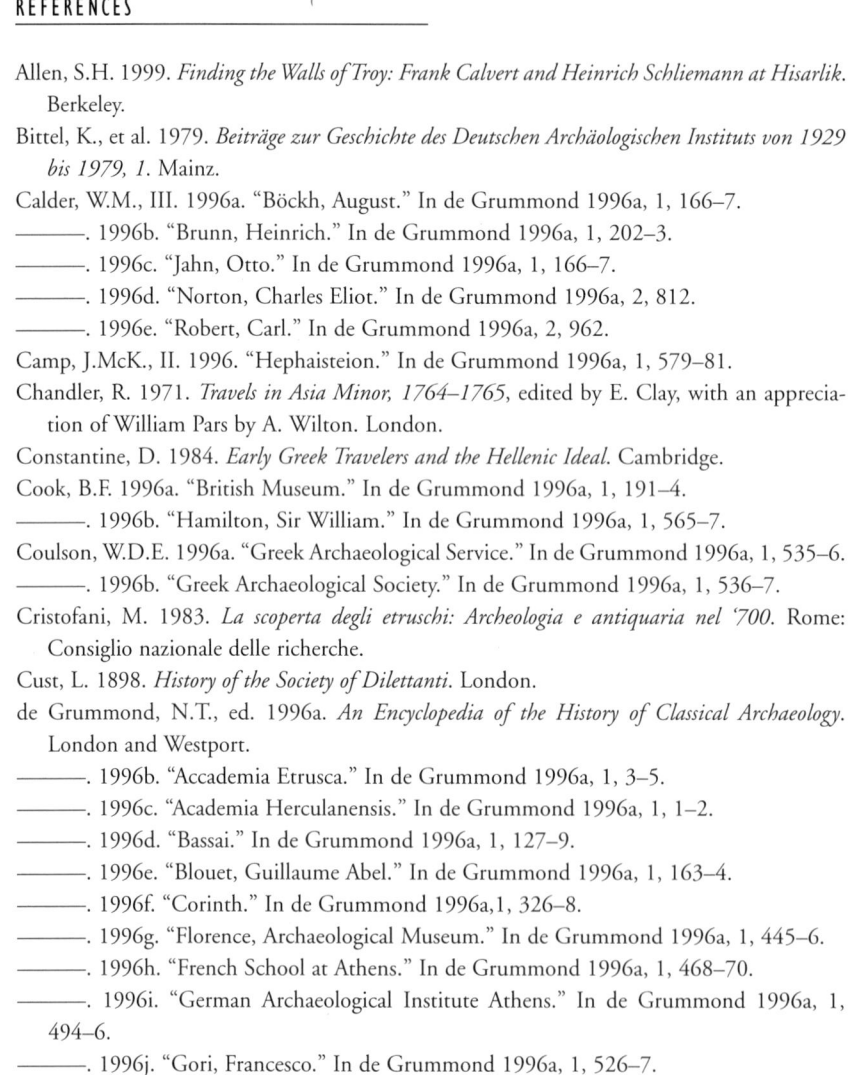

REFERENCES

Allen, S.H. 1999. *Finding the Walls of Troy: Frank Calvert and Heinrich Schliemann at Hisarlik.* Berkeley.
Bittel, K., et al. 1979. *Beiträge zur Geschichte des Deutschen Archäologischen Instituts von 1929 bis 1979, 1.* Mainz.
Calder, W.M., III. 1996a. "Böckh, August." In de Grummond 1996a, 1, 166–7.
———. 1996b. "Brunn, Heinrich." In de Grummond 1996a, 1, 202–3.
———. 1996c. "Jahn, Otto." In de Grummond 1996a, 1, 166–7.
———. 1996d. "Norton, Charles Eliot." In de Grummond 1996a, 2, 812.
———. 1996e. "Robert, Carl." In de Grummond 1996a, 2, 962.
Camp, J.McK., II. 1996. "Hephaisteion." In de Grummond 1996a, 1, 579–81.
Chandler, R. 1971. *Travels in Asia Minor, 1764–1765,* edited by E. Clay, with an appreciation of William Pars by A. Wilton. London.
Constantine, D. 1984. *Early Greek Travelers and the Hellenic Ideal.* Cambridge.
Cook, B.F. 1996a. "British Museum." In de Grummond 1996a, 1, 191–4.
———. 1996b. "Hamilton, Sir William." In de Grummond 1996a, 1, 565–7.
Coulson, W.D.E. 1996a. "Greek Archaeological Service." In de Grummond 1996a, 1, 535–6.
———. 1996b. "Greek Archaeological Society." In de Grummond 1996a, 1, 536–7.
Cristofani, M. 1983. *La scoperta degli etruschi: Archeologia e antiquaria nel '700.* Rome: Consiglio nazionale delle richerche.
Cust, L. 1898. *History of the Society of Dilettanti.* London.
de Grummond, N.T., ed. 1996a. *An Encyclopedia of the History of Classical Archaeology.* London and Westport.
———. 1996b. "Accademia Etrusca." In de Grummond 1996a, 1, 3–5.
———. 1996c. "Academia Herculanensis." In de Grummond 1996a, 1, 1–2.
———. 1996d. "Bassai." In de Grummond 1996a, 1, 127–9.
———. 1996e. "Blouet, Guillaume Abel." In de Grummond 1996a, 1, 163–4.
———. 1996f. "Corinth." In de Grummond 1996a,1, 326–8.
———. 1996g. "Florence, Archaeological Museum." In de Grummond 1996a, 1, 445–6.
———. 1996h. "French School at Athens." In de Grummond 1996a, 1, 468–70.
———. 1996i. "German Archaeological Institute Athens." In de Grummond 1996a, 1, 494–6.
———. 1996j. "Gori, Francesco." In de Grummond 1996a, 1, 526–7.
———. 1996k. "Haller von Hallerstein, Carl Christoph." In de Grummond 1996a, 1, 561–2.

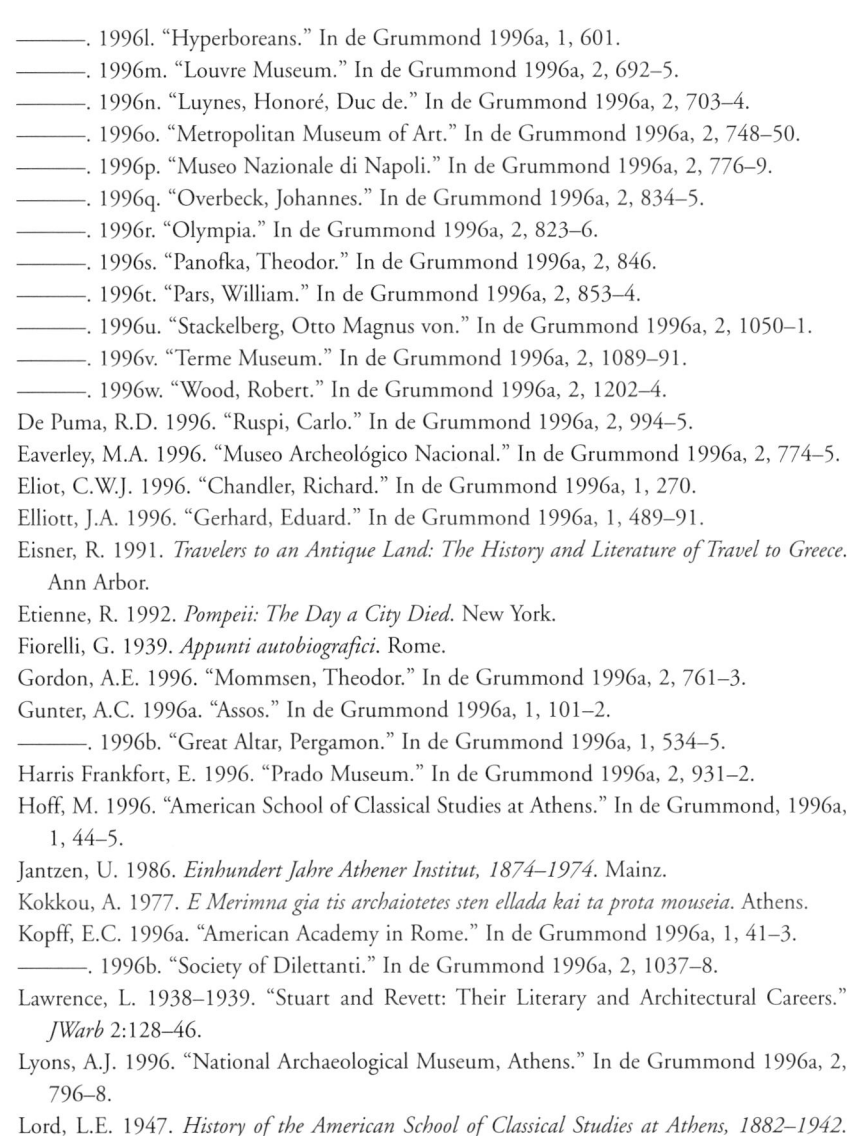

———. 1996l. "Hyperboreans." In de Grummond 1996a, 1, 601.
———. 1996m. "Louvre Museum." In de Grummond 1996a, 2, 692–5.
———. 1996n. "Luynes, Honoré, Duc de." In de Grummond 1996a, 2, 703–4.
———. 1996o. "Metropolitan Museum of Art." In de Grummond 1996a, 2, 748–50.
———. 1996p. "Museo Nazionale di Napoli." In de Grummond 1996a, 2, 776–9.
———. 1996q. "Overbeck, Johannes." In de Grummond 1996a, 2, 834–5.
———. 1996r. "Olympia." In de Grummond 1996a, 2, 823–6.
———. 1996s. "Panofka, Theodor." In de Grummond 1996a, 2, 846.
———. 1996t. "Pars, William." In de Grummond 1996a, 2, 853–4.
———. 1996u. "Stackelberg, Otto Magnus von." In de Grummond 1996a, 2, 1050–1.
———. 1996v. "Terme Museum." In de Grummond 1996a, 2, 1089–91.
———. 1996w. "Wood, Robert." In de Grummond 1996a, 2, 1202–4.
De Puma, R.D. 1996. "Ruspi, Carlo." In de Grummond 1996a, 2, 994–5.
Eaverley, M.A. 1996. "Museo Archeológico Nacional." In de Grummond 1996a, 2, 774–5.
Eliot, C.W.J. 1996. "Chandler, Richard." In de Grummond 1996a, 1, 270.
Elliott, J.A. 1996. "Gerhard, Eduard." In de Grummond 1996a, 1, 489–91.
Eisner, R. 1991. *Travelers to an Antique Land: The History and Literature of Travel to Greece.* Ann Arbor.
Etienne, R. 1992. *Pompeii: The Day a City Died.* New York.
Fiorelli, G. 1939. *Appunti autobiografici.* Rome.
Gordon, A.E. 1996. "Mommsen, Theodor." In de Grummond 1996a, 2, 761–3.
Gunter, A.C. 1996a. "Assos." In de Grummond 1996a, 1, 101–2.
———. 1996b. "Great Altar, Pergamon." In de Grummond 1996a, 1, 534–5.
Harris Frankfort, E. 1996. "Prado Museum." In de Grummond 1996a, 2, 931–2.
Hoff, M. 1996. "American School of Classical Studies at Athens." In de Grummond, 1996a, 1, 44–5.
Jantzen, U. 1986. *Einhundert Jahre Athener Institut, 1874–1974.* Mainz.
Kokkou, A. 1977. *E Merimna gia tis archaiotetes sten ellada kai ta prota mouseia.* Athens.
Kopff, E.C. 1996a. "American Academy in Rome." In de Grummond 1996a, 1, 41–3.
———. 1996b. "Society of Dilettanti." In de Grummond 1996a, 2, 1037–8.
Lawrence, L. 1938–1939. "Stuart and Revett: Their Literary and Architectural Careers." *JWarb* 2:128–46.
Lyons, A.J. 1996. "National Archaeological Museum, Athens." In de Grummond 1996a, 2, 796–8.
Lord, L.E. 1947. *History of the American School of Classical Studies at Athens, 1882–1942.* Cambridge, Mass.
Marchand, S.L. 1996. *Down from Olympus: Archaeology and Philhellenism in Germany, 1750–1970.* Princeton.
McFadden, E. 1971. *The Glitter and the Gold.* New York.
Mejer, J. 1996. "Thorvaldsen, Bertel." In de Grummond 1996a, 2, 1100–2.
Meritt, L.S. 1984. *History of the American School of Classical Studies at Athens, 1939–1980.* Princeton: Princeton University Press.
Michaelis, A. 1879. *Geschichte des Deutschen Archäologisches Instituts 1829–1879.* Berlin.

Morris, S.P. 1996. "Aigina." In de Grummond 1996a, 1, 12–4.
Parslow, C. 1995. *Rediscovering Antiquity: Karl Weber and the Excavation of Herculaneum, Pompeii, and Stabiae*. Cambridge.
Petrakis, S.L. 1996. "Expédition scientifique de Morée." In de Grummond 1996a, 1, 420–1.
Petrakos, V. 1987. *He en Athenais Archaiologike Hetaireia: he historia ton 150 chronon tes, 1837–1987*. Athens.
Picard, C. 1948. "L'oeuvre de l'École française d'Athènes." *RHist* 199:1–21.
Ramage, N.H. 1990. "Sir William Hamilton as Collector, Exporter, and Dealer: The Acquisition and Dispersal of his Collections." *AJA* 94:469–80.
———. 1992. "Goods, Graves and Scholars: 18th-Century Archaeologists in Britain and Italy." *AJA* 96:653–61.
La redécouverte de Delphes. 1992. Paris
Richardson, L. jr. 1996a. "Fiorelli, Giuseppe." In de Grummond 1996a, 1, 441–2.
———. 1996b. "French School at Rome." In de Grummond 1996a, 1, 470–1.
———. 1996c. "German Archaeological Institute, Rome." In de Grummond 1996a, 1, 492–4.
———. 1996d. "Herculaneum." In de Grummond 1996a, 1, 584–6.
———. 1996e. "Instituto di Corrispondenza Archeologico." In de Grummond 1996a, 1, 608–10.
———. 1996f. "Pompeii." In de Grummond 1996a, 2, 908–14.
Ridgway, F.R.S. 1996. "Villa Giulia." In de Grummond 1996a, 2, 1167–8.
Ridley, R.T. 1992. *The Eagle and the Spade: The Archaeology of Rome during the Napoleonic Era, 1809–1814*. Cambridge.
———. 1996a. "Commissario dell'Antichità." In de Grummond 1996a, 1, 319–20.
———. 1996b. "Fea, Carlo." In de Grummond 1996a, 1, 435–7.
———. 1996c. "Napoleon Bonaparte." In de Grummond 1996a, 2, 792–4.
Rowe, P. 1996a. "Stuart, James." In de Grummond 1996a, 2, 1062–3.
———. 1996b. "Revett, Nicholas." In de Grummond 1996a, 2, 952–3.
Schweiger, I.A. 1996. "Ludwig I." In de Grummond 1996a, 2, 700–1.
Sheftel, P.S. 1979. "The Archaeological Institute of America, 1879–1979: A Centennial Review." *AJA* 83:3–17.
———. 1996. "Archaeological Institute of America." In de Grummond 1996a, 1, 61–3.
Stiebing, W.H. 1993. *Uncovering the Past: A History of Archaeology*. Oxford.
Stoneman, R. 1987. *Land of Lost Gods: The Search for Classical Greece*. Norman, Okla.
Teviotdale, E.C. 1996a. "Berlin." In de Grummond 1996a, 1, 152–5.
———. 1996b. "Glyptothek." In de Grummond 1996a, 1, 513–5.
Traill, D.A. 1995. *Schliemann of Troy: Treasure and Deceit*. New York.
———. 1996. "Cesnola, Luigi Palma di." In de Grummond 1996a, 2, 267–8.
Tsigakou, F.-M. 1981. *The Rediscovery of Greece: Travellers and Painters of the Romantic Era*. London.
Valentine, L., and A. Valentine. 1973. *The American Academy in Rome, 1894–1969*. Charlottesville.
Vanderbilt, K. 1959. *Charles Eliot Norton: Apostle of Culture in a Democracy*. Cambridge, Mass.

Vickers, M. 1996. "Cockerell, Charles Robert." In de Grummond 1996a, 1, 295–6.
Wasano, J.K. 1996. "Museum of Fine Arts, Boston." In de Grummond 1996a, 2, 779–81.
Whitehill, W.M. 1970. *The Museum of Fine Arts, Boston: A Centennial History.* Cambridge, Mass.
Wickert, L. 1959–1980. *Theodor Mommsen, Eine Biographie, 1–4.* Frankfurt.
———. 1979. *Beiträge zur Geschichte des Deutschen Archäologischen Instituts von 1879 bis 1929.* Mainz.
Yegül, F. 1991. *Gentlemen of Instinct and Breeding: Architecture at the American Academy in Rome, 1894–1969.* New York.

NOTES

[1] This article, dealing with the historical and intellectual background for the founding of the AIA, does not attempt to break new ground by utilizing the archives of the organization, as do many of the contributions to this volume. Instead, it is intended to synthesize accepted historical data to establish the climate in which the AIA originated. Most of the general topics and specific individuals and events referred to in this article may be found discussed, with bibliography, under the appropriate headings in de Grummond (1996a). Many of these entries will be indicated in the parenthetical notes, though by no means can all relevant articles be cited comfortably here.

[2] On early travelers to Greece in general, see Constantine 1984; Eisner 1991; Stoneman 1987; Tsigakou 1981.

[3] An excellent review of the intellectual background for the activities of the Germans in Italy during this period may be found in Marchand 1996, 51–65.

[4] Schliemann's tendencies to fabricate aspects of his life and his discoveries have been documented by Traill (1995) and Allen (1999). Well known are such acts as asserting that his wife was at Troy at the time of the discovery of the Treasure (she was actually in Athens), and including in the Treasure a number of items that had already been drawn and prepared for publication before the discovery (Traill 1995, 111–2, 120).

— 2 —

Charles Eliot Norton and the Archaeological Institute of America

◈

Elizabeth Lyding Will

Two previous studies of events surrounding Charles Eliot Norton's (1827–1908) founding of the Archaeological Institute of America have appeared in Institute publications: Anne V. Dort's brief but perceptive account in the 1954 *Archaeology* (Dort 1954) and the more detailed article by Phoebe Sherman Sheftel in the *American Journal of Archaeology* for 1979, the year of the AIA centennial (Sheftel 1979). Sheftel's article, in particular, left little to be said in its summary of the actual founding and of the chief events of the Institute's subsequent history (fig. 2.1), but over 20 years have passed since its publication. Interest in and knowledge about Norton's career have increased, particularly in recent years, and it seems appropriate to look again at Norton's founding of the Institute and at how he imparted to the organization his own unique energy, spirit, and outlook.[1] The very uniqueness of the AIA among the learned societies of America is arguably an extension of Norton's rare versatility. All of his accomplishments, in fact, are stamped with his many-faceted personality, which was seen in various lights in his own time and continues to be discussed and debated energetically today, positively and negatively, more than 90 years after his death in 1908. In taking stock of the AIA at the beginning of the 21st century and in trying to understand it more clearly, it seems useful to look at Charles Eliot Norton the person, both as he was viewed in his own time and also as he is remembered today.[2]

Fig. 2.1. Charles Eliot Norton in later life. (Courtesy of Arnold D. Jones).

Norton's fame and influence in his own time were so great that he became a household word. In 1892, Edwin Arlington Robinson (1869–1935) called him "by all odds the greatest man in America" (Townsend 1996, 881 and n. 5; cf. Workman 1989, 578; Turner 1999, 319, 354, 369, etc.). One must interpret Robinson's words in the light of Boston's status at the time as the intellectual and cultural center of America. Green (1966, 123) refers to Norton and his uncle, George Ticknor (1791–1871), as "masters of ceremonies of [Boston's] cultural life, issuing the invitations, effecting the introductions, determining the decorum, decreeing the activities." Norton's fame has diminished, fluctuated, and changed in character with the passage of time, probably in part because the very diversity of his interests makes it difficult to remember him as we remember certain of his numerous friends and students for their more focused creative accomplishments: Henry Wadsworth Longfellow (1807–1882) for poetry, and James Russell Lowell (1819–1891) for poetry and essays; John Ruskin (1819–1900) and Matthew Arnold (1822–1888) for criticism; Thomas Carlyle (1795–1881) for history and essays; Henry James (1843–1916), William Dean Howells (1837–1920), and Charles Dickens (1812–1870) for novels; William James (1842–1910) for psychology and philosophy; Charles Darwin (1809–1882) for the theory of evolution; Frederick Law Olmsted (1822–1903) for landscape design; Isabella Stewart Gardner (1840–1924) for a museum. All those individuals were indebted to Norton for support and advice, but what they created is easier to analyze and understand than is the range of Norton's many creations. One can hold a printed poem or novel or scientific or critical treatise in one's hands. One can look at it. One can enter a museum. Norton was creative, too, but in dozens of directions, many of them somewhat intangible. He did not, however, spread himself thin. What he did was done thoroughly and precisely, and he remained closely involved with his creations, as he did with the AIA, to the very end. In spite of being at times a semi-invalid, even from childhood,[3] he was possessed of great strength and energy and strong commitment to the causes important to him. He saw to them all. Organizer, founder, innovator, disseminator, grassroots activist, master of what one today calls "outreach," he acted on his concerns, and his position of intellectual and cultural preeminence contributed materially to the success of his undertakings. Though in some ways limited by the rather provincial assumptions of the Boston Brahmin establishment to which he belonged, Norton shared with contemporary Modernists an interest in expanding American epistemological horizons. In the same spirit, he was also producing authoritative scholarship on literature and architectural history; editing collections of letters; co-founding or co-editing journals like *The North American Review, The Nation,* and *The Atlantic Monthly;* and contributing to other journals. Norton's bibliography (the books, articles, and reviews listed by decades in small print) consumes 10 pages in Vanderbilt's 1959 biography and almost 14 pages in Turner's 1999 list. His fine arts courses at Harvard enrolled hundreds and were hugely successful. Somehow Norton also served devotedly as the single father of six children and the center of a close circle of famous friends in this country and abroad. Carlyle referred to him once as "the most human" of his friends. Ruskin, though eight years his senior, called him "my first real tutor."

Norton's fame is still alive today, not only as founder of the AIA, but disseminated among the various areas in which he was active. In Ashfield, Massachusetts, his summer home (fig. 2.2), he is remembered with pride as co-founder, with George William Curtis (1824–1892), of the famous Ashfield Dinners, inaugurated in 1879, the same year in which the AIA was founded (Vanderbilt 1959, 196–9; Gulick and Gulick 1990, passim). He is also remembered as founder of the Dante Society of

Fig. 2.2. Norton's summer home in Ashfield, "The Locusts," as it looks today. (Photo by E.L. Will)

America (1881) and the first president (1897) of the Boston Society of Arts and Crafts. In the area of scholarship, his name is mentioned very frequently in recent publications. A current writer on John Donne remembers Norton as "America's first Donne scholar" (Haskin 1989, 871). In his time, he was also regarded as "America's foremost Dante scholar" (Haskin 1989, 882). Workman (1989, 575) wrote, "Dante scholarship, as distinct from interest, begins with Norton." In 1959, Vanderbilt (p. 173) says of his prose translation of the Divine Comedy, "It remains today our standard prose version." Medievalists praise the important role he played in the development of medievalism in America (Workman 1989, 585). His chief scholarly work, published in 1880, *Historical Studies of Church Building in the Middle Ages: Venice, Siena, Florence* is still praised (Duffy 1996, 102). Scholars still discuss Norton's editions of his letters from Ruskin (Spear 1982, passim; Workman 1989, 582–4) and of Carlyle's correspondence (Haskin 1989, 884–5). They also regularly mention him still as a sponsor and advisor of Henry James (Townsend 1996, 82) and of Isabella Stewart Gardner (Shand-Tucci 1997, 38–9). He is still remembered as one of Harvard's most popular and influential professors (Russo 1990, 304; Cohn 1993, 33; Townsend 1996, 81; Turner 1999, 375–7, passim) and as the founder there of the first Fine Arts department in the country. Each of the areas in which he was influential thinks of him in connection with itself rather than as part of a spectrum of other interests, though there is no doubt that Norton's personal pride in the AIA and his involvement in its affairs to the end of his life give that accomplishment a special aura that sets it apart from many of his other achievements. In reviewing scholarship on Norton, even in fields not related to archaeology, one is surprised by how often his connection with archaeology and his founding of the Institute are mentioned (Vanderbilt 1959, 147–8; Green 1966, 135; Workman 1989, 576; Duffy 1996, 102, to cite four references from four decades of the last half of this century, and Turner 1999 is a treasury of references to the early history of the AIA).

Norton's prestige must have been of great importance to the success of the AIA in its early years. His anticipation, also, of problems the organization might and did face in the future helped to set the Institute on a firm foundation.[4] In analyzing Norton's effect in other respects on the AIA, one should think first of his stated goals in founding the Institute. Quoting his words in *AJA* 7 (1903), 351: "In April, 1879, a circular was issued stating that it was proposed to establish a society for the purpose of furthering and directing archaeological investigation and research . . . This circular had been drawn up by me, and I had obtained for it the signatures of eleven persons representing the scholarship, the intelligence, and the wealth of our community. The chief motive which led me to undertake this task was the hope that, by the establishment of such a society, the interests of classical scholarship in America might be advanced, and especially that it might lead to the foundation of a school of classical studies in Athens." Norton had been aware of archaeology for many years. There had been his trip to the site of Mahabalipuram in India in 1849 (Turner 1999, 71). His fifth publication, in fact, "Ancient Monuments in America," a long review article in the 1849 *North American Review,* makes clear his belief that only through archaeology can "the dark subject of the origin of American civilization" be clarified.[5] In addition, he had always been impressed and moved by the civilization of ancient Greece. The courses he offered at Harvard in art history and architectural history had intensified that interest. He felt that exposing Americans to the culture of Greece, a first order of business for the new Institute through the founding of a school of classical studies in Athens, would help to arrest the downward spiral toward materialism and tastelessness that he saw around him in his native country (Winterer, this volume; Turner 1999, 298, refers to the School in Athens as "the first American institute in a humanistic field"). An agnostic, he found in art and architecture a substitute for religion. Turner (1985, 252) calls Norton and Matthew Arnold "orthodox priests" of the "Religion of Culture," preaching "art as a means of moral as well as spiritual grace." Norton's was almost a missionary zeal. His propensity for outreach was inherent in his proposal to form the AIA. It was outreach toward Greece, and outreach toward America. The unique structure he gave the AIA, including the School in Athens, the local societies of the AIA, its mixture of lay and professional members, his support of the founding of the *AJA,* the initially informal lecture program: these were ways in which Norton not only imbued the AIA with an almost messianic purpose but also sought to give reality to his feeling that America must strive to rediscover its European cultural roots. Many of his contemporaries, a century after the American Revolution, had felt culturally rootless and had withdrawn to Europe or to a mythical West. They were looking for an alternative to what some saw as a "barbaric America." Norton, too, had gone to Europe

Fig. 2.3. Norton (right), and George William Curtis ca. 1880. (Courtesy of Arnold D. Jones)

with his family, but his wife's death in Germany in 1872 after the birth of their sixth child, Richard, brought him to his senses. Abetted by his inherited Puritanical conscience and the scholarly Unitarianism in his background (his father, Andrews Norton, was called the "Unitarian Pope" by Carlyle: Brooks 1936, 39), he had decided to return home to fight for higher intellectual and moral standards, as well as for order in his own life. The formation of the Fine Arts Department at Harvard and the structure Norton gave to the AIA, a structure that survives intact today, were ways in which he gave substance to that decision, a substance that grew out of and reflected his own many-sidedness.[6]

The famed Ashfield Dinners, founded three months after the AIA, were a similar bugle call to Americans. Norton and his friend George William Curtis, political editor of *Harper's Weekly* (fig. 2.3), co-founded the Ashfield Dinners to benefit Sanderson Academy, which still exists in the village. These dinners drew large audiences and national attention in the press. They became an annual event, attracting speakers such as Booker T. Washington

(1856–1915), James Russell Lowell, and William Dean Howells. Guests came from a wide area. Topics were social, political, and educational. Sumptuous food and lively band music provided a change of pace (Vanderbilt 1959, 196–9; Fessenden unpublished tape, 1985; Gulick and Gulick 1990, passim). The occasions were rather like AIA local societies writ large and had a similar, almost apostolic purpose. Ostensibly the dinners benefited the Academy, but they had the goal also of raising America's consciousness about contemporary issues, just as the AIA and the School in Athens were designed as means of increasing American awareness of the past. Norton's penchant for reforming American ideals and standards as he saw them had increased, especially after the deaths of his more moderate friends, Lowell in 1891 and Curtis in 1892. He was particularly critical of imperialism and of the Spanish-American War, and his 1898 and 1899 speeches at Ashfield on those topics ultimately played a part in the demise of the dinners, which ended in 1903 (Gulick and Gulick 1990, 18–21; cf. Norton and Howe, 1913, 455–7; Fessenden unpublished tape, 1985).

In the early 1880s, Norton joined his old friend, Frederick Law Olmsted, in a difficult but ultimately successful ecological struggle to preserve Niagara Falls from industrial development. Cohn comments (1993, 24): "Norton understood the symbolic value of Niagara as the equivalent of history—nature's analogue of the ruin—for the United States in the nineteenth century." Later on the same page, she quotes from his letter to Olmsted, "The real value of the Falls is moral not material . . . their beauty is not a mere show for the eyes." Such feelings are clearly in line with Norton's moral goals in founding the AIA and in teaching art and architectural history.[7]

After Norton's death, his fame, as we have noted, diminished or underwent change. By the middle of the century, Van Wyck Brooks, in two popular books, *The Flowering of New England* (1936) and *New England Indian Summer* (1950), presented a somewhat negative view of Norton, criticizing him as a "Jeremiah." "To lay down the law was his nature" (Brooks 1950, 250–1). Vanderbilt 1959, 227–8, followed by Workman 1989, 579–80 (an essay review of Bradley and Ousby's 1987 edition of the Ruskin/Norton correspondence), challenges this caricature of Norton, and it is gratifying to note that most of the scholarly studies produced during the last 30 years have sought, as we have tried to suggest, to restore a balanced evaluation of Norton's contributions to American

Fig. 2.4. Norton's home, "Shady Hill," in Cambridge. It was razed in 1960, according to Marshall, n.d., p. 21. (Courtesy of Arnold D. Jones)

scholarship and to its cultural and intellectual history. One hopes that these studies will lead to a fuller understanding of Norton. Hostility toward Norton is out of step with current scholarship, but it still occasionally gets into print. For example, W.M. Calder III (1996) first makes the misstatement that, soon after founding the AIA, Norton "sponsored the founding of the American Academy in Rome" (by which Calder must mean the American School of Classical Studies at Athens, which opened in 1882; the American School of Classical Studies at Rome, out of which the American Academy in Rome later grew, was founded in 1895. See also n. 8 below). Calder then concludes his entry with this statement: "A dilettante, unashamedly subjective, never a scholar, Norton exerted wide, if sometimes deleterious, influence even outside his discipline. He preferred European travel and study over specialist training. His extensive publications are not read today by scholars." We have commented, however, on Norton's continuing reputation as a major scholar of Dante, Donne, and Medieval architecture, and we have noted the frequent references to his work in current scholarship. By "deleterious influence even outside his discipline," Calder perhaps has in mind Norton's outspoken hostility to the Spanish-American War and the criticism he incurred as a result. The

Charles Eliot Norton and the Archaeological Institute of America   57

justification for that war is, however, still a matter of lively discussion and debate among historians. In any case, Turner's new biography of Norton should lay to rest permanently the more persistent exaggerations, and even untruths, that have become part of the Norton mythology. It will both increase interest in Norton and contribute materially to an accurate perception of him.

By seeking to understand Norton as objectively as possible, we in the AIA can hope to reach a better comprehension of the Institute's past, its present, and its future. We have not perhaps been so aware as we might have been of the distinctive position our organization holds among American learned societies and of the debt we owe our founder for our uniqueness and success. Norton's influence on his times, his individuality, the astuteness with which he structured the Institute, and not least his many years of devotion to it gave great strength to the AIA and to the entire discipline of archaeology, both in North America and throughout the world.[8]

Fig. 2.5. The Norton family plot in Mount Auburn Cemetery, on the edge of Cambridge. The gravestone of Norton and his wife, born Susan Ridley Sedgwick (1838–1872), and of their son, Eliot (1863–1933), is second from the left. The gravestone of Norton's father, Andrews Norton (1786–1853), and his mother, born Catherine Eliot (1793–1839), and of other family members is to the rear. (Photo by E.L. Will)

REFERENCES

Bradley, J.L., and I. Ousby, eds. 1987. *The Correspondence of John Ruskin and Charles Eliot Norton.* Cambridge.
Brill, B. 1987. "My Dear Mr. Norton." *The Gaskell Society Journal* Summer:30–40.
Brooks, Van W. 1936. *The Flowering of New England, 1815–1865.* New York.
———. 1950. *New England Indian Summer.* New York.
Calder, W.M., III. 1996. "Norton, Charles Eliot." In de Grummond 1996, 2, 812.
Cohn, M.B. 1993. "Turner, Ruskin, Norton, Winthrop." *Harvard University Art Museums Bulletin* 2:9–86.
de Grummond, N.T., ed. 1996. *An Encyclopedia of the History of Classical Archaeology.* London and Westport.
Dort, A.V. 1954. "The Archaeological Institute of America: Early Days." *Archaeology* 7:195–201.
Duffy, T.P. 1996. "The Gender of Letters: Charles Eliot Norton and the Decline of the Amateur Intellectual Tradition." *New England Quarterly* 69:91–109.
Dyson, S.L. 1998. "Dubious Deals." *Archaeology* 51:6.
Emerson, E.W., and W.F. Harris. 1912. *Charles Eliot Norton: Two Addresses.* Boston.
Fasanelli, J.A. 1967. "Charles Eliot Norton and His Guides: A Study of his Sources." *Journal of Aesthetics and Art Criticism* 26:251–8.
Fessenden, R. 1985. "Academy Dinners and National Politics." Unpublished tape, lecture presented to the Ashfield Historical Society.
Green, M. 1966. *The Problem of Boston: Some Readings in Cultural History.* New York: W.W. Norton.
Gulick, B., and E. Gulick. 1990. *Charles Eliot Norton and the Ashfield Dinners, 1879–1903.* Ashfield.
Haskin, D. 1989. "New Historical Contexts for Appraising the Donne Revival from A.B. Grosart to Charles Eliot Norton." *English Literary History* 56:869–95.
Kelsey, F.W. 1919. "Richard Norton." *Art and Archaeology* 8:329–35.
Lutz, T. 1991. *American Nervousness 1903.* Ithaca.
Marshall, E.S. undated but after 1960. Biographical Sketch of the Life of Elizabeth Gaskell Norton. Unpublished.
Norton, C.E. 1903. "The Founding of the School at Athens." *AJA* 7:351–6.
———. 1849. "Ancient Monuments in America." *North American Review* 68:466–96.
Norton, S., and M.A. DeWolfe Howe. 1913. *Letters of Charles Eliot Norton with Biographical Comment.* Boston.
Russo, J.P. 1990. "The Harvard Italophiles: Longfellow, Lowell, and Norton." In *L'esilio romantico: forme di un conflitto,* edited by J. Cheyne and L. Crisafulli Jones, 303–24. Bari.
Rybczynski, W. 1999. *A Clearing in the Distance: Frederick Law Olmsted and America in the Nineteenth Century.* New York.
Shand-Tucci, D. 1997. *The Art of Scandal: The Life and Times of Isabella Stewart Gardner.* New York.

Sheftel, P.S. 1979. "The Archaeological Institute of America, 1879–1979: A Centennial Review." *AJA* 83:3–17.

Spear, J.L. 1982. "'My darling Charles': Selections from the Ruskin-Norton Correspondence." In *The Ruskin Polygon,* edited by J.D. Hunt and F.M. Holland, 236–79. Manchester.

SPNEA. 1990. "The Norton Bequest." *SPNEA* 52 (Fall):1–2, 7–8.

Townsend, K. 1996. *Manhood at Harvard.* New York.

Turner, J. 1985. *Without God, Without Creed: The Origins of Unbelief in America.* Baltimore.

———. 1999. *The Liberal Education of Charles Eliot Norton.* Baltimore: Johns Hopkins University Press.

Vanderbilt, K. 1959. *Charles Eliot Norton: Apostle of Culture in a Democracy.* Cambridge, Mass.

Wellek, R., and A. Warren. 1956. *Theory of Literature.* New York.

Workman, L.J. 1989. "My First Real Tutor: John Ruskin and Charles Eliot Norton." *New England Quarterly* 62:572–86.

NOTES

[1] I would like to thank Mr. Arnold D. Jones of Ashfield, Massachusetts, a great-grandson of Professor Norton, for his kindness in discussing the Norton family with me, in allowing me to read letters and make copies of several photographs in his collection, and in giving me a copy of Esther S. Marshall's unpublished *Biographical Sketch of the Life of Elizabeth Gaskell Norton (*Marshall*,* unpublished and undated*).* Mr. Jones still lives in "Lilliput Lodge," the Ashfield house Norton intended for Lowell, who died before he could occupy it. Professor Barbara E. Will has also been of great help in providing me with references to many of the books and articles about Norton, or in which Norton is mentioned, that have been published during the last 30 years. I would also like to thank Mrs. Harriet Pike of Ashfield, who arranged for me to meet Arnold Jones and gave me a tape of a lecture, "Academy Dinners and National Politics," delivered by Russell Fessenden (whose parents were Ashfield neighbors of Norton) to the Ashfield Historical Society in 1985. I also thank the late Professor Homer A. Thompson, and Professors Helen H. Bacon, Phyllis W. Lehmann, and Katherine Geffcken for sharing with me their insights on Charles Eliot Norton and Richard Norton, and I am grateful to Professor Frederic Will, Dr. Linda Benson, and Dr. Diana Wolfe Larkin for valuable suggestions. I also thank Professor Susan Heuck Allen for her editorial patience and consideration. Last but by no means least, I had the good fortune to correspond and talk with Professor James Turner, whose extensive biography of Norton, *The Liberal Education of Charles Eliot Norton,* was published by the Johns Hopkins University Press in late 1999. Professor Turner, as I mention in the text, was gracious enough to read this chapter and to clarify for me, from his vast knowledge of Norton, some matters about which I was unsure. After his book's appearance, the editor of this chapter kindly permitted me to incorporate a few references to the book into the chapter.

[2] In the process, however, we need to recognize that Norton himself would have opposed

our effort to see him in what he created. He espoused, and may have been partly responsible for the origin of, the concept often called the "biographical fallacy," a cornerstone of the New Criticism that reached its height in the middle of the 20th century, long after his day. For the classic mid-century view of biographical interpretation of literary and artistic creations, see Wellek and Warren 1956, esp. ch. 7. Norton's attitudes are well summarized by Haskin 1989, 870–1, 885–7. (Haskin also discusses (p. 890) Norton's possible influence in this respect on his distant cousin, T.S. Eliot.) Privacy was of great importance to Norton. Cf. Spear (1982, passim) on his suppression, in his 1904 edition of Ruskin's letters to him, of about a third of the letters. See also Workman 1989, esp. 582–4. Cf. Brill 1987, 39–40, on the topic of Norton's correspondence with the British writer, Elizabeth Gaskell (1810–1865). What Spear calls Norton's "acute sense of propriety" was inherited by his daughter, Sara (1864–1922), whose edition of his letters (Norton and Howe 1913) reflects family discretion. His daughter Elizabeth (1866–1957) is described by her biographer as reluctant to discuss her father's friends and unwilling to talk about her childhood (Marshall, unpublished and undated, 15).

[3] He is identified, for example, as "a neurasthenic Bostonian" in a recent book on American nervousness (Lutz 1991, 176). On Norton's neurasthenia, cf. also Duffy (1996, 94–5) and Turner (1999, 136).

[4] Emerson and Harris 1912, 51–2. Harris adds, "He met every situation with a sane radicalism; the dominant note was ever: 'We want nothing but the best.' The best always costs a great deal of money, but where the treasury was empty, he still insisted, with far-seeing courage, on the best."

[5] Thirty years later, however, shortly after the founding of the Institute, during what became a long controversy between members who backed American archaeology and those who supported work in classical lands, Norton, though favoring classical archaeology, sought to be impartial and served as a mediator between the two groups, both of which he felt the AIA should support. I am very grateful to Norton's biographer, Professor James Turner (above, n. 1), for explaining Norton's position to me; cf. Turner 1999, 286. It was not until 1907 that the Institute established the School of American Archaeology in Santa Fe. (For a different view of Norton's position in the controversy, see Sheftel 1979, 5–6, 11–2).

[6] Duffy (1996, 99) notes that Norton "drew both strength and comfort from the gender ambiguity of the antebellum amateur intellectual tradition." Before the Civil War, the purely masculine literary tradition of the 18th century separated into two different spheres, a practical, political, "masculine" sphere, and a sympathetic, socially aware, "feminine" sphere. Norton identified with both groups before the war. On the socially aware side, he had been horrified, on a visit to Charleston in 1855, by his observation of the evils of slavery: Turner 1999, 123–4. He was later to keep photographs of Lincoln and John Brown on the mantel of his home in Ashfield: Brooks 1936, 454. With the end of the Civil War, however, Duffy suggests that Norton developed a "new masculinist orientation." Cf. Townsend 1996, 82. This attitude, Duffy feels, carried over into Norton's scholarship, which became less imaginative and more structured and orderly. "Order," Duffy says (p. 102), "was also the mission of the Archaeological Institute of America, an organization Norton founded to regularize classical scholarship." Norton's motives in founding

the AIA were undoubtedly somewhat more complicated than is generally assumed. This is perhaps an appropriate place to mention that Dort (1954, 195) explicitly says at the beginning of her brief history of the AIA: "These two objectives, to secure for America its due share in the field work in the lands of antiquity, and to bring great works of Classical art to this country, were clearly the primary motives in Professor Norton's mind." Spear (1982, 258–9) in discussing letters from Ruskin to Norton, comments: "Norton had an open commission from Ruskin to buy antiquities while in the south of Italy, and his surviving letters to Ruskin during 1871 record a string of purchases, including: 'thirty small Greek vases, cups, etc., from Corfu or Samos, but one from Athens,— . . . and a lovely little Greek statue found in a Temple of Neptune . . . of a wingless Fortune, standing on a globe' (29 March 1871)." Professor James Turner, however, whose biography of Norton has just appeared (see footnote 1 above), assures me that he has read every extant piece of Norton's correspondence and that, notwithstanding the Norton mythology to the contrary, there is no written evidence that Norton was himself a collector of antiquities or that he was engaged in the antiquities trade. He says it is true that Norton made the 1871 trip to southern Italy, during which he collected for Ruskin the objects just mentioned. He also advised Isabella Stewart Gardner, for example, about her collection of paintings, manuscripts, and books. But he was not a "collector of antiquities." Dyson (1998, 6) also denies that Norton engaged in the acquisition of antiquities.

[7] For a recent discussion of Norton's relationship with Olmsted, see Rybczynski 1999.

[8] Sara Norton points out in her edition of his letters (Norton and Howe 1913, 99) that while he lived there was a feeling "that Norton was himself the Institute," which was on occasion referred to as the "Archaeological Institute of Shady Hill," the name of the Norton home in Cambridge (fig. 2.4). And it is appropriate to add here that archaeology and the Institute were also a family matter for Norton. His oldest son, Eliot (1863–1932), who later became a prominent lawyer in New York City and also wrote a book about one of his father's heroes, Abraham Lincoln, took part in the AIA's first expedition to Assos in 1881. His youngest son, Richard (1872–1918), studied at the American School of Classical Studies at Athens and, among other publications, contributed a chapter to Charles Waldstein/Walston's *Argive Heraeum*. From 1899 to 1907, to his father's great pride, Richard Norton was Director of the American School of Classical Studies at Rome, which had been founded by the AIA in 1895 and later became part of the American Academy in Rome. Richard Norton also directed the excavations at Cyrene in 1910–1911 under the auspices of the AIA and the Boston Museum of Fine Arts. In 1914, he published *Bernini and Other Studies in the History of Art*. His career was cut short in 1918, when, at the age of 46, he died of an infection in France during the First World War. Kelsey 1919 gives further details. He is buried with his father and mother, his siblings, and his paternal grandparents in an elegantly simple family plot in Mount Auburn Cemetery, on the edge of Cambridge (Fig. 2.5). Richard's only child, Susan (1902–1989), who died in Washington D.C., left most of her possessions to the Society for the Preservation of New England Antiquities (SPNEA) in Boston. The bequest included many personal objects that had once belonged to her grandfather, Charles Eliot Norton (*SPNEA* 1990, passim).

— 3 —

"Americans in the East":[1] Francis Henry Bacon, Joseph Thacher Clarke, and the AIA at Assos

Susan Heuck Allen

In 1878 Charles Eliot Norton, eager for the United States to stake its claim to a major archaeological site in the Mediterranean, watched as European powers scrambled to plant their flags at ancient sites in Greece and Turkey. He needed reconnaissance to determine the most appropriate site for America's first fieldwork in classical archaeology, yet there were no senior classical archaeologists in America to whom Norton might entrust such a critical venture. For this mission he ultimately decided to support two young architects, Joseph Thacher Clarke (1856–1920) and Francis Henry Bacon (1856–1940). Norton viewed Clarke as a worthy pioneer, for he had been educated in Munich, then a major training ground for Americans in search of advanced education in classical archaeology. That Clarke had studied architecture, not archaeology or classics, at the Munich Polytechnic made little difference since he had developed an interest in ancient Greek architecture through the inspiration of art professor Franz von Reber (1834–1919) and gained firsthand experience of the architectural sculptures of the Temple of Aphaia on Aigina at the Glyptothek in Munich (Austin 1942, 1–2). In 1876 Clarke returned to Boston to practice architecture. With "elements of scholarliness in his makeup far in advance of his contemporaries . . . great things were predicted of him . . . in the way of learning and scholarship" (Austin 1942, 1). Norton was impressed by his "assurance and exhibition of erudition," in large part the result of his German education, and he quickly made Clarke his protégé.

Bacon had some field experience from helping his father survey the Boston-Maine Railroad Extension in his late teens,[2] and also had studied architecture at the Institute of Technology (MIT) with William Robert Ware (1832–1915), vice president of the Boston Society of Architects where Clarke was a junior member.[3] By 1877, at age 21, Bacon was working as a draftsman in New York, "moonlighting" for McKim, Mead, and Bigelow. Ware described him as a gentleman of "fine taste and generosity of appreciation," and probably introduced him to both Clarke and Norton (Ware to CEN, 10 September 1880, AIA Archives, box 6.2). The young men's talents were complementary: Bacon was an impeccable draftsman and experienced field surveyor, while Clarke exuded confidence and had a synthetic mind and scholarly ambitions. Both sought adventure, though neither had much money.

With Norton's strong support, Clarke appealed to the Society of Architects on 8 February 1878 for financial aid "to write a history of Doric Architecture" (Bacon to Moran; Austin 1942, 2–3, 15). Although Clarke's "youthful dogmatism and attempted show of knowledge" did not impress the membership, Ware's mentor and president of the Society, Edward Clarke Cabot (1818–1901) (*Dictionary of American Biography*, 3, 394), wished to "know more of the principles underlying the development of Greek Architectural forms" in order to inform, correct, and inspire contemporary Neo-Classical practitioners (Cabot to CEN, 20 March 1884, AIA Archives, box 3). Thus, the Society awarded Clarke a matching grant to cover part of the expenses for a research trip to study monuments of the Doric style in Greece and Turkey. After Norton supplemented it further (Friskin n.d., 8), Clarke invited Bacon along to make "sketches and drawings of all the temples and sites" (Bacon to Moran). That summer, after a month of research at the British Library, the young architects bought a 20-foot sloop which they named the *Dorian* and spent the autumn sailing her from England to Belgium, through the canals of Holland, and up the Rhine. After wintering in Munich, they continued down the Danube to the Black Sea and Constantinople, where they arrived in May (fig. 3.1) (*Levant Herald* 16 May 1879). Without Bacon's seamanship, learned during summers on the coast of Maine, the trip would have been impossible as "Clarke was a poor sailor, unacquainted with the handling of boats, and was seasick most of the time" (Austin 1942, 12).

To establish his protégé in the academic world, Norton quickly published Clarke's first scholarly article on the method of lighting Greek temples in the

Fig. 3.1. Francis Henry Bacon at the tiller and Joseph Thacher Clarke on deck aboard the Dorian in Constantinople harbor, 1879. (Bacon 1912, 73)

Papers of the Harvard Art Club (Norton 1879, 3–4; Clarke 1879).[4] In forwarding a copy to John Ruskin (1819–1900), Norton wrote that he was "much interested" in its author who was at that time "on a plucky expedition to study up the ruins of Doric architecture." Norton informed Ruskin that he [Norton] was trying to "get up an Archaeological Society, in the hope of encouraging classical studies; . . . and of training some of our College-bred boys to take part in investigations in Greek regions, and regions farther east. What do you think of Sardis as a point of attack,—with the untouched burial mounds of the Lydian kings, and with all the wealth of Croesus to tempt us? I am tempted, too, by Orchomenos and by Samos. But one can hardly put the spade down wrong" (20 May 1879, in Bradley and Ousby 1987, 428–9). After being rebuffed by the Greeks the year before in his request for permission to excavate at Delphi (AIA Archives, box 1), Norton reopened communication with General John Meredith Read (1837–1896), U.S. minister to Greece (1873–1879) and a member of the Archaeological Society in Athens, concerning the possibility of conducting American-sponsored excavations in Greece (23 June 1879, AIA Archives, box 1).

While the AIA was convening in June 1879, Bacon was visiting Troy where he met Heinrich Schliemann (1822–1890). There he and Clarke began their ambitious odyssey to visit every known Greek temple in Asia Minor and Greece. Following Troy, they stopped at Samothrace and then spent two days at Assos on the western coast of the Troad investigating the ruins, especially those of the early Doric temple to Athena on the summit. After visiting Samos and Delos, they reached Athens, where they continued to study and sketch Greek architecture, including the nearby remains of the Temple of Aphaia on Aigina. Meanwhile, Norton had announced to prospective members of the AIA that an expedition was "already on foot," a "comprehensive examination . . . of great value," suggesting it "might seem deserving of aid from the society" (minutes, 10 May 1879, AIA Archives, box 1.1). The AIA offered the architects money to extend their tour to Corfu, Magna Graecia, and Sicily, requesting "a report on the archaeological aspects of the sites visited," with the actual state of the remains. At this point, Bacon demurred and returned home, for despite their accomplishments, the men's personal relationship had so deteriorated after their 4,000-mile journey that they parted (Friskin n.d., 8; AIA 1880, 14–5; Bacon 1912, 123, 133; Clarke to CEN, 26 February 1880, AIA Archives, box 5.12). Clarke, however, accepted the money and agreed to the terms, but instead of undertaking the reconnaissance for future excavations left for Munich where he continued to work with von Reber. While there, Clarke wrote up an account of their experiences, which Norton presented to the AIA (Clarke 1880).

Norton was uncertain about where to begin excavating. In his annual address to the AIA membership in 1880 he spoke of "several trained archaeologists" and young men at Harvard "who would prepare themselves with the best classical teachers for the work." He disclosed that William James Stillman (1828–1901), American consul in Crete (1865–1869), a pioneer archaeological photographer, painter, and anti-Turkish war correspondent who had resided in the Mediterranean for almost two decades, was ready to excavate on Crete for the AIA (Tomlinson 1991, 25–39). The AIA executive committee, however, preferred to excavate at Epidaurus and, if that were not "successful after preliminary investigations," at Assos. Norton reported that antiquities could not be brought out of Greece, but that "with proper management everything could be brought away from Turkey" (minutes, 15 May 1880, AIA Archives, box 1.1). At the same time Norton showcased Bacon's drawings and Clarke's account of sites that "offered promising ground for exploration" and looked forward to "a report upon their actual condition" (AIA 1880, 15).

Clarke was aware of his patron's interest in Assos, for Norton had discussed its potential with his Harvard students as early as 1875 (Wheelwright 1952, 7; HBL). In his report to the AIA, Clarke focused on only two Greek archaeological sites: Samothrace and Assos, contrasting the former, excavated between 1873 and 1875, funded by the Austrian government, and ably published (Conze 1880), with Assos, where, aside from early probes of its unique temple on the acropolis, the entire site was "virgin soil." What had been published about the site was mostly inaccurate for there had been no proper excavations. Thus, it promised much sculpture. With little earth covering the finds on the exposed promontory, results would be quick and inexpensive. Moreover, in addition to the temple, there were extensive fortification walls, a large necropolis, Roman theater, and domestic architecture. Knowing Norton's preference for a site in Greece, Clarke cleverly emphasized the Greekness of Assos: its situation rivaled that of the Parthenon and Sounion and its environs were as beautiful as those of Athens. Here he had an ulterior motive since his own interests lay with the Doric order, which was amply represented at Assos, but not at Sardis or Samos where the temples were of the Ionic order and, thus personally uninteresting to Clarke. Clarke strongly recommended a "comprehensive and thorough publication of the remains of antiquity at Assos" and noted that his opinion was "shared by eminent European authorities who have had the opportunity of examining its acropolis" (1880, 153, 160–1). Ultimately, the AIA agreed that Assos "merited more extensive investigations" and abandoned plans for other sites (AIA 1880, 14–5; Norton 1898, v).

Germany's recent success with "big archaeology" at Olympia had inspired the AIA, but those excavations had brought little but glory back to Germany because of Greece's stringent antiquities laws (Allen, Introduction, this volume). In contrast, the relatively liberal antiquities laws of the Ottoman empire had resulted in major German acquisitions from Pergamon (Marchand 1996, 95–6). These lenient laws likewise promised sculptures for

American museum collections, so the executive committee of the AIA staked its claim, and in June 1880 Norton requested the permit for Assos. Clarke would lead the team. Thanks to Ware's intervention, Bacon, the experienced surveyor and draftsman, agreed to be associate director. "With the hope of making a valuable contribution to knowledge, and of quickening, and deepening interest" in the classical world, the committee allotted funds and endorsed the proposed excavations at Assos. Norton personally hoped for a "scientific result, giving us a distinct knowledge of the general characteristics of a site of Greek occupancy" (minutes, 28 December 1880, AIA Archives, box 1; AIA 1880, 23–4; 1881, 28).

In January 1881 Bacon prepared for the great adventure. No less than Luigi Palma di Cesnola (1832–1904), former U.S. consul on Cyprus and director of the Metropolitan Museum of Art in New York, counseled Bacon on practical matters and how to deal with Greeks and Turks. En route to Assos, Bacon stopped in Paris to draw the sculpted frieze fragments from the Temple of Athena at Assos, which the French had removed in 1838 and later placed in the Louvre. Upon arrival at the site itself in March, he began to survey the mountainous terrain and eventually produced a masterful plan, four ft. square (fig. 3.2a, b).

Seven competent assistants culled from more than 50 applicants supplied volunteer labor for the excavation. Initially they included Maxwell Wrigley, engineer and architect who had worked with Bacon in New York;[5] Charles Howard Walker (1857–1936), who had studied architecture with Ware at MIT; and geologist Joseph Silas Diller (1850–1928) of Harvard. Three of Norton's Harvard students also came: Edward Robinson (1858–1931),[6] Charles Wesley Bradley (1857–1884),[7] and William Cranston Lawton (1853–1941),[8] the last two of whom were to study the inscriptions, since by his own later admission, Clarke was wholly ignorant of Greek in 1880 (Lawton to CEN, 1 November 1881; Robinson to CEN, 14 November 1881; Clarke to CEN, 22 April 1886, AIA Archives). Norton's eldest son Eliot (1863–1932), about to enter Harvard, also joined the group (AIA 1881, 28–9). The eighth and most experienced member was recruited by chance. John Henry Haynes (1849–1910) had already worked on Crete and in Athens with Stillman, whom Norton had authorized to excavate Knossos and the Idaean Cave as the AIA's "agent" and sent out without a permit. Since it never came, Clarke was able to recruit Haynes, whom Stillman had already trained in photography, to work at Assos.

Fig. 3.2a. Francis Henry Bacon's plan of Assos. (Clarke 1882, pl. 1)

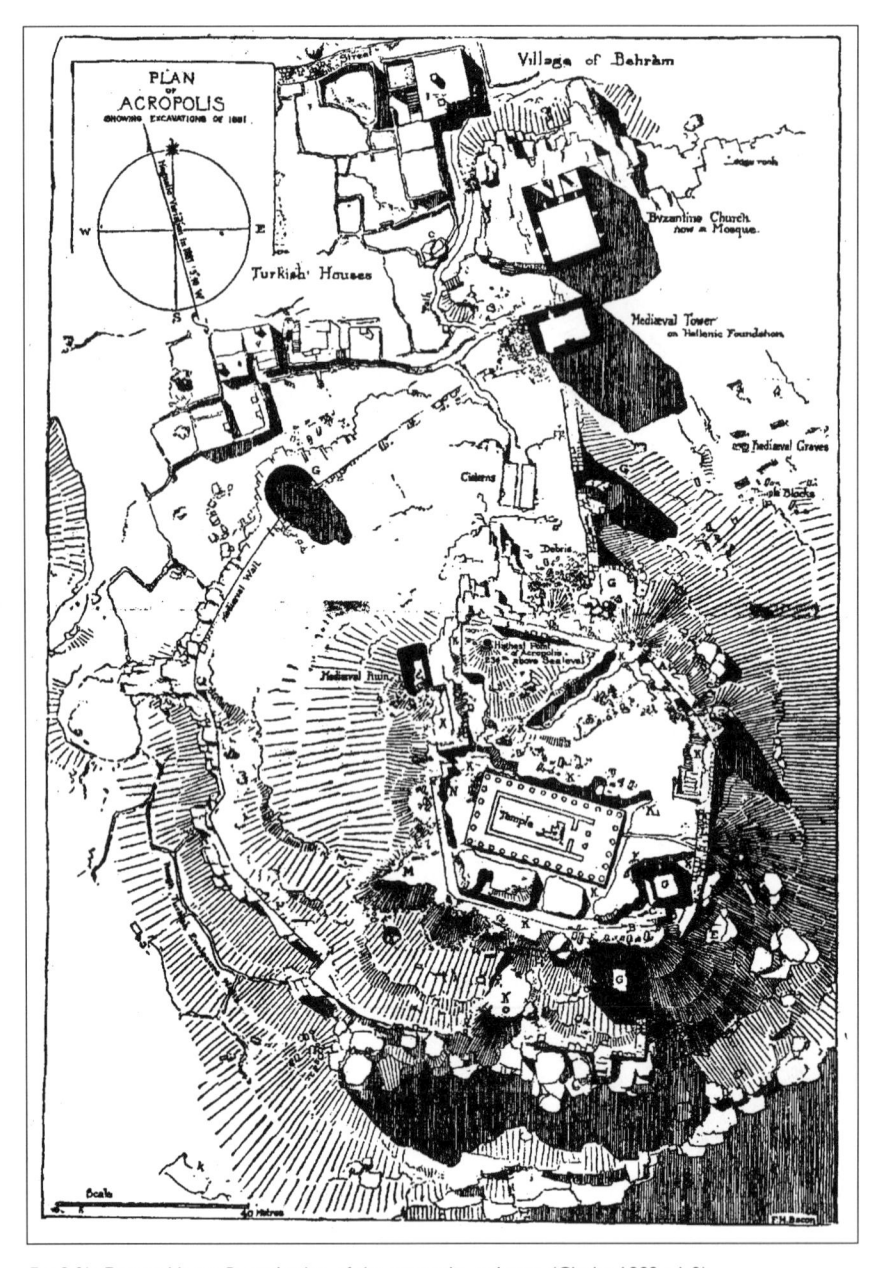

Fig. 3.2b. Francis Henry Bacon's plan of the acropolis at Assos. (Clarke 1882, pl. 2)

Apparently Norton did not learn from his failure at Knossos and once again naively sent American excavators into the field without securing a permit in advance, but this time the consequences were more serious, as the young men went to an inhospitable, remote site where none spoke the native language. Moreover, although the archaeologists arrived in March, began surveying in mid-April, and had the *firman* (permit) on 13 May, they did not begin to excavate until August because Clarke, the director, was absent.

As an expedition leader, the 25-year-old Clarke had not a fraction of Stillman's experience. Unable or unwilling to cope with the problems of dig management, he abandoned the men early into the season for "that nest of pagans . . . gay Parisian Smyrna"[9] where he remained, apparently squandering AIA funds and provisions, for the better part of two months while the situation for the excavation team at Assos deteriorated disastrously.

Clarke's lack of professionalism and moral irresponsibility were matched only by the volunteers' loyalty to Norton and Bacon. Unapprised by the absent Clarke of his whereabouts, Bacon bore all responsibility, negotiated with local authorities, and made do with little money and no medical supplies. During the summer months all suffered from fever and malnutrition and at one point they survived on bread, boiled weeds, an occasional egg, and condensed milk while "there were stores of provisions in Smyrna" (Robinson to CEN, 14 November 1881; Stillman to CEN, 26 March 1882, AIA Archives; Ramsay 1897, 294–5). When he was present, Clarke appropriated one room of their two-room "excavation house" for himself, forcing the rest of the team, including Bacon, into the other where they slept on the floor "with vermin" (Bacon to parents and Katherine Bacon, 13 April 1881, Duke; Lawton to CEN, 1 November; Robinson to CEN, 14 November 1881, AIA Archives).[10]

Ironically, Eliot Norton never actually excavated at Assos, for although he was there for more than three months, ground was not broken until 1 August, more than a month after he departed. Clarke appeared briefly at the site in mid-June to escort Eliot to Smyrna for his trip home, but remained there ostensibly for the acquisition of equipment. In July he abdicated even this minor task and summoned Bacon to do it. After acquiring the gear, Bacon finally retrieved Clarke, but by then five months had elapsed since the time of Bacon's arrival. Clarke blamed delays on the permit process (1882, 16), but this could not account for his absences in June and July. The euphoria of early spring was gone and Clarke had alienated the group. Some feared a "rebellion," "outbreak," or "explosion" and wished to notify Norton, but others counseled silence lest "the first work of the Americans in the East should end in a disgraceful break up" (Lawton to CEN, 1 November 1881, AIA Archives).

By the middle of the first season Bacon's survey was the only significant accomplishment of the expedition. When Clarke finally returned to the site, Bacon buried his own problems with him and focused on improving relations between Clarke and the volunteers. As Clarke gave wildly contradictory orders, Bacon counseled him until he became more reasonable. When the excavators finally began digging, they struck the temple stylobate in their first pit (Bacon to parents, 5 August 1881, Duke). Later they moved to the southern slopes of the lower town where they investigated the stoa, gymnasium, theatre, and "Street of the Tombs," though Clarke admitted that it was "little more than a preliminary investigation" (Clarke 1882, 34–43, 123–30). Clarke kept the general chronicle of their work and concentrated on the acropolis, but rarely visited the site and abdicated responsibility for all but the temple. By contrast, Bacon documented the general topography, managed excavations at the rest of the extensive site, and supervised the work, climbing the hill four times a day (Bacon to parents, 22 August 1881, Duke). Later all agreed that Bacon had held the group together and provided the only method and plan for excavating (Lawton to CEN, 18 December 1881; 16 July 1882; Walker to CEN, 18 December 1881; Robinson to CEN, 14 November 1881; Haynes to Stillman, 26 January 1882, AIA Archives).

In Boston, interest in the expedition was great and the Museum of Fine Arts (MFA) displayed Bacon's great plan on which it marked the monthly progress of the dig (AIA 1881, 32). Yet at the end of the 1881 season the future of American involvement at Assos was uncertain, for the funds necessary for continuing were not in place. Following Clarke, Norton chided the executive committee, suggesting that if they did not continue, "the Germans probably would" (minutes, 20 October 1881, AIA Archives, box 1.1). He held a special general meeting of the AIA in November at which he presented results of the first season and displayed Bacon's drawings. Meanwhile, Clarke addressed the American Institute of Architects. The *American Architect* printed Clarke's speech (19 November 1881 [10: 308] 237) and wrote: "the extent and importance of the work achieved by the Expedition was a complete surprise to most of those present and excited great interest" (26 November 1881 [10: 309] 251). According to Ware, Bacon's drawings "powerfully contributed to the great interest it excited" (to CEN, 30 November 1881, AIA Archives). In London the *Athenaeum* claimed that Clarke's report showed that Texier's plans of the city and temple were "not merely incorrect, but imaginary" and his coming book would be "of unusual interest to all students of classical antiquity" (31 December 1881 [2827] 905–6). These accolades were not lost on Norton.

At the same time, however, Norton received serious private complaints that Clarke's incompetence in the field and moral and professional unsuitability would compromise the work.[11] Assos was threatened from within. The directors' architectural backgrounds along with their reconnaissance experience had been an asset to the AIA, but their youth was not. Though the volunteers praised Bacon, they begged Norton to replace Clarke, whom they accused of being a "libertine," a "charlatan," and an "unmitigated evil," with "an archaeologist of real training," someone older with more experience and integrity. Robinson wrote Norton that "Haynes was the only man in Assos whose judgment about pottery, cutting of stone, etc. was of any value at all" and Clarke would not listen to him. Moreover, the work at Assos was mere "digging," not "scientific archaeology . . . that of boys doing their level best without any experienced hand to guide them" (14 November 1881, AIA Archives). Bacon himself refrained from criticizing Clarke on the grounds that the work of the Institute could not be done if confidence were taken from him (Lawton to CEN, 16 July 1882, AIA Archives).

Norton treated with "contemptuous silence" private criticisms of Clarke's personal and professional life and continued to support him. Stillman rebuked Norton for his own lack of "experience of the East" and unwillingness to seek advice of those more seasoned (10 December 1881, AIA Archives). Stillman counseled him not to ignore the volunteers' complaints or "put their appeals aside as prejudice," that, if aired publicly, would mean "general disgrace to the Institute and its management and the failure of the whole work of the School [the American School of Classical Studies at Athens (ASCSA)] . . . for which Mr. Clarke is proposed as head!!" Clarke was "a pretender, charlatan" [who would] "in the end make the Institute and [Norton's] work the laughing stock of scientific Europe. . . . He is heavy enough to sink you all" (to CEN, 24 January, 11 February, and 26 March 1882, AIA Archives; *Athenaeum* 31 December 1881 [2827] 905–6). Stillman threatened that Norton himself would "not be held blameless personally or professionally" (20 December 1881, AIA Archives). To Stillman,

Clarke merited "nothing but dismissal" (24 January 1882, AIA Archives), but instead Norton focused on Clarke's achievements. He had discovered seven new fragments of the epistyle and, under Bacon's sober influence had produced an "able and learned" report, "illustrated by the exact and beautiful drawings of Mr. Bacon." Not surprisingly, it focused on the temple, "the investigations of the other structures of the city, . . . still imperfect, and requiring to be completed by the labors of the present year" (AIA 1882, 38, 41). To Norton, Clarke's timely Assos report (1882), underwritten by the Harvard Art Club and the Philological Society of Harvard College, gave evidence not only of his "high qualities as an investigator, but also of his possession of learning adequate to enable him to set forth the discoveries made by the expedition in a manner fitted to meet the demands of modern scholarship" (Norton 1898, v).

The volunteers from the first season refused to work again for Clarke, so in 1882 there was a completely new, salaried staff. With the directors' experience of a first field season and a smaller, more mature and better-trained group, the new team brought professionalism to their work. As with the Germans at Olympia and Pergamon, they focused on religious and public monuments. Bacon began on his own in March, working on the stoa and Roman theatre, and later reconstructing the Greek bridge, the gymnasium, and the Street of the Tombs (fig. 3.3). Clarke arrived in April with German architect Robert Koldewey (1855–1925), who took responsibility for the agora, the bouleuterion, and the Greek bath (Clarke 1898, 3). As a favor to Norton and the AIA, Haynes, who was teaching at Robert College in Constantinople, returned and photographed the excavations (e.g., the cover photograph), but was plagued by problems with supplies.

Marked improvement over the previous season characterized all aspects of the excavation. In 1883 John Robert Sitlington Sterrett (1851–1914), a Munich Ph.D. and student at the newly established ASCSA, took over work on the inscriptions (AIA 1883, 24–5).[12] The Americans continued to benefit from the benevolent guidance of British expatriate Frank Calvert (1828–1908), diplomat and resident excavator of the Troad who since 1881 had guided members of the expedition around archaeological sites in the Troad (Lawton 1882, 145–7, 151, 159). As U.S. consular agent at the Dardanelles (Çanakkale), Calvert assisted the excavators in all of their dealings and occasionally excavated with them (Clarke 1898, 17; Allen 1999, 214). Early on he helped Diller with his geological studies (Diller 1882,

Fig. 3.3. Francis Henry Bacon's drawing of a vaulted tomb in the Street of the Tombs (Clarke, Bacon, and Koldewey 1902/1921, 287).

195–6, 202). Later he put Clarke in touch with Schliemann's colleague, pathologist Rudolf Virchow (1821–1902), who published the skulls from the Assos graves (Virchow 1884).

Increasing the impact of the Assos expedition at home, Bacon sent casts of the new temple sculptures to augment the MFA's plaster cast collection and some of his own drawings to colleagues for exhibition at the newly formed Architectural League of New York. Meanwhile, Norton acknowledged Bacon's critical role by raising his salary to equal Clarke's and in 1884 published Bacon's 1882 visit to Sardis (in Norton 1884) and later asked him to write an article on Assos. But "academic (scholarly) archaeology never interested" Bacon (Austin 1942, 11), to whom "the mores" and lives of the ancient Greeks were more appealing (Bacon 1886, 850–60).

Norton and the AIA wished the Institute's fieldwork to follow the German model of an architecturally oriented large-scale excavation, but Assos had no direct government subsidies like the imperially-sponsored German excavations at Pergamon or Olympia, where the Germans employed at least 500 workers and spent the equivalent of $200,000 from 1875 to 1881 (Marchand 1996, 85, 87). It became clear that the AIA lacked both the commensurate institutional expertise and financial resources, as insufficient funds raised from private subscriptions were the cause of frequent delays (Clarke 1898, 20–1). The cost of three years of excavation at Assos totalled only $19,121.16, of which $3,344.53 went to excavation and the rest to staff salaries, household supplies, maintenance, transportation of equipment, antiquities, and agents of the AIA as well as dealings with the Ottoman authorities (Clarke 1898, 38–9; AIA Archives, box 1.2).

Compared to the Germans, the young Americans had neither the comparable authority nor the depth of experience in the field, and Clarke's squandered first season necessitated a second and part of a third, which ceased with the expiration of their permit in May 1883. At Olympia the Greek government had built a road to the site to facilitate German operations and provided police to ensure against pilfering, while at Assos, even as they excavated, the Americans enjoyed little assistance from the Ottoman authorities and could not prevent villagers from removing ancient cut stones from freshly exposed walls (AIA 1881, 26–7).

This lack of experience and authority proved devastating when it came time to bring the antiquities home. After first thinking that the AIA should let the Louvre have the temple sculptures (Clarke, quoted in Brimmer to

CEN, 20 November 1881, AIA Archives, box 3.2), Clarke waffled and suggested "smuggling Assos objects out of the country" (to CEN, 19 February 1883). Norton wrote to Aristarchi Bey, a specialist on Ottoman antiquities legislation then serving as minister to the United States who had promised to intervene with his government on behalf of the American excavators (AIA 1883, 23). Naively Norton wished "not to have the antiquities divided; that is [for the Ottomans] to cede the temple sculptures and inscriptions to the Institute" (minutes, 31 March 1883, AIA Archives, box 1.2) and advised the excavators "to deal with scrupulous honesty with the Turks and to comply literally with the terms of the firman, . . . in spite of the example of other expeditions" (AIA 1883, 23–4). In 1878, for example, Carl Humann (1839–1896), the German excavator at Pergamon, had hidden finds from the Ottoman authorities until he had purchased the land of the site. Once ownership was secure, Humann had a right to two-thirds of the finds and began exporting 350 tons of marble sculpture to Germany (Marchand 1996, 95, 201–2).

According to Ottoman law, two-thirds of the finds were to go to the Ottoman authorities (as government and landowner) and one-third to the AIA (as excavator). Ottoman commissioner Demetrios Baltazzi Bey was appointed to handle the division and a verbal agreement was quickly reached (AIA 1884, 23–4; Clarke 1898, 25–30). Clarke agreed to the division, but departed from Turkey before it had been written down and carried out. In anticipation, Norton held a special meeting of the AIA where he announced that the Institute had secured "40 to 50 cases coming: the best sculpture of the temple; . . . all of the inscriptions (except the rare bronze one); a large number of terracottas; all the coins and considerable number of miscellaneous articles found in the tombs and a large number of architectural fragments (so that it would be possible to erect at the Museum of Fine Arts, a complete order of the temple)" (minutes, 6 October 1883, AIA Archives, box 1.1).

The AIA paid dearly for Clarke's haste and arrogance, for only 13 cases of antiquities were accounted for in Clarke's precipitous agreement and none included certain architectural fragments that the AIA wanted. To complicate matters further, Haynes later reported to Norton that "Clarke's bruskness of manner" had insulted Hamdi Bey (1842–1910), director of the Imperial Ottoman Museum from 1881 until his death. Clarke had offered the director "an affront to his dignity" as though "Hamdi Bey as an antiquarian and his museum [were] beneath his notice." Feeling "greatly injured,"

Hamdi Bey was "down on American expeditions" and not inclined to help (4 September 1885, AIA Archives). This undoubtedly accounts for the discrepancy in the number of cases anticipated by Norton and the number actually shipped.

The State Department instructed General Lewis Wallace (1827–1905), U.S. minister to Constantinople (1881–1885) and author of *Ben Hur*, to exert pressure in Turkey to secure objects desired by the AIA, yet he neglected to come to their aid (AIA 1883, 24), demonstrating not only that the AIA lacked authority with its own diplomats, but also that the U.S. lacked the strong arm of international politics to carry out its wishes. Norton complained to the U.S. Secretary of State that the Americans had received "vastly less than the one third which by right belonged to the Institute," noting further that "our Legation . . . would seem to have adopted the official habits ascribed to Ministers of the Sublime Porte itself." (CEN to Frederick Frelinghuysen, 16 December 1884, AIA Archives). Wallace matched Norton's acidity, disparaged the AIA enterprise, and blamed it all on Clarke's haste (13 January 1885 to CEN, AIA Archives).

Clarke had secured frieze blocks of Herakles and the human-legged centaurs and the heraldic sphinxes which the AIA had agreed to present to the MFA, but forfeited many prizes left unmentioned in the agreement. As a result, Bacon shipped only the specified antiquities on 20 October 1883 (AIA Archives, box 2.2). Other cases of fragments, desired by the AIA but retained by Turkey, included the complete order from the Temple of Athena as well as moldings from the Street of the Tombs, capitals from the stoa, fragments from the Greek bath, and portions of the two chief mosaics found in the lower town (minutes, 10 December 1884, AIA Archives, box 1.2; Clarke 1898, 17). With $2,000 pledged by the MFA, the Americans had hoped to purchase additional frieze slabs owned by the Ottomans in order to augment their own share, but the Turks refused to sell. In fact, the AIA was lucky to secure any of the sculptures found, for in 1884 a new Ottoman antiquities law prohibited the export of *all* antiquities from Ottoman soil (Reinach 1884, 335–44; Young 1905). In the end, the contested temple capitals and cornice blocks were left on the quay by local authorities where 20 years later Bacon found them "half-covered with dirt and trodden by dogs and camels, etc." (Bacon to CEN, 26 June 1904, "Assos Days"). Throughout the next century they were built into the renovated port buildings and breakwater, where they can be seen today.

While waiting for exportation problems to be solved, Bacon escorted his teacher, William Ware, throughout the Troad,[13] where he was hosted by Frank Calvert. Since their arrival in 1881, both Bacon and Clarke had been captivated by the members of a European commercial aristocracy who enjoyed comparative freedom as foreigners in the Ottoman empire. At the straits Bacon met Alice Mary Calvert (1858–1949), niece of the Americans' resident mentor, who fit neatly into the society with which he was smitten. They became engaged in September 1883 and married in 1885. In expectation of the event, Bacon returned to Boston where he completed the Assos drawings by spring, 1884.

Norton was gratified by positive firsthand accounts from eminent visitors to Assos. In April 1883 Calvert escorted William Watson Goodwin (1831–1912), director of the new ASCSA, and British classicist Richard Jebb (1841–1905) to Assos. Jebb pronounced the new epistyle blocks destined for Boston as "the most important links yet found between Oriental and Greek art" and noted that the temple plan had been "for the first time completely and scientifically discovered." He praised the "admirable" preliminary report and noted that the AIA "may well feel gratified by the result of an enterprise commenced under its auspices" (AIA 1884, 39–45). Thanks partly to Calvert, the excavations had not simply been architecturally oriented, but also comprised skeletal and topographical studies such as those undertaken by Virchow, Diller, Lawton, and Haynes. Acknowledging its debt, the AIA recognized Calvert for his help (Allen 1999, 214–5, 349; Ware to CEN, 9 January 1885, AIA Archives).

At home kudos awaited the returning excavators whose work had surpassed all expectations, an enthusiasm that might have been tempered had they known that they were not going to receive all the pieces promised by Clarke. On 31 October 1883 the AIA presented a public talk on Assos and the ASCSA, which drew 750 people to MIT (*Science* November 16 [2: 41] 646–50). To the Boston Society of Architects the Assos excavations had shown "the Greek Architect experimenting with forms," had given "the best lesson yet derived from Greek antiquity in the grouping of buildings; . . . the only examples of the . . . Greeks . . . in domestic and civic works; and . . . brought nearer to our sympathies and comprehension that spirit which the conditions of modern architecture require as a corrective and purifying force." Praising Bacon and Clarke for their "valuable acquisition to our knowledge of Greek Architecture," president Cabot offered support for the next volume, desiring drawings "as full and complete as possible" (to CEN, 20 March 1884, AIA Archives, box 3).

1884 boded well for Bacon and Clarke. The AIA unanimously voted them life members (minutes 17 May 1884, AIA Archives, box 1.3). In April Clarke was elected Corresponding Member of the German Archaeological Institute (Clarke to CEN, 10 February 1885, AIA Archives) and Norton arranged for him to represent the AIA on the Wolfe Expedition to Mesopotamia, but at the last minute Clarke balked (to CEN, 17 August 1884, AIA Archives, box 5.12). Instead, Haynes and Sterrett accompanied William H. Ward (1835–1916) to Mesopotamia (Haynes to CEN, 29 October 1884, 7140 NP/HL; minutes, 11 October 1884, AIA Archives, box 1.1). Clarke hoped to land a teaching job, but his lack of an advanced degree and training in philology were serious impediments to an academic position. Repeatedly, he asked Norton to find him a lectureship at Harvard, a consulship in Smyrna, or superintendence of the ASCSA (2, 15 April 1885; 28 February 1886, 15 February 1888, AIA Archives), but he was never able to parlay Norton's favors into a university position because of the increasing professionalization of the field (Allen, Introduction, this volume).

Despite their glorious accolades, neither Bacon nor Clarke was destined to devote his life solely to archaeology. Rather, these men and their excavation were caught on the cusp of the change from amateur to professional in the discipline of American classical archaeology. Once Bacon finished his Assos drawings, he abandoned archaeology and architecture for the more lucrative field of interior and furniture design[14] where his keen eye and experience as architect and draftsman at Assos informed his classicizing style. Yet, after his marriage to Calvert's niece in 1885 Bacon's professional association with the Troad assumed a deeper dimension because his wife never acclimated herself fully to New England. He subsequently "wore a path across the ocean," returning to the Dardanelles in 1889, 1892, 1895, 1904, and with increasing frequency after 1907 when his wife resumed her residence in Turkey. By contrast, Clarke would never return.

Meanwhile, Clarke tried to secure gainful employment as an archaeologist, arranging and cataloguing Assos antiquities at the MFA which, while numerous, were not what the MFA had expected; for example, a complete order of the temple for reconstruction. Instead Clarke catalogued 156 sculpted or inscribed fragments of marble or stone, 344 pieces of pottery, 27 of glass, 3 of gold, 57 of metal, and 851 coins, not to mention a fish vertebra, wild boar's tusk, and camel tooth (AIA 1885, 25; Whitehill 1970, 64 and museum register).[15] In March 1884 Clarke lectured on *entasis* for what later became the Baltimore society of the AIA. At the Johns Hopkins University he gave "A Plea for Practical Archaeology," and spoke on Assos and Cyrene.[16] He repeated these for Alexander Graham Bell and others in Washington, D.C. and New York, since several embryonic archaeological societies were considering mounting their own expeditions to the Cyrenaica in 1884 (Clarke to CEN, 5, 21 March 1884; minutes, 10 December 1884, AIA Archives), but the money could not be raised (Ware to CEN, 13 March 1884, AIA Archives, box 3.2). Thus, although Norton wanted to keep Clarke in the field for the AIA, the Cyrene expedition was postponed (10, 17 August 1884, AIA Archives).

Slowly, Clarke began to slide. He reworked his Johns Hopkins lecture for publication (1889, 89–103) but wrote nothing on Assos. In 1885 only Bacon was nominated to honorary membership in the Boston Society of Architects for "his distinguished services on the Assos Expedition" (Austin 1942, 9–10). The historian of that Society wrote that Clarke had "slipped" and committed "an affront to the officers of the Archaeological Institute and of the Boston Society of Architects, for the outcome seems to have resulted in the tacit understanding among the leaders . . . to utterly ostracize Clarke by ignoring all mention of his name and behavior forevermore."[17] It is difficult now to sort out which mistake it was, but Clarke finally abandoned the United States and settled in England where he, too, married in 1885. He continued to draw a salary from the AIA for Assos until May 1886[18] when, after taking up photography at Assos through Haynes, he met inventor George Eastman (1854–1932). Thus, Clarke began work as Eastman's patent expert and troubleshooter in Europe (Ackerman 1938, 59), spending his scholarly acumen as Eastman's agent by advising him on art purchases (Brayer 1979, 2). But the cost was dear, for he could no longer focus on Assos or archaeology. When his subsequent fieldwork in Italy was aborted in 1887,[19] Clarke immediately headed for Cyrene on a prospecting expedition for the Baltimore society.[20] Perhaps because of renewed AIA interest in Delphi (Sheftel, this volume), nothing came of it. When in 1888 Norton again offered him a fieldwork position, this time in Egypt, Clarke refused because of the protracted publication of Assos. In 1888 he published his last article[21] and Cyrene later went to Norton's youngest son Richard (1872–1918).

The publication of Assos suffered from the fact that the principal investigators left the field to earn livings in other professions, and Norton recorded his frustration in successive AIA annual reports (e.g., AIA 1885, 41). But Clarke had also become mired in an exhaustive "learned apparatus" and "pedantic style" (to CEN, 12 August 1886, AIA Archives). In 1888 he vowed to avoid "unnecessary excursions into the field of scholarship" and "to restrict the work as much as possible to actual description, reducing the encyclopedic character by presenting only the most essential references" (to CEN, 11 March, 15 July 1888, AIA Archives). An AIA representative passing through London likened him to a "Yankee working with the minuteness of a German professor" (J.P. Peters to CEN, 31 August 1888, AIA Archives), but by 1889 Norton admitted, "it is impossible to say when the final Report by Mr. Clarke on the Investigations at Assos will be completed" (AIA 1889, 36). In 1890 when Norton left the AIA presidency, it had still not appeared.

When it became clear that Clarke had completely abdicated, Norton asked Bacon to take over and he agreed. Fortunately for the AIA, Bacon's character and choice of spouse aided the publication of the Assos reports. Because of his continued association with Calvert[22] and his repeated presence in the Troad, Bacon was able, despite his occupation and own professional commitments, to keep abreast of the archaeological world, particularly in Athens and Turkey.

At Bacon's instigation, Norton offered Clarke his "sincerest sympathy with his trials and disappointments," but officially requested "as Late President and Vice President" of the AIA, all of the drawings in Clarke's custody "at once" (28 December 1894, AIA Archives). Embittered, Clarke, in turn, blamed business trips for his failure to follow through and lamented "the necessity of earning a living by hand to mouth work in other fields" (Clarke to CEN, 19 January 1895, AIA Archives, box 6.5), but by 1896 he had surrendered all of the Assos material to Bacon. The task of moving it to publication, however, was more daunting than Bacon had envisioned. He relied on his former Assos colleague Robert Koldewey, who had drawn a salary from the AIA until 1885 and journeyed to Boston to confer with him about reconstructions for the agora in 1896, but by 1898 Koldewey was thoroughly committed to Babylon, where he excavated until 1917 (Kuklick 1996, 144–5; Marchand 1996, 114). So Bacon alone had to decipher and ink Clarke's and Koldewey's notes and drawings (to CEN, 25 February 1895, AIA Archives).

Meanwhile, appreciation for and interest in Assos was waning. When Wilhelm Dörpfeld discovered two epistyle blocks there in 1896 and offered them to the AIA for publication, Norton's own son Richard dismissed the Assos sculpture as "the work of a provincial school in a country where the Fine Arts never attained the noblest development" (CEN 1897, 514). Norton and Bacon managed to publish Clarke's notes on the temple in 1898, but Norton himself acknowledged that the 1898 volume (mostly written in the 1880s) was "partial and imperfect" as a result of "a series of calamities" for which Clarke was "in no wise responsible. . . . It is a matter of serious regret that a full record of the results of the expedition should not be made by the person most competent to describe the discoveries and exhibit their importance" (Norton 1898, vi). Bacon vented his frustration with Clarke's selective study of only that which interested him personally, the temple and its sculptures, "leaving untouched the other interesting monuments of the ancient city, namely the Agora, with the surrounding buildings, the Theater, Gymnasium, the Fortification Walls, as well as the Street of the Tombs with its many exedras, sarcophagi, and monuments, and the Greek and Roman mosaic pavements!" (Bacon, epilogue to "Assos Days"). Internationally, scholars criticized America for undertaking "the splendid work of excavating the provincial city of Assos and then dropp[ing] it" and unfairly disparaged the lack of thoroughness of the 19th-century American excavation "where no private house, and not even the immediate neighborhood of the provincial temple, was entirely excavated" (quoted in Sterrett 1911, 36, 45–6).

From the beginning, AIA financing for Assos was problematic, and funding for the beleaguered publications fared no better. After Clarke's 1898 volume, Bacon brought out the second in two installments, the latter of which was delayed because of lack of money. The first, chiefly of text, appeared in 1902, a year after Cabot, former president of the B.S.A., had died. Before bringing out the second, Bacon traveled first to England to consult with Clarke and then to Assos to verify their conclusions (1904 Journal). After Norton's death in 1908, Bacon asked Norton's former student, New York banker and AIA patron James Loeb (1867–1933) for a $3000 loan for the second. Although Bacon had finished it by 1916, Loeb became impatient and the war in Europe intervened, doubling the price of paper and printing (Bacon to Frederick W. Shipley, 22 December 1916, AIA Archives). In 1918, AIA acting general secretary wrote that "this long delayed and troublesome enterprise . . . will be a serious reflection on American scholarship

Fig. 3.4. The Agora at Assos restored, by Francis Henry Bacon. (Clarke, Bacon, and Koldeway 1902/1921, 127. Courtesy of Brown University Library)

if this report is not published very soon" (to William F. Harris, 7 December, AIA Archives, box 20). Finally in 1921, a year after Clarke died in obscurity, Bacon published the folio of plates mostly at his own expense. For his "gift" he was listed as a Patron of the Institute from that year to his death in 1940, although the AIA discharged its debt to Bacon during the presidency of Louis Eleazar Lord (1875–1957) in 1936.[23]

Both of the volumes that Bacon shepherded to publication bear his indelible stamp. Unlike Clarke, who never shared authorship with his colleague, Bacon generously cited both Clarke and Koldewey as co-authors and even put Clarke's name first. Rather than the exhaustive scholarly commentary, which only Clarke could have provided, the folios reflect Bacon's strengths: carefully measured map-plans, restorations in perspective of parts of the principal monuments (fig. 3.3), and elevations. One review praised Bacon's "peculiar and most beautiful style . . . one of the most, if not the most satisfactory that has ever been attempted for the rendering and interpretation of ancient Classical architecture" (Butler 1921, 17) (fig. 3.4).

As a draftsman and architect Bacon always stressed the importance of full-size moldings, especially early Greek ones since they were useful for architects,[24] and believed that "when you draw a full size of a good Greek original, you shake hands with the man who made it" (Bacon to Moran). For this reason he included many of the architectural details that the late Cabot had requested almost four decades earlier. Yet the volume, which would have been useful for architects, had come too late, for the classicizing style in architecture, which Bacon had helped influence in the 1880s, was by that time falling victim to the austerity of International Modernism (Thomas 1990, 29, 664).

After 1927 Bacon retired at the Dardanelles, where he endured two wartime evacuations, earthquakes, the Depression,[25] and a successive loss of freedom for foreigners (Allen 1999, 242–4). Although crippled in 1923, Bacon kept alive his archaeological connections (fig. 3.5) and was made a member of the Archaeological Society of Berlin. Again he found pleasure in his association with the ASCSA, to which he donated the family's surviving Calvert-Schliemann correspondence (Allen 1999, 360, n. 50) and his own portfolios of full-size moldings and rubbings of Greek architectural details and inscriptions.[26] He also became a close friend of Carl Blegen (1887–1971), who had renewed excavations at Troy in the 1930s. To help Blegen, Bacon designed a dig house (not adopted) and also furniture to be used therein (Bacon 1934–1939 Journal; to Blegen, 27 February 1932, Blegen Papers, ASCSA Archives). In 1937 and 1938 he and Blegen hosted

Fig. 3.5. Francis Henry Bacon and a marble sima fragment from the Temple of Athena Ilion in the garden of the Calvert house at the Dardanelles. (Allen 1996, pl. 20b)

each other on opposite shores of the Aegean (Allen 1999, 361, n. 55). But circumstances there overwhelmed him. After suffering the collapse of his world and seizure of property in Turkey, Bacon died, a virtual "prisoner . . . in Chanak," in 1940 (Rosalind Reed to Bacon, 4 December 1937, Bacon 1934–1939 Journal).

William Bell Dinsmoor (1886–1973), AIA president from 1936 to 1945, delayed the January 1940 issue of the *AJA* to include his appreciation of "a most beloved figure among a past generation of American archaeologists… "Uncle Bacon" to many . . . one of the most accomplished of architectural archaeologists, . . . [whose] sympathetic handling and delicate technique in pencil" was unrivaled and whose drawings "served as models for imitation . . . at Harvard and Columbia" (1940, 117; to Stephen B. Luce, 19 February 1940, AIA Archives, box 31.9). Within a month Columbia University and the Boston Society of Architects exhibited his "unique line drawings, which combined esthetic feeling and disciplined imagination with great clarity and accuracy" as a way of mourning his passing and celebrating his legacy (AIA Archives, box 31.9; Bragdon 1940, 189). Through his instruction and encouragement of younger scholars, such as AIA gold medalists Lucy Shoe Meritt and Homer Thompson (1906–2000), Bacon raised the standard of archaeological draftsmanship in America and influenced a generation of American classical architects, including his younger brother Henry (1866–1924), architect of the Lincoln Memorial, who contributed a rendering of Francis's restoration of the tomb of the Assos monument of Publius Varius to the 1921 folio (Bacon 1886, 857; Clarke, Bacon, and Koldewey, 1902/1921, 229). Thus, Bacon's drawings were key both to igniting American interest in excavating classical sites and influencing the idealism seen in classicizing architecture in America from the 1880s on (Thomas 1995–1996, 29).

The AIA recognized Bacon as its "earliest and most energetic pioneer. Had it not been for Bacon's enterprise and perseverance, the Archaeological Institute of America would not have been able to undertake, just at the beginning of its career, such an important work as the excavations at Assos" (AIA *Bulletin* 31 (1940), 41–2). Although Clarke's passing went unmentioned by the AIA, Bacon generously recalled his partner's strengths, "it was entirely owing to his energy and forceful character that the Assos expedition took place" (Austin 1942, 15). Dinsmoor honored both for "carrying out the first city excavation in Greek lands . . . [and producing] the pictorial record of a small provincial town of ancient Greece . . . [which] will never be superseded" (1940, 117). Though neither joined the professional ranks of AIA archaeologists, they both helped secure a place for the AIA in the competitive Aegean arena of classical archaeology, and Bacon set professional standards for architectural plans and renderings for his own and future generations.

REFERENCES

Primary Sources by Location

Athens, Greece: American School of Classical Studies at Athens (ASCSA), Archives: Bacon molding profiles, Blegen papers, and Stillwell papers (unpublished).

Çanakkale, Turkey: Private collection: Bacon 1934–1939 Journal (unpublished).

Massachusetts: AIA Archives, Boston University, Boston, Mass.; Massachusetts Institute of Technology, Cambridge (MIT): Bacon "1904 Journal" (unpublished), "Log of the Dorian" (partially published); Houghton Library, Harvard University, Cambridge: Norton Papers (NP); L.O.K. Congdon: Bacon "Assos Days (An Archaeological Expedition to Asia Minor. Letters and Journals of Francis Henry Bacon 1881–1882–1883)" (partially published).

New York: Avery Architectural and Fine Arts Library, Columbia University in the City of New York: William Robert Ware Collection, Division of Drawings and Archives: Bacon Drawings.

North Carolina: Duke University, Special Collections: Bacon Letters. (unpublished).

Secondary Sources

Ackerman, C. 1938. *George Eastman.* Boston.

Archaeological Institute of America (AIA). 1880. *First Annual Report of the Executive Committee, with Accompanying Papers, 1879–1880.* Cambridge, Mass.

———. 1881. *Second Annual Report of the Executive Committee, 1880–1881.* Cambridge, Mass.

———. 1882. *Third Annual Report of the Executive Committee, 1881–1882.* Cambridge, Mass.

———. 1883. *Fourth Annual Report of the Executive Committee, 1882–1883.* Cambridge, Mass.

———. 1884. *Fifth Annual Report of the Executive Committee, 1883–1884.* Cambridge, Mass.

———. 1885. *Sixth Annual Report of the Executive Committee, 1884–1885.* Cambridge, Mass.

———. 1887. *Eighth Annual Report of the Executive Committee, 1886–1887.* Cambridge, Mass.

———. 1889. *Tenth Annual Report of the Executive Committee, 1888–1889.* Cambridge, Mass.

Allen, S.H. 1996. "'Principally for Vases, etc.': The Formation and Dispersal of the Calvert Collection." *Anatolian Studies* 46:145–65, pls. 18–21.

———. 1999. *Finding the Walls of Troy: Frank Calvert and Heinrich Schliemann at Hisarlik.* Berkeley.

———. Forthcoming. "Francis Henry Bacon: An Appreciation." In *Francis Henry Bacon's Log of the Dorian and Assos Days*, edited by S.H. Allen, L.O.K. Congdon, and H.B. Landry.

Austin, W.D. 1942. "A History of the Boston Society of Architects in the 19th Century." Chs. 10–12. Boston Athenaeum. unpublished.

Bacon, F.H. 1886. "American Explorers in Assos." *Century Magazine* 25, n.s. 3:850–60.

———. 1912. Extracts from "The Log of the Dorian." *Architectural Review* 1:7, 73–6; 1:8, 76–86; 1:9, 97–9; 1:10, 100–15; 1:11, 121–4; 1:12, 124–36.

Bradley, J.L., and I. Ousby, eds. 1987. *The Correspondence of John Ruskin and Charles Eliot Norton.* Cambridge.

Bragdon, C. 1940. "Francis H. Bacon, 1857 [sic]–1940: An Appreciation." *Architectural Forum* 72 (March 1940):189–90.

Brayer, E. 1979. *George Eastman, Collector.* Rochester, NY.

Briggs, W.W. jr., ed. 1994. *Biographical Dictionary of North American Classicists.* Westport, Conn.: Greenwood Press.

Burke, D.B. 1986. *In Pursuit of Beauty: Americans and the Aesthetic Movement.* New York: Rizzoli.

Butler, H.C. 1921. "The Investigations at Assos conducted by the Archaeological Institute of America." *Art and Archaeology* 12:17–26.

Calvert, F. 1865. "Contributions to the Ancient Geography of the Troad: On the Site and Remains of Cebrene." *Archaeological Journal* 22:51–7.

Clarke, J.T. 1879. *The Hypaethral Question, an Attempt to Determine the Mode in which the Interior of a Greek Temple was Lighted. Papers of the Harvard Art Club* 1. Cambridge, Mass.

———. 1880. "Archaeological Notes on Greek Shores 1." In *First Annual Report of the Executive Committee, 1879–1880*, 93–163. Cambridge, Mass.

———. 1882. *Report on the Investigations at Assos, 1881.* Papers of the Archaeological Institute of America, Classical Series 1. Boston.

———. 1889. "A Plea for Archaeological Instruction." In *Methods of Teaching History*, edited by G.S. Hall, 89–103. Boston.

———. 1888. "Gargara, Lamponia, and Pionia: Towns of the Troad." *AJA* 4:291–319.

———. 1898. *Report on the Investigations at Assos, 1882, 1883*, pt. 1. Papers of the Archaeological Institute of America, Classical Series 2. New York.

Clarke, J.T., F.H. Bacon, and R. Koldewey. 1902 and 1921. *Expedition of the Archaeological Institute of America. Investigations at Assos. Drawings and Photographs of the Buildings and Objects Discovered during the Excavations of 1881–1882–1883.* Cambridge, Mass.

Congdon, L.O.K., ed. 1974. "The Assos Journals of Francis H. Bacon." *Archaeology* 27:83–95.

Conze, A. 1880. *Neue archäologische Untersuchungen auf Samothrake.* Vienna.

De Long, D.G. 1981. "William R. Ware and the Pursuit of Suitability." In *The Making of an*

Architect, 1881–1981: Columbia University in the City of New York, edited by R. Oliver, 28–33. New York.

Diller, J.S. 1882. "Notes on the Geology of the Troad. Appendix 4." In *Report on the Investigations at Assos, 1881*, by J.T. Clarke, 180–215. Papers of the Archaeological Institute of America, Classical Series 1. Boston.

Dinsmoor, W.B. 1940. "Francis H. Bacon 1856–1940." *AJA* 44:117.

Dyson, S.L. 1998. *Ancient Marbles to American Shores: Classical Archaeology in the United States.* Philadelphia.

Friskin, R.C. n.d. "I had a Father, too, or the Mustard Seed." unpublished.

Kuklick, B. 1996. *Puritans in Babylon.* Princeton.

Lawton, W.C. 1882. "Notes on Bunarbashi and other Sites in the Troad. Appendix 2." In *Report on the Investigations at Assos, 1881*, by J.T. Clarke, 143–65. Papers of the Archaeological Institute of America, Classical Series 1. Boston.

Marchand, S. 1996. *Down from Olympus: Archaeology and Philhellenism in Germany, 1750–1970.* Princeton.

Norton, C.E. 1879. "Introductory Note." In *The Hypaethral Question,* by J.T. Clarke, 3–4. Papers of the Harvard Art Club 1. Cambridge, Mass.

———. 1882. "Introductory Note." In *Report on the Investigations at Assos, 1881*, by J.T. Clarke, vii–viii. Papers of the Archaeological Institute of America, Classical Series 1. Boston.

———. 1884. "A Visit to Sardis." *Harpers* April. 68, 407: 672–9.

———. 1898. "Introductory Note." In *Report on the Investigations at Assos, 1882, 1883,* pt. 1, by J.T. Clarke, v. Papers of the Archaeological Institute of America, Classical Series 2. New York.

Norton, R. 1897. "Two Reliefs from Assos." *AJA* 1:507–14.

Ramsay, W.M. 1897. *Impressions of Turkey During Twelve Years' Wanderings* London.

Reinach, S. 1884. "Chronique d'Orient." *Revue Archéologique.* 3rd ser. 3:335–44.

Riordan, R. 1883. "The Architectural League of New York." *Century Magazine* 32 ns. 10:698–708.

Roth, L.M. 1983. *McKim, Mead & White Architects.* New York.

Sterrett, J.R.S. 1911. *A Plea for Research in Asia Minor and Syria Authorized by Men Whose High Achievements and Representative Character Make the Project a Call for Humanity at Large for Light in Regard to the Life of Man in the Cradle of Western Civilization.* Ithaca.

Swales, F.S. 1924. "Master Draftsmen, V: Francis H. Bacon." *Pencil Points* 5 (September):38–54.

———. 1924. "Henry Bacon as Draftsman." *Pencil Points* 5 (May):43–6.

Thomas, C. 1990. "The Lincoln Memorial and its Architect, Henry Bacon (1866–1924)." Ph.D. diss, Yale University.

———. 1995–1996. "Francis H. Bacon. Master Draftsman as Archaeologist." *The Classicist* 2:28–33.

Tomlinson, R. 1991. *The Athens of Alma Tadema.* Wolfeboro Falls, NH.

Virchow, R. 1884. *Über alte Schädel von Assos und Cypern.* Abhandl. Der Königl. Preuss. Akademie der Wissenschaften zu Berlin.

Wheelwright, J.T. 1952. "The Origin of the Lampoon." In *The Harvard Lampoon: Seventy-fifth Anniversary, 1876–1951*. Cambridge, Mass.

Whitehill, W.M. 1970. *Museum of Fine Arts Boston: A Centennial History*, vol. 1. Cambridge, Mass.

Young, G. 1905. *Corps de droit Ottoman: Recueil des codes, lois, reglements, ordinances, et actes les plus importants du droit contumier de l'empire Ottoman*. Oxford.

NOTES

[1] William C. Lawton to Norton (CEN), 1 November 1881, AIA Archives. Former AIA Executive Director Mark Meister provided me support and permitted me to publish materials from the Archives where former AIA staff members Margo Muhl Davis, Priscilla Murray, and Wendy O'Brien assisted me. All AIA letters are from box 6 unless otherwise stated. Stephen Nonack of the Boston Athenaeum allowed me to quote from Austin's memoir, all of which citations come from chapter 10. Unless specified, all Bacon letters were written by or to Francis Henry Bacon and are published with the permission of Kendall Bacon and Candace Bacon Cordella. Clarke's excavation diaries, personal, and professional papers are lost, but Helen Landry (HBL) shared with me a memoir written by his daughter, Rebecca Clarke Friskin, (Friskin, n.d.). Lenore O.K. Congdon (LOKC) has been a true support and corrected my manuscript. I thank the special collections librarians for permission to cite letters from the Duke University Special Collections (Duke), the Norton Papers (NP) at the Houghton Library (HL), Harvard University, and the John Hay Library, Brown University.

[2] "Notes for the Historian," in Bacon to Horace Moran, 25 October 1936, in Bacon 1934–1939 Journal, henceforth Bacon to Moran.

[3] Ware began his pioneering course in architecture at MIT in 1866 (*Dictionary of American Biography* 19, 452; De Long 1981, 28–33).

[4] At the same time Clarke worked on his translation (1882) of von Reber's *Ancient Art* (von Reber to CEN, 2 March, 19 June, 19 August 1879, NP/HL).

[5] Wrigley's leg was amputated in 1881 as a result of injuries at Assos (Ware to CEN, 30 November 1881; 16 April, 11, 30 June 1882, AIA Archives, box 6.7).

[6] Robinson became Curator of Classical Archaeology at the MFA in 1885, Director of the MFA in 1902, and Director of the Metropolitan Museum in New York in 1910.

[7] Bradley, trained in reading inscriptions and making squeezes at the British Museum, had his health broken by fever and malnutrition at Assos (Bradley to CEN, 31 October 1881; Robinson to Stillman, 24 January 1882, AIA Archives) and died young as a result.

[8] He contributed an appendix to Clarke (1882, 143–65), later taught Greek and Latin at Bowdoin and Bryn Mawr, and served as secretary of the AIA (Briggs 1994, 348–9).

[9] Stillman to CEN, 24 January, 25 March 1882; Lawton to CEN, 1 November 1881, 16 July 1882; Robinson to CEN, 14 November 1881; Haynes to Stillman, 26 January 1882, AIA Archives; (Smyrna quote: Bacon to parents, 20 May, 15 July, 5 August 1881, Duke). For Clarke's experiences in Smyrna, see Allen (forthcoming).

[10] It is unusual that Eliot Norton, well aware of Clarke's dalliances (Lawton to CEN, 1 November, and Bradley to CEN, 15 December 1881, AIA Archives), did not communicate the seriousness of its implications to his father, but he left before the worst deprivations occurred. Perhaps delicacy of feeling prevented the 17-year-old from informing his father of Clarke's moral negligence.

[11] Lawton to CEN, 1 November 1881; Robinson to CEN, 14 November 1881; Haynes to Stillman, 26 January 1882, AIA Archives (Allen forthcoming). Although he was supposed to photograph from May to October 1881, Haynes was never given a camera.

[12] Sterrett later taught Greek at Amherst College, the University of Texas, and Cornell University (Dyson 1998, 65–6).

[13] Ware served on the Managing Committee of the ASCSA from 1885 to 1915 and designed its first building (Lord 1947, 11, 27–30). At the Calverts' estate he posed next to a grave stele, later bought by the MFA (Allen 1999, 358, n. 26). Ware recounted his trip to the Boston Society of Architects on 5 October 1883 (Austin 1942, 9–10).

[14] Through Norton, Bacon worked first with Henry Hobson Richardson (1838–1886) and then moved on to A.H. Davenport, one of Richardson's collaborators, where he worked from 1884 until Davenport's death in 1908 (Burke 1986, 418). Then Bacon established his own firm, FHB Co., which "had a practical monopoly of what used to be called 'the carriage trade'" (Bragdon 1940, 189–90). Often working with McKim, Mead and White, Bacon designed classicizing furnishings for the New York University Club (1896–1900), the White House in 1902, the Secretary of the Treasury's Offices in 1910, the Caucus Room of the Russell Senate Office Building in 1910–1911, members' benches for the U.S. House of Representatives in 1913, and the Shrine of the Declaration of Independence for the Library of Congress in 1923 (Swales 1924, 50–1; Bragdon 1940, 189–90; Roth 1983, 219, 223, 267–72, figs. 237, 238, 288; Thomas 1995–1996, 32).

[15] Quoted with permission of John Herrmann, MFA Curator of Art of the Ancient World.

[16] In Baltimore Clarke saw Alfred Emerson (1859–1943) who, like Clarke, was an American raised in Munich. But unlike Clarke, this pioneer archaeologist had a Munich Ph.D. in classical archaeology (1880) and a post-doctoral position at Princeton. He taught Greek, Archaeology, and Latin first at Johns Hopkins and later at the ASCSA, Cornell, Miami University, and Lake Forest (*The Nation* 24 July 1884 [995] 72; *NYT* 20 October 1943).

[17] In fact, a rumor circulated that he was dead (Austin 1942, 9–10).

[18] Although he published the translation of von Reber's *New Catalogue of the Old Pinacotheke* as his own, he admitted to Norton that his mother had done it (25 November 1884, AIA Archives). Later, mother and wife translated von Reber's *History of Medieval Art* (1887), likewise misleadingly credited to Clarke. His wife typed, drew, and photographed for him until she was overwhelmed by the births of two children in 16 months and the death of Clarke's mother in 1887 (Clarke to CEN, 9 February 1886, AIA Archives, box 5.12).

[19] After the AIA voted $1000 to investigate Magna Graecia in 1886, the Baltimore society raised an additional $2000 and entrusted the project to Clarke and Emerson, who surveyed the Doric temple of Hera Licinia at Croton and began to excavate with permission from the landowner, but without that of the government, which subsequently shut them down (AIA 1887, 40–6; AIA 1889, 40; Dyson 1998, 74–6).

[20] Their reconnaissance in Cyrenaica is recounted in *The Nation* 21 April 1887 [1138] 342; as well as Friskin, n.d., 9. A.L. Frothingham, Jr.'s letters to CEN, of 26 April and 5 June 1887 betray Clarke's desire to dig there and the Baltimore society's agreement to fund the work (AIA Archives, box 5.6).

[21] Clarke (1888, 293, fig. 9) simply imposes Calvert's analysis of the political spheres of the southern Troad (Calvert 1865, 52) on a map. The sites discovered came from Haynes's 1881 topographical study with Diller (Haynes to CEN, 28 November 1881, AIA Archives, box 6.5), never credited to Haynes in Diller (1882, 182–7) or Clarke (1888, 291–319). The scholarly apparatus was Clarke's.

[22] In 1889 Bacon helped Calvert sell antiquities to the Chicago Art Institute (LOKC), in 1903 to the MFA, and in 1905 to the Worcester Art Museum (Allen 1999, 241–2).

[23] Although the AIA owed Bacon more ($4901.13), Bacon insisted that Loeb's loan be paid off first. This was done (Ralph van Deman Magoffin to George H. Chase, 12 November 1925, AIA Archives, box 23.5). Lord visited Bacon at the Dardanelles and described him as "really destitute" to life members (7 February 1934, AIA Archives, box 31). Finally, Lord noted the debt discharged (to Frederick Calvert Bacon, 13 March 1936, AIA Archives, box 31). For Bacon as Institute Patron, see (AIA *Bulletin* 31 [1940], 42). See Congdon in Allen, Congdon, and Landry (forthcoming) for a history of publication.

[24] Bacon criticized ASCSA architect Gorham Stevens (1876–1973) for his publication of the Erechtheum because it omitted full-size molding profiles (Bacon to Moran).

[25] From 1885 to 1923, the Bacons changed their residence 16 times, gradually moving their possessions to Turkey where they retired in 1928. Decimated by the Depression, Bacon's company was liquidated by his son in 1939.

[26] Bacon to Richard Stillwell, (ASCSA director, 1932–1935), 21 May 1933, Stillwell Papers. His moldings are in the ASCSA Archives. Other Bacon drawings are in the archives of the Avery Architectural and Fine Arts Library, Columbia University.

— 4 —

The American School of Classical Studies at Athens: Scholarship and High Culture in the Gilded Age

Caroline Winterer

The Archaeological Institute of America was founded at an important moment in late 19th-century American intellectual life, when ideals of scholarship and erudition were rapidly transforming. This was the dawn of the age of the university, when the small, religiously oriented colleges of the antebellum era gave way to the great universities of today, with Ph.D.-granting programs, specialized scholarship, proliferation of academic disciplines, and a secular and cosmopolitan outlook. Some of the founders of the AIA were themselves representative of this new breed of investigator: the specialized, scientifically oriented career scholar of the university era. Yet the AIA was also home to another, older ideal of learning that had flourished for centuries in Europe and America: the scholar as man of letters, with a general knowledge base steeped in classical learning.

The 20th century places these two ideals in institutional opposition to one another. We reserve general learning and high culture for the undergraduate college, and advanced, specialized erudition for the Ph.D.-granting graduate program. But were these ideals always in conflict? In the late 19th century, they were not. Indeed, Charles Eliot Norton, the first president of the AIA and a Harvard art historian, resolutely opposed the narrowing of learning while also supporting the results of modern, specialized scholarship (Turner 1999). We might call this belief the "ideal of cultivated erudition":

the conviction that the highest scholarship must always rest on a rich base of cultured, general learning.

The ideal of cultivated erudition flourished in the AIA's first archaeological training school, the American School of Classical Studies at Athens (ASCSA), founded in 1881 (Lord 1947; Sheftel 1979; Dyson 1998). The ASCSA was the first of the AIA's institutions abroad, being joined in 1894 by the American Academy in Rome, whose early pedagogical goals drew on the same idealized classicism that animated the Athens school (Valentine and Valentine 1973; Yegül 1991, 3–13). The Athens school, however, as the earliest of the schools, deserves special notice among those interested in how the AIA and its schools can illuminate the broader scholarly landscape of Gilded Age America. First, the school was one of the first generation of American graduate training programs, when these were still an educational novelty. The school was an attempt by AIA members to remedy what they called "the comparative neglect among us of ancient studies and especially of those relating to the archaeology of Greece, in which is comprised the study of the origin and development of those arts which gave just expression to the Greek intelligence and sentiment, and afford such an image of national life and character as no other people has left of itself in its works." No universities or colleges at the time provided regular instruction in this field, even though "to encourage a cultivation of it . . . might well be considered as among the chief aims of an enlightened scheme of education" (AIA 1880, 23).

The school also created what was still a rarity in America: a national intellectual venture that would transcend the merely local. The AIA itself was such an organization, and the Athens school could possibly go even further by linking the archipelago of American colleges and universities in a commonality of purpose. The school's managing committee was composed of classical scholars from around the country: John Williams White (1849–1917) of Harvard as chairman; William Sloane (1850–1928) of Princeton; Lewis R. Packard (1836–1884) of Yale; Henry Drisler (1818–1897) of Columbia College; and Basil Lanneau Gildersleeve (1831–1924) of Johns Hopkins (AIA 1882, 54). The committee enlisted support and subscriptions from 12 American universities, which the AIA saw as "natural feeders" for the Athens school (Seymour to Norton, n.d. [1895?], AIA Archives). "The close union of colleges in the promotion of a common object," wrote the founders, "is a spectacle unique in this country, where the relations between colleges are far too slight." (AIA 1884, 11).

Third, the ASCSA reflected the slow divergence of the field of classical archaeology from its parent discipline, philology. The study of texts had long dominated European and American classicism. Although a lively interest and trade in the physical remains of antiquity had flourished—coins, sculpture, pots—these were believed to be less authoritative than texts as avenues to accurate knowledge of antiquity (Grafton 1991; Levine 1991; Haskell 1993). Indeed, in American higher education until the mid 19th century, students focused to the exclusion of all else on classical texts rather than art or artifacts (Winterer 2002). It was not until the late 19th century that other aspects of antiquity began to be taught in colleges and universities, gradually diluting classical philology with pedagogical innovations like slide shows, sculpture galleries, and maps. This new, broader approach to understanding antiquity spread across the disciplines in the newly formed "humanities" of the post-Civil War era, in disciplines such as literature, philosophy, and history that sought to give students a dose of high culture through the study of antiquity broadly construed (Turner 1996). Art history, for example, did not appear in the American college curriculum until Charles Eliot Norton began to teach it at Harvard in 1874 as a broad-gauged study that aimed to use art as a path to understanding past civilizations in their entirety (Turner 1999, 256–7; Hiss and Fansler, 1934). The Athens school reflected this shift toward the visual as an equally reliable source of information about the classical world. After visiting the Athens school in 1883, the Princeton art history professor Alan Marquand (1853–1924) praised its attention to archaeology in a letter to Charles Eliot Norton: "I was particularly pleased to find the School from the start dealing with archaeological questions and not expending all its energy on language" (Marquand to Norton, 31 March 1883, AIA Archives).

Most importantly for our purposes, the ASCSA can illuminate an important intellectual moment in the late 19th century, when a group of scholars believed that it was possible to train specialized scholars while also hewing to the kind of broad, humanistic learning that had characterized erudition in Europe and America for centuries. The school's founders hoped to maintain classical learning in the intellectual arsenal of the educated American, and classical antiquity as a touchstone of moral, political, and aesthetic guidance. Yet they also recognized the importance of disciplinary specialization and embraced the idea of science as a method of inquiry leading to objective truth. The curriculum and programmatic statements of the school in the early decades continually restated the importance of the ideal of cultivated erudition.

As it turned out, the ideal of cultivated erudition embodied in the Athens school—that the highest scholarship rested on a base of cultured generalism—did not flourish in American postcollegiate training programs in the 20th century. Instead, graduate programs became institutionally separate from the undergraduate college. In graduate school, students mastered a small province of knowledge and received a degree, the Ph.D., certifying specialization and research competence rather than cultivated erudition. But in the late 19th century, it was by no means clear that this form of advanced study would eventually dominate the landscape of higher education. Graduate study was still a new idea, and many experiments were attempted. The ASCSA should interest us, then, as an effort by an influential group of scholars to usher an older style of humanistic learning into the modern era, to keep classical learning at the core of erudition while also admitting the results of modern scholarship.

Classicists in the Age of Science

Classicists, both now and in the past, are often cast as educational conservatives, but in fact throughout the 19th century in America, they were vocal and energetic pedagogical and scholarly innovators. William Watson Goodwin (1831–1912), Eliot Professor of Greek Literature at Harvard from 1860 to 1901 and first director of the school at Athens, in 1883 addressed the common misperception that classicists were a stale lot, mired in the past just as their colleagues in other, new disciplines were entering the modern age of science and specialization. "It is often amusing to hear some well meaning people who undertake to enlighten the public about classical education talk about this as a department in which methods of teaching never change and everything is essentially musty and antiquated, while in all other departments the spirit of modern improvement reigns supreme. In point of fact, there is no study in which greater and more radical changes have been made in this country within the last generation than in this" (Goodwin 1884, 11).

At the core of classicists' concerns in the mid to late 19th century was the desire to keep Greece and Rome as relevant entities in the age of canals and rails, when it seemed that antiquity was slipping from the grasp of many

Americans. Whereas in the 18th century, classically imbued statesmen such as Thomas Jefferson (1743–1826) and John Adams (1735–1826) regularly deployed the counsel of the ancients, by the mid 19th century classicism in American political culture had begun to ebb. Moreover, within the college curriculum itself, new studies such as modern languages and chemistry began to displace Greek and Latin, which had dominated the curriculum for two and a half centuries. These subjects promised greater immediate social utility and an equal capacity to train the mental and moral faculties. Amid these assaults, classicists maintained that antiquity was not only relevant, but necessary: ancient Rome and Greece could inspire 19th-century Americans to reach for higher intellectual and ethical truths that would purge them of the spirit of relentless acquisition that polluted the factory age. The spirit of antiquity, they promised, could ennoble Americans corrupted by materialism and machines. Greece especially assumed new importance in the 19th century as the source of new possibilities of self-perfection: to study and observe the remains of the Greek past was to cultivate one's intellectual and aesthetic nature. Such beliefs animated the study of antiquity not only in America, but in England and Europe as well (Turner 1980; Jenkyns 1980; Marchand 1996). James Russell Lowell (1819–1891), man of letters and a trustee of the Athens school after 1886, expressed this pervasive, idealized view of Greece in 1886 in a letter to Walker Fearn (1832–1899), the U.S. Minister to Greece:

> Yes, I have been at Athens—*et ego in Arcadia*—and shall never outwear the impression I brought away. Pardon what looks like a pun when I say that as I stood gazing at the Acropolis, many new sensations were born in me by a very natural parthenogenesis. . . . I am glad to hear that you are happy there. It is good to be so anywhere, but in Athens must be best of all! (Lord 1947, 24).

I have argued elsewhere that such beliefs arose in America in the early 19th century, and contributed to a humanist revolution in higher education between 1820 and 1860 that radically transformed the study of classical antiquity in the colleges (Winterer 2002). The outcome of this revolution was that by 1860, the study of classical antiquity in American colleges was very different from what it had been just a century before. Instead of focusing on the minutiae of Greek and Latin grammar, students took a broad approach to antiquity, studying its literature, history, and artifacts in pursuit of a kind of secular perfection embodied in the ideal of "high culture." The undergraduate college indeed became a hothouse of high culture and Hellenism. Students encountered antiquity not only in their classroom texts, but also in the vogue for Greek play productions that took campuses by storm after 1881, and in the museums of classical antiquities that sprang up at a number of colleges and universities after mid-century (Norman 1882; Pluggé 1938). The undergraduate college had become a bastion of high culture by the late 19th century, and classical antiquity had been well-established as a road to that culture.

The triumph of the college of liberal culture in the late 19th century occurred also, however, at the dawn of the age of science and specialization, when for the first time advanced study became feasible in American higher education. Philology was fracturing into a number of smaller disciplines, each with its own specialized practitioners and journals. The *American Journal of Philology*, for example, was founded in 1880 by the Johns Hopkins University philologist Basil Lanneau Gildersleeve, while in 1885 the AIA began to produce its own more archaeologically oriented journal, the *American Journal of Archaeology*.

It was in this environment that late-century classical scholars in America sought to define the "science" of classical scholarship. Looking to Germany, they held up the Halle philologist Friedrich Augustus Wolf (1759–1824) as the father of the "science of classical philology, " because he had unified the disparate approaches to antiquity in the study of "Greek and Roman culture" as a whole, giving it what the University of Michigan Latinist Francis Willey Kelsey (1858–1927) called "a scientific coherence and consistency." In a science of classical philology, argued Kelsey, sources needed to be "critically examined," subjected to "rigid tests" for the "facts of language" and the "truth or falsity of statements" (Kelsey 1908, 372–3). The Dartmouth College classicist John Henry Wright (1852–1908) concurred, calling "exactness and discrimination" those qualities that made a study scientific (Wright 1886, 19).

Lauding the science of classical antiquity on the one hand, these Gilded Age classical scholars also feared excessive specialization because it would divorce classicism from general life. "I have spoken of classical philology as a science," wrote Francis Kelsey, "but do not misunderstand me, I mean no pyramid of bricks." No matter how much information scientific scholarship added to the edifice of knowledge, classicists needed to remember what

Kelsey called "the higher mission" of the classical scholar in America: "that he is to his day and generation an interpreter not of an isolated group of phenomena, but of a civilization, which in its better moments rose to ideals that are akin to those of our day because we have them as an inheritance" (Kelsey 1908, 385). Gildersleeve, who in so many ways seemed the archetypal modern scholar, with his Göttingen Ph.D. (1853) and his pioneering graduate courses at the new Johns Hopkins University, like Kelsey mocked what he termed "the supersubtle genius of the present day," who made college work excessively specialized and language a "dry and thirsty land" (Gildersleeve 1960 [1883], 133–4). In the late 1860s, he expressed his twin concerns for his discipline: "As on the one hand the classical philologians must not divorce themselves from general culture, so on the other they must see to it that they do scientific work and have scientific work done, that they live in a scientific atmosphere." (Gildersleeve 1960 [1878], 76). Gildersleeve, like many in his generation of classicists, stood at the historical moment when learning began to splinter into two worlds: one of specialized, "scientific" scholarship, the other of cultivated generalism. Encapsulating the ambivalence of his day, he wrote in 1880 to Johns Hopkins University president Daniel Coit Gilman (1831–1908): "If we dissociate classical philology from our general life, it has no hope of a future." (Briggs 1987, 120).

Cultivated Erudition: The American School of Classical Studies at Athens

It is thus the unique position of classicism as the traditional bedrock of erudition that makes its fate in the late 19th century so important. It also explains why classical scholars remained an energetic group of pedagogical reformers. The school at Athens reflected its founders' concerns about specialization and generalism, science and high culture, and shows their attempts to navigate between the twin perils of dilettantism and pedantry. Its role was ambidextrous: it was simultaneously intended to allow college graduates to pursue higher studies unavailable in America, but also to fertilize the ground of classical study more broadly. The school embodied the ideal of cultivated erudition: that advanced work in classical study must always rest upon a solid foundation of general culture.

In part this animus flowed from the relatively backward position of American classical scholarship compared to European. Since 1846, the

French had supported a school of classical study in Athens, the Germans established theirs in 1878, and the British were planning one of their own. The French and German schools were staffed by renowned archaeologists, filled with students, and housed large libraries—all at the expense of the home government. By contrast, America looked like a classical wilderness. Harvard's John Williams White, chairman of the school's managing committee from 1881 through 1887, observed of the school that "It cannot hope immediately to accomplish special work in archaeological investigation which will put it on a level with the German and French schools." The duty of the ASCSA nevertheless was one "of special importance": "an American school in particular should at the first not so much aim at distinguished achievements as seek to arouse in American colleges a genuine interest in classical archaeology in general" (AIA 1884, 113). The school would expose young Americans directly to ancient Greek remains for a year, after which they would return enriched to the United States, there to "stimulate intelligent interest in antiquity" (AIA 1887, 48–9). This sense of cultivating an impoverished soil was repeated like a mantra; in 1888 it appeared again as a reminder that the "chief aim of the School, for the present, is not the education of trained specialists . . . so much as the animation of classical studies in America by the vivifying study of the remains of ancient life in Greece, and to bring home to our country as a living force the artistic sense and culture of old Greece" (AIA 1888, 24).

But it was not only a keen sense of America's lowly place on the international scholarly scene that propelled such ruminations. It was also the sense that the school had two equally important constituencies of students to serve: the future professional and the cultivated generalist. William Watson Goodwin described both of these in his report of the work of the first year of the school in 1882–1883.

The first class of students, he explained, were those "who have a definite object in view, such as professional study of Greek architecture, or special study of Greek art or of some department of antiquities which can best be studied at Athens" (Goodwin 1884, 9). A year at Athens would allow these future professionals to work on specialized topics independently, training them in the ability to perform original research that was becoming a requirement of modern scholarship. The founders of the school were especially concerned that these young researchers be given ample opportunity to pursue archaeological topics rather than traditional textual ones, for it was in classical archeology that Americans could hope to begin to rival the Europeans. Only Greece itself furnished the monuments, inscriptions, topography, and opportunities to participate in excavations. Such aspirations were in keeping with the growing number of graduate-level courses in classical art and archaeology available in American universities during the Gilded Age, beginning sporadically in the early 1870s until by 1898 over 17 universities offered continuous graduate training in classical art history and archaeology, with course offerings far more specialized than those available at the undergraduate level (Hiss and Fansler 1934, 35–7, passim).

A number of students in the early years of the school fit into this first class of those who sought pre-professional training. One of these was J.R.S. Sterrett (1847–1923), who went on to head the Department of Greek at Cornell after 1901. Sterrett had been a member of the AIA's first archaeological expedition, the excavation of Assos, between 1881 and 1883 (Allen, ch. 3, this volume). He had already received the Ph.D. from Munich in 1880, and spent the 1882–1883 academic year at the school at Athens editing the inscriptions found at Assos (AIA 1886, 15). There were several other students in this first year in the Athens school who went on to professional careers in classical study: Harold North Fowler (1859–1955), Paul Shorey (1857–1934), and James Rignall Wheeler (1859–1918). Fowler, who received a Harvard A.B. in 1881, went on to earn a Ph.D. from Bonn in 1885. His work during the 1882–1883 year at the Athens school led to a published thesis on the Erechtheum. Wheeler, who received a Ph.D. from Harvard in 1885, produced a thesis on the theater of Dionysus at Athens; after 1895 he was professor of Greek literature and archaeology at Columbia. Paul Shorey, who went on to receive a Munich Ph.D. in 1884, wrote a thesis that was entirely textual, focusing on Theocritus. A professor of Greek at the University of Chicago from 1892 to 1927, Shorey became one the most influential classical scholars of his generation, as well as a vocal critic of the drift away from humanism in American education and society. Clearly these students used the school as a stepping stone to a later career as professional classical scholars. Goodwin, the director during that first year, proudly reflected that the school offered a year of "systematic study" as beneficial as "a year spent at one of the great universities of Europe." It would produce students who would "enlarge the bounds of science" and "bring their own work and our school into notice" (Goodwin 1884, 9–10).

Yet equally important to the mission of the school was the second group of students, whom Goodwin described as "the general students of classic antiquity, who come rather for general cultivation in Greek studies than for special research in a particular department" (Goodwin 1884, 10). Here was an idealized view of the possibilities offered by ancient Greece: Greece was the fountainhead of civilization, the source of timeless canons of taste and beauty, the site of both "instruction and inspiration" (Goodwin 1884, 12). The school at Athens would expose college graduates not to the old gerund-grinding mode of classical study, but to antiquity as "the road (and the only sure road) leading to the higher level of literature and art and beyond" (Goodwin 1884, 11). Classical study was "the foundation of literary culture," exposing students to "the best and choicest of the treasures of antiquity" (Goodwin 1884, 12). Like many others, Goodwin saw actual contact with antiquities, rather than just texts, as a quasi-religious experience that would help to cultivate students:

> I am sure that no one can dwell in daily sight of the dark rock of the Acropolis, crowned with the stately Parthenon, meeting his eyes at every turn in the crowded streets of the modern Athens as it met the eyes of the ancient Athenians, and become familiar with the calm beauty and dignity of this favorite home of Athena, without feeling that merely to live under its shadow is in itself an education (Goodwin 1884, 8–9).

This second group could use Athens as a grand illustration of literary and historical passages, one that would inoculate them against the money-grubbing concerns that awaited them in industrializing America.

Such sentiments were repeated a number of times over the next two decades at the school. The ASCSA's director from 1888 to 1892, Charles Waldstein (1856–1927), reminded readers in 1890 that the "encouragement of a general interest in classical antiquity" at the school was intended for those "not intending to pursue this as their chief vocation in life," and "not specially prepared for higher archaeological investigation" (ASCSA 1890, 31). Every year the regulations of the school explicitly stated that American students living or just traveling in Greece might enroll as students and enjoy the school's privileges. (ASCSA 1884, 20). Thus while students like Paul Shorey and Harold North Fowler were producing original, specialized researches, Franklin H. Taylor, their fellow student in 1882–1883, produced a thesis entitled "The Value of Modern Greek to the Classical Student," a study that required little specialized work (Lord 1947, 42).

In the 20th century, the twin hopes embodied within the Athens school would prove increasingly incompatible in graduate education in America. As Stephen Dyson (this volume) has argued, professional classicists became increasingly divorced in their interests and goals from those of amateur archaeologists in the AIA. This failure reflected the larger drift in American intellectual life from 19th-century ideals of scholarship, when the scholar's hope was to bring specialized research to the service of the cultivation of the general public. The early history of the American School of Classical Studies at Athens has importance as a relic of a fading world, when classical knowledge marked the educated citizen and general education was esteemed more than narrow specialization.

REFERENCES

Archaeological Institute of America (AIA). Archives. Boston University.
———. 1880. *First Annual Report of the Executive Committee, with Accompanying Papers, 1879–1880.* Cambridge, Mass.
———. 1882. *First Annual Report of the Committee on the American School of Classical Studies at Athens, 1881–82.* Cambridge, Mass.
———. 1884. *Third Annual Report of the Committee on the American School of Classical Studies at Athens, 1883–84.* Cambridge, Mass.
———. 1886. *First, Second, and Third Annual Reports of the Managing Committee of the American School of Classical Studies at Athens. 1881–84.* Cambridge, Mass.
———. 1887. *Fifth and Sixth Annual Reports of the Committee on the American School of Classical Studies at Athens, 1885–87.* Cambridge, Mass.
———. 1888. *Seventh Annual Report of the Committee on the American School of Classical Studies at Athens, 1887–88.* Cambridge, Mass.
———. 1890. *Ninth Annual Report of the Committee on the American School of Classical Studies at Athens, 1889–90.* Cambridge, Mass.
Briggs, W.W., Jr., ed. 1987. *The Letters of Basil Lanneau Gildersleeve.* Baltimore.
Dyson, S.L. 1998. *Ancient Marbles to American Shores: Classical Archaeology in the United States.* Philadelphia.
Gildersleeve, B.L. 1960 [1878]. "Classics and Colleges." In *Essays and Studies Educational and Literary,* 43–84. New York.
———. 1960 [1883]. "Grammar and Aesthetics." In *Essays and Studies Educational and Literary,* 127–57. New York.
Goodwin, W.W. 1884. *Report of the Director of the American School of Classical Studies at Athens for the Year 1882–'83.* Washington, D.C.

Grafton, A. 1991. *Defenders of the Text: The Traditions of Scholarship in an Age of Science, 1450–1800*. Cambridge, Mass.

Haskell, F. 1993. *History and Its Images: Art and the Interpretation of the Past*. New Haven.

Hiss, P., and R. Fansler. 1934. *Research in the Fine Arts in the Colleges and Universities of the United States*. New York.

Jenkyns, R. 1980. *The Victorians and Ancient Greece*. Oxford.

Kelsey, F.W. 1908. "Is There a Science of Classical Philology?" *Classical Philology* 3:369–85.

Levine, J. 1991. *The Battle of the Books: History and Literature in the Augustan Age*. Ithaca, NY.

Lord, L. 1947. *A History of the American School of Classical Studies at Athens 1882–1942: An Intercollegiate Project*. Cambridge, Mass.

Marchand, S. 1996. *Down from Olympus: Archaeology and Philhellenism in Germany, 1750–1970*. Princeton.

Norman, H. 1882. *An Account of the Harvard Greek Play*. Boston.

Pluggé, D. 1938. *History of Greek Play Production from 1881 to 1936*. New York.

Sheftel, P.S. 1979. "The Archaeological Institute of America, 1879–1979: A Centennial Review." *AJA* 83:3–17.

Turner, F.M. 1981. *The Greek Heritage in Victorian Britain*. New Haven.

Turner, J. 1996. "The Relocation of Religion and the Invention of the Humanities." Paper presented at Princeton University Conference on Higher Education, March 1996.

———. 1999. *The Liberal Education of Charles Eliot Norton*. Baltimore.

Valentine, L., and A. Valentine. 1973. *The American Academy in Rome, 1894–1969*. Charlottesville.

Winterer, C. 2002. *The Culture of Classicism: Ancient Greece and Rome in American Intellectual Life, 1780–1910*. Baltimore.

Wright, J.H. 1886. *The College in the University and Classical Philology in the College. An Address at the Opening of the Eleventh Academic Year of the Johns Hopkins University, October 7, 1886*. Baltimore.

Yegül, F.K. 1991. *Gentlemen of Instinct and Breeding: Architecture at the American Academy in Rome 1894–1940*. New York.

— 5 —

"Sending out of Expeditions": The Contest for Delphi

Phoebe A. Sheftel

The contest for the promising site of ancient Delphi highlights both the high ambitions and serious challenges faced by the Archaeological Institute of America in its early years. From its very beginnings excavation was an essential element of the organization's mission, and Charles Eliot Norton engaged in a constant search for suitable sites. When the possibility arose for getting the permit for Delphi, he led the campaign to prevail over competing French interests. The struggle dragged on for five years, and in the end the prize escaped his grasp. Norton found himself embroiled in disagreements within the American scholarly community on the appropriateness of pursuing the site to the possible detriment of other European scholars. His fundraising difficulties, ultimately blamed for the failure to gain the site, created a dawning awareness that having a great goal and an important site did not translate into automatic funding from a donor pool that was attracted by competing needs. Finally, the loss of the site cut short a simmering internal disagreement over who would control the excavation, the AIA or Charles Waldstein (1856–1920), then director of the American School of Classical Studies at Athens.

When it was apparent that the French had secured the site, Norton urged the Institute to prepare a full account of the Delphi episode. He noted that "the record of these doings will be of importance in the history of the Institute, and of interest as indicating the possibilities of general public support for such undertakings. It is an irreparable loss that we have suffered; one which will seem greater as time goes on than it does now. And had the public responded more promptly to our appeal, it need not have occurred" (Norton to Seth Low, 18 March 1891, AIA Archives, box 7). He was clearly smarting from defeat, but whether the consequences were as dire for American archaeologists as he imagined is better judged from the record of the last 100 years. Nevertheless, the story of the contest for Delphi, as seen by the American players, gives an interesting insight into the Institute as a young organization. This is the story that Norton wanted told.[1]

During two extended trips to Europe in 1846 and 1869, Norton grew to appreciate the value of learning from original materials. In his position as a teacher, he saw America's cultural education hampered by a lack of access to primary sources of information. Responding to this deficiency, he and the other founders of the AIA spelled out their goals in the first *Annual Report* as "promoting and directing archaeological investigation and research . . . sending out of expeditions for special investigation . . . aiding the efforts of independent explorers . . . and the publication of reports of the results of the expeditions which the Institute may undertake or promote" (AIA 1880, 6). From the very beginning, Norton hoped that the work of the AIA "might be as creditable as that of the Dilettanti Society in England" (Minutes of the formation meeting, 10 May 1879, AIA Archives, box 1).

Archaeological societies in Europe focused their early efforts on assembling large collections of artifacts (sarcophagi, pottery, etc.). The fact that Norton had traveled in Europe and seen museums bulging with objects gathered from a variety of sources, scientific and otherwise, must have enhanced his belief that America should respond in kind, or soon be left behind with little of significance to excavate and display in its own recently founded museums, such as the New York Metropolitan Museum of Art (1872) and the Boston Museum of Fine Arts (1876). The growing field of archaeology threatened to become even more crowded, with countries such as Greece producing scholars of merit and protecting the value of their own patrimony since 1835.

In 1880 the AIA launched two significant expeditions, giving balanced recognition to the two areas competing for the organization's support. Norton's first AIA presidential report in May of that year had hinted at plans for an excavation in the Mediterranean (AIA 1, 1880, 9). A fundraising goal was set at $8000 and the promise of objects was offered in return for institutional contributions. In July of 1880 Norton appointed Adolph Bandelier

(1840–1914) to work on advancing the "knowledge of the past and present conditions of the aboriginal races in New Mexico and its neighborhoods" (Norton to Bandelier, 19 February 1880, AIA Archives, box 1). For that undertaking Bandelier was awarded a stipend of $1200. Meanwhile, Turkey was targeted as the most attractive Mediterranean country in which to excavate, largely because the Turks still allowed finds to be removed. (Allen, ch. 3, this volume) The excavations at the ancient site of Assos in Turkey, begun in 1881, received considerably more funding than those in America, commensurate with AIA interest in classical antiquities. While both excavations yielded plentiful and exciting remains, the experience of dividing the Assos objects with the Ottoman government gave the new organization a quick lesson in dealing with the politics of national interest. Persuasion, negotiations, and money were not entirely successful in securing all the objects deemed desirable for the Boston Museum. (Allen, ch. 3, this volume)

No other expeditions were sent out during Norton's tenure as AIA president between 1879 and 1890, but the Institute did sponsor several independent research projects, including studies at Knossos and Gortyna on Crete (1881) and a survey of Babylonian sites (1884–1886) (Allen, ch. 3; Silberman, this volume). Even the local societies played a role in supporting exploration. The New York society joined the Metropolitan Museum in a survey of Hittite sites in eastern Turkey (1887) and the Philadelphia society contributed to the University of Pennsylvania's excavation at Nippur (1888–1889).

Most interesting, however, is the story of the excavation that did not take place. For playing in the political arena on a grand scale, nothing quite matches the story of the American and French contest for the prize of Delphi. This episode confronted the AIA with issues that remain significant even today: the clash of the quest for pure learning with political realities, the importance of stable funding, the challenge of conveying the value of archaeology to the layperson, and the critical role of persistent and visionary leadership. Between 1886 and 1891 the Americans, French and Greeks tried every maneuver possible to settle their conflicting claims to the site of Delphi, with the dispute even spilling over into the company of American archaeologists and the governing council of the AIA.

The minutes of the AIA's formation meeting on 10 May 1879 contain the first hint of what was to come. The year before, the Harvard Club, through Norton, had written to the Greek government asking about sites to excavate; Delphi was high on the list, even though the French had bought land for a small excavation at the site in 1861 and were known to be seeking the concession. The reply was generally encouraging, except as it related to the coveted site, "at which place the Greeks themselves have begun to make investigation" (Minutes of the formation meeting, 10 May 1879, AIA Archives, box 1). Norton was undeterred and kept the subject alive, at least among his associates. Some years later Shakespearean scholar Horace Howard Furness (1865–1930) posed a prescient question in a letter to Norton: "The thought of excavations at Delphi makes the brain whirl, and yet where are we to find the man whose purse reaches the required depth?" (Furness to Norton, 18 December 1886, AIA Archives, box 7). The idea appeared to have met a swift death, when five weeks later Norton received a communication from University of Michigan professor Martin D'Ooge (1839–1915) announcing, "Delphi is lost—to our School" (D'Ooge to Norton, 29 January 1887, AIA Archives, box 7). The school referred to was the American School of Classical Studies at Athens (ASCSA) (Winterer, this volume). He had just learned that the French and the Greeks had been negotiating over the site, and suggested that contributors to the AIA's effort might be persuaded to divert their funds to a small study of Sikyon planned for that summer.

There the matter appears to have rested for nearly two years, until December of 1888, when United States consul general to Greece Walker Fearn (1832–1899) wrote John Williams White (1849–1917), professor of Greek at Harvard, with news that must have pleased Norton: "I am at length able to report that Delphi is open to us—provided the required funds can be obtained" (Fearn to White, 15 December 1888, AIA Archives, box 7). This apparent reversal of fortune was occasioned by the report that the French Chamber of Deputies had rejected the proposed Graeco-Gallic commerce treaty—a treaty that the Greeks had hoped to secure by linking it to the promise of excavation at Delphi. Fearn guessed that it would cost up to $100,000 to buy the modern town covering the site and reminded White that a condition of the excavation would be that all the finds stay in the country.

When the effort to acquire the excavation rights eventually fell through, critics of the AIA's quest for the site particularly railed against the way Norton and the AIA had played into the Greeks' hand by presenting themselves as competitors to the French. But if the Greek government could not use the site in negotiations for a treaty they dearly wanted, they could certainly turn it into a shrewd business exercise in extracting money from American millionaires. The Greeks decided that the excavators would have to buy the whole town at the site, despite the fact that part of it sat on bedrock and obviously had no archaeological value; "this squalid neo-Hellenic palimpsest" was how Fearn referred to it (Fearn to James Russell Lowell, 31 December 1888, AIA Archives, box 7). By the spring of 1889 Charles Waldstein reported to Norton that he had secured the Greek minister's promise that the AIA could have Delphi if they raised the money to buy the site (Waldstein to Norton, 9 May 1889, AIA Archives, box 7).

The next several years brought high hopes and threatening disappointments. Rumors flew. William Robert Ware (1832–1915) reported to Norton that he had heard that the Archaeological Society in Athens had "raised a group in Vienna and will do Delphi themselves" (Ware to Norton, 26 March 1889, AIA Archives, box 7). But the French were still in the competition and when they were unable to raise the money, a compromise was proposed whereby the French and the Americans would become partners in the site. This idea was dismissed by Augustus Chapman Merriam (1843–1895), who curtly proclaimed that the French "have no right to hang on to Delphi by the skirts and try to keep others away for an indefinite series of years" (Merriam to Norton, 14 May 1889, AIA Archives, box 7). In another letter, written on the same day, William J. Stillman (1828–1901) urged Norton to withdraw from the whole matter and get the benefit of a "spontaneous renunciation" (Stillman to Norton, 14 May 1889, AIA Archives, box 7). In early March he had sent a letter published in *The Nation,* which criticized the Americans for breaching common courtesy in vying for the site and suggested that their reputation for "having millions [of dollars] to throw away" would only encourage the Greeks to demand exorbitant prices for future excavations (Stillman 1889). Four months later, Stillman reported that the Archaeological Society in Athens had urged the government not to give the site to the AIA, "the reasons for which are conclusive but not flattering"; he cryptically noted in his letter that he was declining to elaborate on the nature of the reasons (Stillman to Norton, 14 September 1889, AIA Archives, box 7).

Stillman kept up this argument for renunciation, telling Norton that he had been misinformed, criticizing him for not talking directly with the French, and warning him that the Americans had been used by the Greek government, whose role in the whole affair was termed "most disgraceful" (Ibid.). Stillman brushed off the suggestion that his personal opposition stemmed from resentment over not being selected as director of the ASCSA and, without equivocating, wrote that by remaining in the contest for the site "we are making ourselves, nationally, accomplices in the dirtiest piece of work on the part of the Greek government that I have ever known any civilized government to be guilty of." (Ibid.) Norton cannot have been pleased to have these internal disagreements undermining his fundraising efforts.

But the Americans were not above their own persuasive tactics. Charles Waldstein first discovered from reading in the Greek newspapers on the day after he arrived in Athens to take up the post as director of the ASCSA, that he had been "sent by the American government to enter upon negotiations for the excavation of Delphi" (Waldstein 1889). He took up the challenge with enthusiasm and later reported that when the Greek prince had expressed great interest at one of the school lectures, he had suggested that both he and the king should become honorary members of the AIA. Waldstein also assured Norton that the Greek Prime Minister, Harilaos Tricoupis (1833–1896), was still pledging to keep the site open for the Americans and discounting the possibility that the treaty with the French would ever be approved (Waldstein to Norton, 20 February 1890, AIA Archives, box 7).

Undeterred by Stillman's complaints, Norton stepped up his fundraising campaign and approached some of America's wealthiest men, but not with universal success, however. Collegiate architect Russell Sturgis (1836–1909) wrote Norton, lamenting that the wealthy, like the Vanderbilts, prefer to support hospitals and asylums: "Like robber-knights they will try to save their souls by building Sunday-schools out of their spoil, but they don't look for any benefit to their hereafter from scholarship and so they won't give" (Sturgis to Norton, 14 December 1889, AIA Archives, box 7).

Others, though, were seen as ripe for the motivational approach. Two months later William W. Goodwin (1831–1912) enthusiastically reported to Norton that he had just met a relative of California Governor Leland Stanford (1824–1893) and gained an entree to work on him to buy the whole site, perhaps in memory of his son, Leland Stanford, Jr. (1869–1884) (Goodwin to Norton, 7 February 1890, AIA Archives, box 7). A follow-up letter contained the encouraging news that Governor Stanford had expressed interest, if the gift could "bring glory to his University and to the name of his son" (Goodwin to Norton, 11 February 1890, AIA Archives, box 7). Meanwhile, another contact suggested that Governor Stanford's wife was the one to approach, as it was she who had the fortune, was "the real sentimentalist of the family," and had been instrumental in getting the Governor "to start his university scheme" (Thomas A. Walker to Norton, March 1890,

AIA Archives, box 7). The records do not indicate whether or not this approach was successful.

One potential benefactor displayed biting wit in declining to contribute. He said he had been asked by so many and preferred "the feeding and clothing and care of the poor and sick close around him to excavations even at Delphi" (H. Saltonstall to Norton, 14 February 1890, AIA Archives, box 7). He went on to express his "sympathy with poor old Pharaoh and his family, who have been pulled out of the graves they made for themselves with so much care, and stuck up in a museum, all withered and shriveled and black, for us irreverent moderns to laugh at. What good does it do, save to satisfy the curiosity of a few, to dig up these poor cusses? Think what might happen if we encourage these things . . . President Harrison may be exhibited to a wondering and indignant population not yet discovered as the champion of the Protective Tariff." (Ibid.) Clearly, this was a marketing challenge for the development office.

By October of 1890 things were looking promising. Financier Cornelius Vanderbilt (1843–1899) had pledged $5000, and $30,000 had been raised in all. In November, new AIA President Seth Low (1850–1916) wrote United States Secretary of State James Blaine (1830–1893) reporting that all the funds were in hand to purchase the site (Low to Blaine, 26 November 1890, AIA Archives, box 7).

With the prestige of Delphi apparently secured for the Americans, AIA internal politics suddenly threatened to derail the whole project. Charles Waldstein, Director of the ASCSA, had realized that it was the AIA, not the School, that was to be in charge of the excavation. In a blistering letter to Seth Low, Waldstein claimed that he had left his post as Director of the Fitzwilliam Museum and Reader in Classical Archaeology at Cambridge University to assume the role of Director of the American School, based primarily on his expectation of excavating Delphi (Waldstein to Low, 28 November 1890, AIA Archives, box 7). He further maintained that donations toward the purchase of the site were a consequence of his role as director. He laid out detailed demands for a contract to run the excavations under his control, with a staff that included professionals in everything from business to epigraphy. Seth Low reminded Waldstein that all the pledges had been made to the AIA directly and vaguely suggested that the Council would consider appointing him director of the excavation (Low to Waldstein, 9 December 1890, AIA Archives, box 7).

The portent of a negative outcome for the project surfaced in early 1891, when word came that the French had signed the treaty with the Greeks. AIA President Seth Low wrote the members of the Institute's Council proposing as the "proper" stance that "we withdraw absolutely pending settlement of French claims" (Low to members of Council, 20 January 1891, AIA Archives, box 7). Norton had earlier tried to dissuade Low from withdrawal, claiming that the Americans were perfectly within their rights to pursue the concession "for the general interests of learning," and underlining his view with a critical assessment of French excavation skills (Norton to Low, 14 January 1890, AIA Archives, box 7). He characterized their work as "lacking in essential features of thoroughness, accuracy, and respect for ancient remains," noting that "their recent work at Delos is open to very serious reproach in these respects" (Ibid.). By late February reports filtered back that Waldstein had told the Greek newspapers that the Americans felt they had been unfairly treated and were withdrawing. William Goodwin wrote Norton, assuring him that they had not been mishandled, and worried that their "friend in the government" would misread the reports (Goodwin to Norton, 23 February 1891, AIA Archives, box 7).

But all was lost in March of 1891 when Seth Low reported that he had received a cable from Waldstein definitely informing him "that the French possess Delphi." He immediately proposed that the contributors be asked to convert their donations to the permanent endowment fund (Low to AIA Secretary William Lawton, 12 March 1891, AIA Archives, box 7).

Immediately the recriminations started. Norton blamed the failure on the public's slow response to the appeal for funds. Stillman despaired of damaged relations with the French and complained that his criticism of the affair led to his being "attacked as unpatriotic, put in Coventry by the friends of our School, and made to pay such penalties as the outraged dignity of our archaeologists could inflict" (Stillman 1891). Low saw the key event in the earlier overthrow of the Greek Prime Minister Harilaos Tricoupis, whom he felt had deceived the AIA with persistent promises of success. He was pleased that the site was to be uncovered and reported that the American and French archaeologists still enjoyed cordial relations. Low saw it in a positive light, pointing out that while Americans "are sometimes said to be a people given over to materialism," the events had shown them to have "an enlightened interest in everything that tends to intellectual and artistic culture." He sought to maintain the members' enthusiasm by pointing to exciting possibilities of excavation at promising sites in Eretria, Sparta, and the Argive Heraeum (Low to members of the AIA, 9 May 1891, AIA Archives, box 7).

From its earliest days the Institute had claimed excavation as one of its primary goals. The usually prompt and generous response of wealthy donors had supported expeditions that produced romantic and appealing stories of adventurous discovery, along with plentiful artifacts for new and growing museums. The Delphi episode, however, injected a jarring note of reality, underscoring the rising costs and political unrest that were to be a constant hazard for professionals in the field. Although the Institute supported later excavations and held on to the dream of expeditions as late as 1968, when an attempt to revive the excavations at Assos was rebuffed by the Turkish government, the organization began increasingly to focus on its other primary goal—publication and the spread of knowledge. Respected publications, scholarly lecturers, and the comprehensive Annual Meeting have built a creditable legacy that would have well satisfied those 11 scholars who signed on to endorse the founding of the AIA one April day nearly 120 years ago.

REFERENCES

Primary Sources

Archaeological Institute of America (AIA) Archives, 656 Beacon Street, Boston University, boxes 1–38 (1879–1951).

Secondary Sources

AIA. 1880. *First Annual Report of the Executive Committee, with Accompanying Papers, 1879–1880*. Cambridge, Mass.

Stillman, W.J. 1889. "The Excavations at Delphi." *The Nation* 48:1239 (28 March) 266–7.

———. 1891. "The Excavations of Delphi." *The Nation* 52:1344 (2 April) 282.

Waldstein, C. 1889. "The Excavations at Delphi." *The Nation* 48:1245 (9 May) 383.

NOTES

[1] The archives of the AIA are a major source of information about this period. I appreciate the access to this collection of letters that gives the American perspective on these events. Perhaps future discoveries in Greek and French ministry archives will illuminate other aspects of the story.

— 6 —

Between Athens and Babylon: The AIA and the Politics of American Near Eastern Archaeology, 1884–1997

Neil Asher Silberman

The sharp cultural boundaries often perceived by scholars dividing the Near East and the Aegean, the worlds of Semites and Hellenes, and the histories of Babylon and Athens are not features of nature, but ideas spawned in the minds of women and men. Such antiquarian boundaries often mark and reinforce modern political motives and intentions, as even the most casual review of power relations between Europe and the Middle East over the last 200 or so years will reveal (Silberman 1982; Bernal 1987; Larsen 1987; Meskell 1998). And in that respect, the archives of the Archaeological Institute of America can provide a unique perspective (Sheftel 1979). The Institute's history, as recorded in documents, letters, annual reports, and newsletters can offer us more than a dry history of the discipline—of money raised, sites dug, and artifacts found. Over the last 118 years of its existence, it can provide vivid illustrations of the ways in which modern views of the past are constantly reshaped by shifting contemporary political conditions—in particular, the fluctuating interests and involvement of Americans and American institutions in the eastern Mediterranean world (Dyson 1998). For since the late 19th century, the leadership of the Archaeological Institute of America has made a number of dramatic policy shifts with regard to the character, depth, and intensity of involvement in Near Eastern archaeology. These changes have been caused by both war and upheaval in the region and by changing scholarly perceptions of the relevance of ancient Near Eastern studies to the understanding of the

Bronze Age Aegean and classical world. No less significant, the AIA's more direct, official relationship with the various modern nations of the Middle East also continues to be in transition even to the present day.

As earlier chapters have demonstrated, the foundation of the Institute in May 1879 in Boston, the "Athens of America," took place at a time when the scholars of other nations were making great archaeological discoveries throughout the Mediterranean. Schliemann, the great archaeological entrepreneur, was making headlines in Greece and Asia Minor. German expeditions were uncovering Olympia. The French were digging in lower Mesopotamia. And the British Palestine Exploration Fund had just completed its massive archaeological survey of Western Palestine. AIA founding father Charles Eliot Norton (1827–1908) was thus motivated by the worry that the United States would be among the last of the world's major powers in adopting—and even harvesting—cultural models from the ancient world (Sheftel 1979, 3–4; AIA 1880, 17–26). The American Southwest, with its impressive archaeological remains, was an obvious field for action (Hinsley 1989), yet the official focus of the Institute always drifted in the direction of Greece. "The superiority of the Greeks," noted the Fifth Annual Report of the Institute Executive Committee in 1884, "had its source in their moral discipline, was the result of adherence to principles of universal application and validity, and is therefore of perpetual service, alike, as an example for emulation and as a criterion of conduct" (AIA 1884, 28). Much has been written about the ideological implications of late 19th-century philhellenism—literary, archaeological, and racial (Turner 1981; Bernal 1987, vol. 1, ch. 7; Marchand 1996; Shanks 1996). Yet for the AIA, which began its excavations at Assos in 1881 and established the American School of Classical Studies at Athens in the following year, involvement in Middle Eastern exploration proved to be just a matter of time and opportunity.

By 1884, in fact, a new field of exploration beckoned (Kuklick 1996, 25–6). The discovery of the exotic remains of the Assyrian and Babylonian empires had been begun earlier in the century by the French and the British. But the 1881 discovery of an Assyrian flood myth—strikingly similar to the biblical account—among the cuneiform tablets from Nineveh established beyond question the relevance of those civilizations to the cultural heritage of the West. And no less a patron of American culture than Mr. J.P. Morgan (1837–1913) of New York City soon began to provide funds for the purchase from art dealers of Mesopotamian antiquities for the Metropolitan

Museum. But the obvious question in that gilded age of big business was: Why not eliminate the middleman and dig the relics directly? To that end, in 1884, the tobacco heiress Catherine Lorillard Wolfe (1828–1887) provided $5000 for a preliminary American reconnaissance of the eastern salient of the Fertile Crescent, and President Norton waxed enthusiastic about its prospects for success. "The whole Mesopotamian region," he wrote in 1884, "becomes from year to year, with the rapid advance in knowledge of Mesopotamian antiquity, of more and more importance in the field of archaeological investigation. It is desirable that the Institute should bear its part in the long and interesting work that still needs to be done in the lands bordering upon the Tigris and Euphrates" (AIA 1885, 43–4).

So with the wholehearted sponsorship of the Archaeological Institute of America, the Wolfe Expedition steamed across the Mediterranean to the Levant and cruised down the Euphrates, led by the indefatigable amateur William H. Ward (1835–1916)—newspaper editor, antiquities collector, and former president of the American Oriental Society (King 1983, 11–2). The delegation braved the political uncertainty of Ottoman Iraq and the suspicion of other European representatives to lay claim to the massive site of Nuffar—the ancient Nippur, one of the richest of Sumerian sites. Yet the intensive exploration of this site would require a more sustained commitment than the AIA, with its Athens school, continuing projects in the American Southwest, and hopes of gaining a concession for a dig at Delphi, was willing to give.

A determining principle thus emerged early in the AIA's history: general sponsorship of Near Eastern projects, rather than direct involvement, better suited the goals of the Institute. In the view of the Institute's leaders and most influential supporters, the recovery and study of classical antiquities were to be the organization's primary task (Dyson 1998). Yet as the senior American archaeological institution working in the eastern Mediterranean, the AIA was also intent on maintaining its position of moral and intellectual authority in the development of the discipline. In the event, individual Institute members, pursuing specific Near Eastern interests became the practical link. Thus the excavation of Nippur was ultimately carried out under the auspices of the University of Pennsylvania and financed by a group whom Ward called "a few gentlemen in Philadelphia, mostly members of the Institute, who are organized as the Babylonian Exploration Fund" (Ward 1888, 61).

In 1899, the Institute again involved itself in American Near Eastern exploration, this time in a more formal relationship with a new American scholarly organization. AIA President Seth Low (1850–1916) joined with the officers of the American Oriental Society and the Society for Biblical Literature to establish an "American School of Oriental Research in Jerusalem" as a parallel to the American School of Classical Studies at Athens established 17 years before (Sheftel 1979, 10–11; King 1983, 25–6). Yet AIA hopes of coordinating American archaeological efforts in a great, eclectic outreach were again to be disappointed by the distinctly different interests and motivations of American Near Eastern archaeology. The goal of the Jerusalem School, for example, was to be frankly ecclesiastical. Its constitution declared that it would "afford graduates of American theological seminaries, and other similarly qualified persons, opportunity to prosecute biblical and linguistic investigations under more favorable conditions than can be secured at a distance from the Holy Land" (King 1983, 27). That strong biblical orientation, with only secondary interest in classical civilizations or influence in the Near East, would make meaningful cooperation with the AIA on field projects and research questions initially quite difficult.

That is not to say that the AIA gave up hope of further exploration in the region—or that it would avoid involvement in Middle Eastern intrigues. In 1910, Richard Norton (1872–1918), the son of former AIA President Charles Eliot Norton, hit upon the idea of planting the American archaeological flag amidst the Hellenistic and Roman ruins of Libya by excavating the massive ancient city of Cyrene (Norton 1911).[1] The expedition, setting up its camp in the modern village of Shahhat, began to excavate structures on the ancient acropolis, but was quickly swept up in a violent whirlwind of tribal warfare and imperial politics. In 1911, the local Ottoman government, already weakened by the effects of the Young Turks' Revolt in Anatolia and the Balkans, had little control over the area of ancient Cyrene. There, tribal rivalries fueled by the passion of the fundamentalist Sanusiyya movement clearly doomed any chance for a tranquil American dig. Norton's assistant and translator, Herbert Fletcher De Cou (1868–1911), was murdered in a dispute with local laborers (Kelsey 1911) and despite Norton's insistence that the excavations continue, the tragedy of errors and misunderstandings did not end. In September 1911, the Italians invaded Libya, occupied Tripoli, and called a halt to the American excavations. The only bright note in this otherwise sorry chapter of AIA exploration was that after diplomatic protest, the Institute received an indemnity of approximately $16,000 from the Italian government for the loss of its excavation concession (Sheftel 1979, 12). Norton's North African adventure had come to an end.

The outbreak of World War I temporarily halted further AIA field projects, yet with the post-war political transformations that occurred throughout the Near East, the Institute hoped to resurrect its program of Near Eastern exploration. With Mesopotamia—now Iraq—placed under the rule of a temporary British mandate, the reconstituted "Mesopotamian Committee" of the AIA authorized Professor Albert Tobias Clay (1866–1925) of Yale in 1920 to investigate the possibilities for the establishment of an American School of Mesopotamian Archaeology in Baghdad (King 1983, 67). Yet once again, the specific interests and expertise of the Biblical and Near Eastern archaeologists pushed them toward institutional independence.

In the post-World War I world, with the establishment of European mandatory governments in Syria, Palestine, Transjordan, and Iraq, the opportunities for extensive archaeological fieldwork throughout the region increased dramatically. Yet the close contacts and local expertise required to initiate and administer this fieldwork necessitated highly focused and fairly autonomous regional organizations—rather than a single distant academic and organizational patron like the AIA. Thus in 1921, the American Schools of Oriental Research (now including the research facilities in both Jerusalem and Baghdad) were independently incorporated in Washington, and AIA oversight became just a polite formality (King 1983, 59–60).

By the 1930s, the focus of the Institute had clearly and permanently been fixed on the operation of the American School of Classical Studies at Athens and the ongoing excavations in the Agora and at Corinth. Yet the AIA sponsorship of the pioneering excavations of Hetty Goldman (1881–1972) at the site of Gözlü Kule near Tarsus from 1934 to 1939 and, after World War II, in 1947–1948, marked the beginning of an era of dramatic change in the archaeological partition between Near Eastern and Aegean archaeology. First came the scholarly advances, reflecting new, more cosmopolitan post-war perspectives on the likely links between the Aegean and the ancient Near East. Goldman's work at Tarsus underlined the connections between the two regions in the Bronze Age (Magness-Gardiner 1997) and the equally pioneering 1947 monograph by Helene Kantor (1919–1993) on *The Aegean and the Orient in the Second Millennium* (reprinted in 1997 by the AIA) helped demolish the logistical and conceptual boundaries between the Aegean and Near Eastern worlds (Kantor 1947; McDonald and Thomas 1990, 304–6). Second, the changing political climate also played a part in the strictly organizational sphere. With the United States emerging from World

War II with ever-deepening global involvements, the AIA joined as a sponsor in the creation of three new research institutes throughout the Near East: the American Research Center in Egypt in 1948 (Patch 1997); the American Research Institute in Turkey in 1964 (Cross 1997); and the American Institute of Iranian Studies in 1968 (Sumner 1997). The trend that had been established as early as the 1884 Wolfe Expedition to Mesopotamia had by now become a fact of the AIA's existence. Continuing excavation and primary interest in the Aegean was combined with institutional and occasional logistical support for American exploration in the Near East.

Throughout the 1960s, while studiously avoiding the political entanglements of the archaeological organizations more directly affected by the ongoing Arab-Israeli conflict, the AIA nevertheless indicated its continued interest in the archaeology of the region. ASOR (the American Schools of Oriental Research) continued to be the primary institutional framework for American fieldwork. Yet its projects figured prominently in the AIA lecture program to its local societies—as a clear reflection both of the directions in which public archaeological interest was moving and in the continuing inclusion of biblical and Near Eastern archaeology in the AIA's sphere of intellectual influence. The Institute's publication in 1967—a year marked by war and a new configuration of the Middle Eastern conflict—of a collected volume of articles on *Archaeological Discoveries in the Holy Land* that had appeared in *Archaeology* magazine further addressed this public interest by bringing together the research of scholars working in both Jordan and Israel (Archaeological Institute of America 1967). And the 1973 election of Professor James Pritchard (1909–1997), who was at the time directing excavations at Sarepta in Lebanon, as AIA president further blurred the once clear-cut disciplinary boundaries of the Institute's work.

The subsequent establishment of a Committee on Near Eastern Archaeology; the publication in the *American Journal of Archaeology* of a series of authoritative review articles on archaeological developments in Turkey, Syria, Israel, and Jordan; continuing professional and institutional connections with ASOR; and even the appointment of the Assyriologist and Near Eastern archaeologist James Muhly as director of the American School of Classical Studies at Athens were all aspects of an intensifying web of relationships that went far beyond the original vision of Charles Eliot Norton, of obtaining antiquarian models for the moral and aesthetic improvement of American society. Growing numbers of classical scholars began to integrate

Near Eastern findings into their own work (e.g., S. Morris 1992; I. Morris 1996). No less important, the involvement of the AIA in research, preservation, ethics, and public outreach throughout the entire Mediterranean reflected the growing involvement of American scholars and private citizens with the region's modern peoples, from Italy eastward to Israel and Jordan, all the way to the war-damaged monuments and museums of Iraq (Zettler 1991).

In 1997, precisely a century since the establishment of the *American Journal of Archaeology* as the publication of record for AIA projects; 113 years since the Institute's first involvement in Near Eastern archaeology; and 118 years since its founding, there was simply no way that Charles Eliot Norton's original estimation about the divide between "Hellenic" and "Semitic" studies could be maintained. The AIA had survived over all these years—by chance, by attitude, or by intention—in remaining above the fray of particular missionary interests or direct political entanglements. And although the systematic exploration of the New World had largely passed on to others, the Institute's gradual recognition of the essential *unity* of the Aegean and Eastern Mediterranean had indeed played—and, it is to be hoped, would continue to play—at least a small part in the internationalization of American intellectual life.

REFERENCES

Archaeological Institute of America (AIA). 1880. *First Annual Report of the Executive Committee of the Archaeological Institute of America, 1879–1880.* Cambridge, Mass.

———. 1884. *Fifth Annual Report of the Executive Committee of the Archaeological Institute of America, 1883–1884.* Cambridge, Mass.

———. 1885. *Sixth Annual Report of the Executive Committee of the Archaeological Institute of America, 1884–1885.* Cambridge, Mass.

———. 1967. *Archaeological Discoveries in the Holy Land.* New York.

Bernal, M. 1987. *Black Athena.* Vol. 1, *The Fabrication of Ancient Greece 1785–1985.* New Brunswick, NJ.

Cross, T.M. 1997. "American Research Institute in Turkey." In *The Oxford Encyclopedia of Archaeology in the Near East* 1, edited by E.M. Meyers, 92. New York.

Dyson, S.L. 1998. *Ancient Marbles to American Shores: Classical Archaeology in the United States.* Philadelphia.

Hinsley, C.M. 1989. "Zunis and Brahmins: Cultural Ambivalence in the Gilded Age." In *Romantic Motives: Essays on Anthropological Sensibility. History of Anthropology,* vol. 6, edited by G.W. Stocking, 169–207. Madison, Wis.

Kantor, H. 1947. *The Aegean and the Orient in the Second Millennium BC*. Bloomington, Ind.

Kelsey, F.W. 1911. "The Tragedy at Cyrene." *Bulletin of the Archaeological Institute of America* 2:111–4.

King, P.J. 1983. *American Archaeology in the Mideast: A History of the American Schools of Oriental Research*. Philadelphia.

Kuklick, B. 1996. *Puritans in Babylon: The Ancient Near East and American Intellectual Life, 1880–1930*. Princeton.

Larsen, M.T. 1987. "Orientalism in the Ancient Near East." *Culture and History* 2:96–115.

McDonald, W.A., and C.G. Thomas. 1990. *Progress into the Past: The Rediscovery of Mycenaean Civilization*. Bloomington, Ind.

Magness-Gardiner, B. 1997. "Hetty Goldman." In *The Oxford Encyclopedia of Archaeology in the Near East*, vol. 2, edited by E.M. Meyers, 424. New York.

Marchand, S.L. 1996. *Down from Olympus: Archaeology and Philhellenism in Germany, 1750–1970*. Princeton.

Meskell, L. 1998. *Archaeology Under Fire*. London.

Morris, I. 1996. "Negotiated Peripherality in Iron Age Greece: Accepting and Resisting the East." *Journal of World-Systems Research*. 2 (12):1–8.

Morris, S. 1992. *Daidalos and the Origins of Greek Art*. Princeton.

Norton, R. 1911. "The Excavations at Cyrene: First Campaign, 1910–1911." *Bulletin of the Archaeological Institute of America* 2.

Patch, D.C. 1997. "American Research Center in Egypt." In *The Oxford Encyclopedia of Archaeology in the Near East*, vol. 1, edited by E.M. Meyers, 91–2. New York.

Shanks, M. 1996. *Classical Archaeology of Greece: Experiences of the Discipline*. London.

Silberman, N.A. 1982. *Digging for God and Country*. New York.

Sheftel, P.S. 1979. "The Archaeological Institute of America, 1879–1979: A Centennial Review." *AJA* 83:3–17.

Sumner, W.M. 1997. "American Institute of Iranian Studies." In *The Oxford Encyclopedia of Archaeology in the Near East*, vol. 1, edited by E.M. Meyers, 91. New York.

Turner, F.M. 1981. *The Greek Heritage in Victorian Britain*. New Haven.

Ward, W.H. 1888. "Expedition for Exploration in Babylonia." *Ninth Annual Report of the Executive Committee of the Archaeological Institute of America, 1887–1888*. Cambridge, Mass.

Zettler, R.L. 1991. "Iraq's Beleaguered Heritage." *Archaeology* 44 (3):38–42.

NOTES

[1] As early as 1884, however, the AIA wished to send an expedition to Cyrene, and in 1887 Joseph Thacher Clarke visited the site as a preliminary reconnaissance (Allen, ch. 3, this volume).

— 7 —

The "Western Idea":
Local Societies and American Archaeology[1]

James E. Snead

American research was an important activity of the Archaeological Institute of America in its formative decades. Distinguished American ethnologists and archaeologists, including Lewis Henry Morgan (1818–1881) and Frederic Ward Putnam (1839–1915) of Harvard's Peabody Museum, were among the founding members of the Institute. The Institute's sponsorship of the fieldwork of Adolph Bandelier (1840–1914) had a profound impact on anthropological studies of the American Southwest (Lange and Riley 1996), and occurred simultaneously with early efforts to establish an American presence in classical archaeology. This breadth of purpose in the early research agenda of the Institute, however, was contentious, and from the beginning the organization's membership was divided between proponents of a largely classical orientation and those supporting greater involvement in American work.

Much of the debate centered upon perceptions of the social role of archaeological research. Classical antiquity was considered to be the progenitor of 19th-century European and American culture, and the study of the monuments and antiquities of the Mediterranean was a means through which this heritage could be emphasized (e.g., Marchand 1996). In contrast, American archaeology had an entirely different significance for the intellectual classes, in part attributable to the absence of genetic and historical connections between the Precolumbian inhabitants of the New World and 19th-century

Euro-Americans (Trigger 1986, 188). This distinction was articulated by Charles Eliot Norton (1827–1908), the first president of the Institute, in his 1879 inaugural address. "While the archaeology of America offers many instructive analogies with the prehistoric archaeology of the Old World," he wrote, "it offers nothing to compare with the historic archaeology of civilized man in Africa, Asia, and Europe" (Norton 1880, 21). While the study of New World antiquities contributed toward a better understanding of humans in general, the greater importance of classical archaeology lay in its promotion of cultural values. Norton's perspective was widely shared within the Institute and became increasingly dominant during the 1880s. Support for American research such as that of Bandelier was left to other organizations, such as the Smithsonian Institution's Bureau of American Ethnology (BAE), and for a decade the Institute concentrated exclusively on the archaeology of the classical world (Sheftel 1979, 5).

At the same time that classical archaeology and overseas research was moving to the center of the scholarly agenda of the Institute, however, the interest of the American public was increasingly drawn towards local work. In the eyes of the average citizen, distinctions between Old World and New World antiquities were ill defined, and their cultural value existed independently of their location or associations. From this perspective the mounds and other ruins in the American heartland occupied a conceptual niche similar to the monuments of the Mediterranean but were far more familiar and accessible. By the late 1870s increasing public awareness of American antiquities was manifested in a variety of ways, including the establishment of archaeological societies and the publication of popular journals of archaeology.[2] Amateur interest in American archaeology, most prominent in the Midwestern states, was eclectic in nature and nationalistic in tone (Hinsley 1996, 192). In 1878 the editor of the *American Antiquarian* announced that "instead of going abroad for antiquities we shall find them at home" (Peet 1878, 45).

The growing difference between scholarly and public perceptions of the value of American archaeology was confronted by the leadership of the Institute in the 1890s, a time when the organization's structure and research orientation were being reevaluated. A mandate to promote popular interest in archaeology and to harness it in support of the Institute's activities emerged, leading both to the development of new national policies and to the establishment of "affiliated societies" throughout the country. As the new affiliated societies became influential in the Institute, American research once again emerged as a subject of debate. While the leaders of the Institute promoted antiquities policy at the national level, the affiliated societies developed their own programs of survey and excavation. This new research agenda, henceforth the "western idea," evolved in the social milieu of the American West at the end of the 19th century and was based on different principles than the fieldwork programs mounted by academic and museum-based archaeologists.

The challenge that the "western idea" represented to the identity of the Institute provoked continuous debate after the turn of the century and provides a window on archaeological thought in America at a critical stage of its history. Rather than a sidelight to the major initiatives of the Institute, the activities of its western affiliates and the furor that surrounded their relationship with the larger association were critical elements in the evolution of the identity of the Institute and the organizational structure of archaeology in the United States. East vs. West and classical vs. American—these themes evolved in ways that provide an important perspective on the development of American archaeology in general at a time when the relatively rigid disciplinary boundaries of today were in the process of formation.

The Creation of the Affiliated Societies

In its initial form, the Archaeological Institute of America was essentially a compact between a group of scholars and members of the New England elite to promote archaeological research. In the years following 1879 funding was amassed and modest field campaigns initiated. As such endeavors expanded, however, it became apparent that much greater levels of financial support would be necessary, and that a "national" presence would promote greater scholarly legitimacy. In 1884 the regulations of the Institute were revised to allow for affiliation with local archaeological societies, which would apply for admittance, and through their dues and contributions would support the initiatives of the larger organization (AIA 1889, 28). The affiliated societies, in turn, gained a limited voice on the governing council of the Institute.

After an initial period of expansion following these reforms, by the early 1890s the membership of the Institute had begun to decline. In 1896 this threat to the success of an increasing array of institutional and research commitments was met by a further elaboration of the affiliated society system, targeting the western states. A common refrain in the annual reports of the 1890s concerned the untapped sources of funding perceived to exist in the west. "It is not to be admitted," reads an 1890 plea for support of excavations at Delphi, "that our West, full of energy and wealth, will fail to do her part" (AIA 1890, 56). While initially emphasizing industrial cities such as Chicago and Detroit, as the century drew to a close this attention focused on the developing commercial centers of the Rocky Mountains and Pacific coast. As these new communities were in general lacking the developed institutional structures of the Northeast, the significance and structure of affiliate societies within them were different from those founded in the first wave of expansion.

By the turn of the century, western interest in local antiquities was developing in a way that resembled developments in the Midwest 20 years earlier, with the establishment of a number of local archaeological societies. The Arizona Antiquarian Society was founded in 1895, followed in 1899 by the Colorado Cliff Dwellings Association and in September 1900 by the Santa Fe Archaeological Society (Wilcox 1987, 16; Hobbs 1946, 87). Membership in these associations was largely drawn from the business classes, for which ruins represented resources with value both as objects of tourism and a source of local distinction. From the perspective of the Institute's leadership, the growing western interest in archaeology was a sign that these communities would respond positively to the establishment of affiliates within their communities, thus increasing support for the organization as a whole.

The process through which affiliated societies were founded is illustrated by a 1902 initiative on the part of Institute President John Williams White (1849–1915) of Harvard. As a preliminary step, written queries were sent to several Harvard alumni in San Francisco asking about their interest in the Institute (Thomas to White, 3 October 1902, AIA Archives, box 10). The following spring Francis Willey Kelsey (1858–1927), the Institute's secretary and a professor at the University of Michigan, sent a printed flier to western alumni of his own institution to stimulate interest in similar fashion. The announcement noted that the Institute proposed "to establish, in several Western cities, Affiliated Societies similar to those which, by means of public lectures and other instrumentalities, have contributed so much to the intellectual life of the East" (Kelsey, 23 April 1903, AIA Archives, box 11). An informal visit to the region by University of Michigan professor Martin D'Ooge (1839–1915) in the summer of 1903 provided additional stimulation (Kelsey to Carroll, 12 January 1906, AIA Archives, box 12).

With a network of contacts established through these preliminary efforts, Kelsey was dispatched on what he called the "western mission" in late fall 1903 (Kelsey to Seymour, 22 February 1904, AIA Archives, box 11). Following a series of lectures and meetings in Colorado, Utah, and California, he reported the establishment of five new affiliated societies (Kelsey to Seymour, 11 May 1904, AIA Archives, box 11). Kelsey's efforts were most notable in Los Angeles, where he participated in the founding of what was soon to be the largest affiliate within the Institute, the Southwest Society. In the process, the cultural goals of the Institute and the widening of its funding base were also enhanced.

The ultimate success of Kelsey's western mission, however, was variable. Despite the public announcement, in the autumn of 1903, of the founding of an affiliated society in San Francisco (*San Francisco Chronicle*, 28 November 1903), the group was largely moribund just a few years later. The Utah society, in turn, was at first crippled by antagonism between Mormon and non-Mormon factions (Kelsey to Carroll, 12 January 1906, AIA Archives, box 12). Repeat visits, such as that made by Mitchell Carroll (1870–1925) in 1906, were required in most cases in order for the initiative to be sustained (Carroll to Seymour, 9 May 1906, AIA Archives, box 11). Despite the role of the Institute in their foundation, however, and its interest in their success, the western affiliates largely shaped their own destiny. In different ways the characteristics of these organizations were shaped by a western ideology of pragmatism to ends unanticipated by the parent organization. This was particularly true in the case of the Southwest Society, which was both a spectacular success and a significant challenge to the policies of the Institute.

The Southwest Society

The Southwest Society was largely a reflection of its founder, Charles Fletcher Lummis (1859–1928). Lummis was a native of Massachusetts, and after attending Harvard took up a career as a writer. In a widely publicized stunt he walked from Ohio to California in 1884, thereafter making his residence on the West Coast and in the Southwest. In addition to his own writings, participation in anthropological expeditions, and founding of various preservationist societies, Lummis also became editor of a magazine called

Land of Sunshine (later, *Out West*), which promoted a pro-western agenda (Fiske and Lummis 1975, 110–11). Flamboyant and eccentric, Lummis was noted for his corduroy suit and strong opinions. His organizational skill and energy also seem to have been widely recognized, and both D'Ooge and Kelsey called upon Lummis in their visits to Los Angeles. Lummis may have been selected to play a leading role in establishing an affiliated society because of his activist reputation, his skills as a publicist, and his Harvard connections, which included friendship with Theodore Roosevelt (1858–1919).

The Southwest Society was officially organized at the time of Kelsey's visit in November 1903 (Dudley 1972, 301). Using what he called "modern business principles," Lummis built up a membership through the use of mimeographs and mass-mailings instead of the personal canvassing more customary of the day (Lummis to Seymour, 24 August 1905, AIA Archives, box 11). J.S. Slauson, a prominent California citizen, presided over the first board of the society, which included the editor of the *Los Angeles Times*, the president of the University of Southern California, and prominent members of the Los Angeles business community. Notably scarce were academic figures, a situation in part caused by the underdeveloped nature of higher education in southern California but also a result of the broader base within the community that the new society enjoyed. From his post as secretary, Lummis worked strenuously to ensure publicity and high attendance for society lectures and also used that information to build his status within the Institute on a national level. A meeting in February 1904 attracted a crowd of between 500 and 600 people, an event Lummis described to the Institute's new president, Thomas Day Seymour (1848–1907), the following day (Lummis to Seymour, 27 February 1904, AIA Archives, box 11). Such activity on the part of an affiliated society appears to have been quite remarkable. Calling Lummis's efforts "worthy of especial mention and commendation," Kelsey pronounced the "western mission" a success (Kelsey to Seymour, 11 May 1904, AIA Archives, box 11).

It was immediately apparent, however, that the motives of Lummis and his associates in the Southwest Society differed significantly from those of the Institute's leadership. While the involvement of the Institute in matters of American antiquities was increasing at the national level, it continued to emphasize classical scholarship as its highest priority. The Institute's principal form of outreach was its public lectures, a program implemented largely as an aspect of the affiliated societies initiative. Museums and collections played no role in this process.

For his part, Lummis built the Southwest Society around what he called the "western idea," a loosely defined concept that emphasized the utilitarian aspects of science and the need of western communities to develop their own, unique identities through cultural heritage (Lummis 1910, 5). The establishment of museums and local research were fundamental to the western idea. As early as 1895, Lummis had expressed, through the editorial pages of *Land of Sunshine*, the need for a museum in California to preserve local archaeology and history (in Dudley 1972, 293). The creation of such a museum was advocated in some of the initial membership letters sent out for the Southwest Society (Lummis to Harvey, 21 January 1904, Lummis Arizona papers). Archaeological and historic research in California and the Southwest were also perceived as having a greater appeal to the membership of the Southwest Society than the overseas projects of the Institute. Lummis, writing to President Seymour, noted: "I find that even the most liberal and progressive of our members look a little cross-eyed at spending their money for a remote archaeological work, yet these same people (and many, many more) would most cheerfully "put up" for the same kind of work which should glorify California—and I mean not merely in the boom sense, but in the higher sense" (Lummis to Seymour, 18 August 1904, AIA Archives, box 11).

In developing the membership of the Southwest Society Lummis played upon local pride and a sense of competition with the easterners who dominated the Institute. "I am mighty anxious," he wrote in one membership drive, "to build up here a membership and a fund which shall jar the Boston dignitaries who think Southern California is populated only by boomers and bandits" (Lummis to Coulter, 21 January 1904, Lummis Arizona Papers).

The first project of the Southwest Society, an initiative to record the Spanish folk songs of Southern California, demonstrated Lummis's understanding of the ambitions of his audience. The program, which he called "catching our archaeology alive," attracted much favorable attention in the community and enhanced membership recruitment (Lummis 1905). Response within the scholarly community was more skeptical. When Lummis lectured on the folk song project to an Institute gathering in Cleveland, one observer described the affair as "not only not archaeological in any sense of the term, but also distinctly unscholarly, undignified, and altogether improper for the occasion" (Platner to Kelsey, 17 December 1904,

AIA Archives, box 11). For the time being, however, the Institute's leaders saw the success of the Southwest Society as promoting their own goals, no matter how unorthodox its leader. Lummis capped off the first year of the Southwest Society's existence in December 1904 with a speech at the Annual Meeting of the Institute in Boston, an event that effectively introduced the new society as an important component of the organization as a whole.

American Work

By the time of Kelsey's western mission, the increasing scientific legitimacy of American work had begun to strengthen the hand of individuals within the Institute who favored greater involvement in New World archaeology. These included Charles P. Bowditch (1842–1921), a wealthy Cambridge businessman with a deep interest in the archaeology of Central America. As a wealthy patron and chair of the Institute's Committee on American Archaeology, Bowditch used his influence to raise the profile of American work within the Institute. In 1900 he funded a scholarship for Central American research, which in 1901 was awarded to Harvard graduate Alfred Tozzer (1877–1954) (Hinsley 1984, 54F). The principal function of the American committee and its subunit, the Committee on the Preservation of the Ruins of American Antiquity, was the promotion of antiquities legislation (Lee 1970; Rothman 1989). Despite the interests of some of the committee's members, fieldwork was not a priority, the official rationale being that increasing governmental and private efforts in American archaeology made it "difficult for the Institute, with its limited means, to enter the field" (White 1901, 10).

In contrast, American fieldwork had been central to the agenda of the western affiliates from the beginning. Western concerns over establishing their own institutions also extended to their obtaining antiquities in the face of competition with other institutions and the federal government. One of the first acts of the Southwest Society was to establish a temporary exhibit even while a site for the permanent museum structure and funding for its construction was being sought ("Southwest Museum," n.d., Lummis Arizona Papers). Befitting the eclectic desires of the founders, initial collections included historic paintings and relics of 19th-century California in addition to prehistoric artifacts (Palmer 1905). With the purchase of the Palmer-Campbell collection of Southern California antiquities, the museum obtained the services of Frank Palmer, who became its first curator.

In 1905 the society mounted its first archaeological excavations, which took place at a site near Redondo Beach, California. This was quickly followed by reconnaissance in the Southwest, dubbed the "First Arizona Expedition" (Palmer 1905). Frank Palmer was placed in charge of both of these efforts, which were conducted at a relatively small scale. In addition to expanding the collections of the new Southwest Museum, the significance of Palmer's expeditions was in establishing the presence of a regional organization in a field previously dominated by governmental and eastern museum-based projects.

The importance of this activity was made clear by Lummis's initial inability to obtain a permit from the Bureau of Indian Affairs for archaeological work on the White Mountain Apache Reservation in Arizona. Informed that representatives of the Smithsonian would be given priority on public lands, Lummis launched a letter-writing campaign to have the decision reversed. "The enclosed will show how the Institute has been buncoed, gold-bricked and generally played with," he wrote Seymour (Lummis to Seymour, 14 August 1905, AIA Archives, box 11). Lummis was able to persuade the Ethnologist-in-Chief of the Bureau of American Ethnology, William H. Holmes (1846–1933), to intercede, and Palmer's work went ahead as planned (Lummis to Holmes, 10 October 1905, Lummis Los Angeles Papers). While the permit difficulties were more a matter of procedures than of law, Lummis was able to manipulate the perception that eastern governmental interests were preventing local organizations from pursuing their legitimate claims to southwestern antiquities.

Maneuvering over access to archaeological resources also placed the western affiliates in competition with each other. The San Francisco Society of the Institute, which had revived under the leadership of the anthropologist Alfred Kroeber (1876–1960), mounted its own modest expedition to eastern Arizona immediately following Palmer's return to Los Angeles. That the Southwest Society was perceived as an opponent in the matter is evident from Kroeber's advice that Joseph Peterson, his agent in the affair, avoid contact with Palmer (Kroeber to Peterson, 2 January 1906, Department of Anthropology Papers). Peterson's efforts were ultimately negligible, but the attempt underscored the importance to the western affiliates of establishing rights to conduct their own fieldwork.

The scope of the First Arizona Expedition was relatively modest, with only Palmer, his son, and one field assistant involved. Based out of Snowflake, Arizona, the party spent several weeks examining prehistoric sites and conducting brief excavations in promising locations. Efforts were largely directed toward obtaining high-quality artifacts, although some architectural features were cleared. In all, Palmer reported examining 80 different ruins. The brief account of the expedition published in *Out West* was short on specifics but featured photographs of the locales and of the more impressive pottery finds (Palmer 1905b). No more detailed description was made available at the time, and the work cannot be said to have made a substantive contribution to scholarship. The publication format, however, was well suited for the membership of the Southwest Society, and the article was later reprinted as a bulletin (Palmer 1907).

Despite limited influence over the Southwest Society, the Institute's leadership became concerned about the professional standards of the Arizona fieldwork. Although the Institute had long encouraged affiliated societies to develop their own projects, no formal mechanism for oversight had been developed. Palmer, for instance, appears to have had no formal archaeological training, and while his work had been placed under the nominal authority of the American Committee this was largely a formality. In January 1906, however, rumors critical of Palmer's activities began to circulate in the east. On Kelsey's authority, a representative was dispatched to oversee and evaluate the Southwest Society's second Arizona expedition, which was to take place in early summer 1906 (Kelsey to Bowditch, 1 June 1906, AIA Archives, box 12).

The emissary was Edgar Lee Hewett (1865–1946), whose involvement with the American work of the Institute was to have dramatic consequences. Hewett was a western educator who had conducted fieldwork and taught archaeology while serving as president of the New Mexico State Normal School (Hewett 1900–1901). After losing his position in 1903, Hewett spent a year studying in Europe and then began a program of southwestern field research on behalf of the Bureau (Hewett to Holmes, 3 April 1905, BAE, Papers). When Alfred Tozzer completed the Bowditch Fellowship and joined the Harvard faculty in 1905, Hewett became the next recipient (Hinsley 1986, 219). Unlike Tozzer, Hewett's talents were in organization, rather than research. Kelsey found these skills useful, and while a research plan involving Central America had been concocted to satisfy Bowditch (Putnam to Hewett, 8 February 1906, Hewett Papers), Hewett spent much of the fellowship year lobbying congress and working on Institute matters at Kelsey's behest.

Hewett joined Palmer and Lummis in Los Angeles and accompanied them to Cañon de Chelly. His evaluation of Palmer's abilities was guardedly optimistic, and he remained with the field party for only a brief time (Hewett to Holmes, 1 June 1906, BAE papers). Despite this assessment, Palmer's report of the summer's activities was greeted with disappointment by members of the American committee (Putnam to Kelsey, 8 November 1906, AIA Archives, box 12). For the Southwest Society, however, a presence in the Southwest was maintained and the collections of the Southwest Museum enhanced. Most importantly, the episode forged a strong bond between Hewett and Lummis, which was to exert considerable influence on the conduct of Institute's American work in the immediate future.

Hewett's role in the passage of the Antiquities Act in June 1906 greatly increased his prestige within the Institute. With the completion of the fellowship at the end of that year, he was appointed to a new Institute post as director of American archaeology (Bowditch to Kelsey, 21 January 1907, AIA Archives, box 13). The circumstances soured relations between Hewett and Bowditch, who thought that the terms of the fellowship had not been adequately met (Bowditch to Hewett, 25 May 1906, AIA Archives, box 12), and set the stage for a series of disagreements between Hewett and other Americanists within the Institute. The creation of a position of director, however, increased the opportunities for the direct involvement of the Institute in the American field. One of Hewett's charges was to investigate the possibilities for founding a School of American Archaeology similar to those already established by the Institute in Rome and Athens. A specific commitment to fieldwork remained tenuous, but Hewett's ambitions for the school and for himself hinged upon the development of a successful research program.

Edgar Lee Hewett's Southwest Program

For fieldwork Hewett turned to the affiliated societies. In earlier years he had brought about the founding of the Santa Fe Archaeological Society (Hobbs 1946, 87) and had been deeply involved with the Institute's Colorado affiliate. He was thus thoroughly aware of the interest in antiquities felt by the western public and the potential this offered for the support of fieldwork. In

Lummis's highly-organized Southwest Society, Hewett found a model for the coordination and funding of a large-scale southwestern research program to be conducted on behalf of the Institute (Hewett to Holmes, 1 June 1906, BAE Papers).

The key to Hewett's fieldwork initiative was to promote modest projects of interest to the members of a local affiliate, who would then be willing to provide financial support. Rather than emphasize austere scientific goals, emphasis would be placed on regional pride and the value of participating in a great national endeavor. Several such initiatives would be in progress during a given field season, resulting in widespread archaeological activity at relatively modest cost. As director, Hewett would provide trained leaders for each of the projects and shuttle between them himself in order to oversee the total effort. Lectures on topics related to the fieldwork would also be provided for the participating affiliates, in order to demonstrate for the membership the fruits of their investment.

Hewett spent the spring of 1907 traveling throughout the west laying the groundwork for the summer's work and investigating possible locations for the proposed School of American Archaeology. Through his connections with the Colorado society, Hewett was able to obtain funding for an archaeological survey in the southwestern part of the state, with some additional excavation in different "cliff dweller" sites at nearby Mesa Verde (Hewett to Lummis, 11 August 1907, Lummis Los Angeles Papers). Hewett also obtained backing for a similar project in Utah, provided by that state's affiliate (Hewett to Cummings, 24 April 1907, Hewett Papers). In the Utah case, the fieldwork was a general effort to document ruins in the southeastern region of the state, coordinated by Byron Cummings (1860–1954) of the University of Utah on behalf of the society (Cummings, "Trodden Trails," Cummings Papers).

Both the Utah and Colorado projects were designed to establish the local affiliates as active participants in studying the archaeological heritage of their own locales. Even though the School was still in the planning stages Hewett arranged for students to participate in the work. This reflected Hewett's own pedagogical background, and the educational mandate of the Institute as well, since the School of American Archaeology was to be modeled after the American schools abroad.[3] Cummings brought students of his own, and three Harvard undergraduates joined the Colorado project for field training (Hewett to Lummis, 23 July 1907, Lummis Los Angeles Papers).[4] While student participation had been a part of Southwest archaeology for some time prior to this (Gifford and Morris 1985, 397; Snead 1999), Hewett's open call for participants marks this episode as the real inauguration of the southwestern field school tradition (e.g., Hewett to Kroeber, 31 May 1907, Department of Anthropology Papers).

With the backing of Lummis, Hewett displaced Palmer as the field agent for the Southwest Society and gained the support of that affiliate for fieldwork as well. When the Colorado and Utah work was finished, Hewett and the Harvard students transferred their operations to northern New Mexico, where a $400 donation from Mary Foy, a member of the board of the Southwest Society, was used to support excavations at the site of Puyé (Lummis to Hewett, 26 April 1907, Lummis Los Angeles Papers). From Lummis's perspective, the Puye work had two functions; the obtaining of specimens for the exhibits of the Southwest Museum, and the establishment of the hegemony of the Southwest Society in the region (Lummis to Hewett, 2 August 1907, Lummis Los Angeles Papers). When the project was complete, 3,000 artifacts were transferred to the Southwest Museum, which published brief reports of the research (Morley 1910).

The success of the entire fieldwork initiative relied on constant and intricate negotiations between the participants. Hewett traveled back and forth between the field parties and also maintained regular contact with his superiors in the Institute. The involvement of the Harvard students was an example of his ability to build strategic alliances both to further his central goals and to counter opposition. The students provided a high-quality, motivated staff at little cost, and Hewett was subsequently able to deputize them to supervise other projects. By drawing them from Harvard Hewett was able to mute criticism about his methods coming from that quarter.[5] Efforts were also made to involve Jesse W. Fewkes (1850–1930), of the Bureau, in the training program, which would have linked practically all of the institutions conducting archaeology in the Southwest together in a common purpose (Hewett to Holmes, 28 May 1907, BAE Papers).

The success of the 1907 field season was also contingent on the application of a research model based upon Lummis's "western idea," through which local interest and pride could be promoted in the support of scientific work. Both the Utah and Colorado societies were enormously stimulated by the summer's activity and enthusiastically extended their financial support to include work the following summer. The Colorado society printed brochures advertising their sponsorship of Hewett's excavations at the Cannonball Ruins, inviting their membership to visit and observe their contributions at work (Colorado society of the AIA 1908, Kelsey Papers). Cummings was able to use the expanding membership of the Utah society to galvanize popular interest in Utah archaeology (Cummings to Hewett, 16 September 1907, Hewett Papers). Through it all Lummis continued to develop the Southwest Museum and the ideology behind it, which desired that Americans be as familiar with the antiquities of their own country as with those overseas (Lummis 1929, 267).

When, after prolonged and acrimonious debate,[6] the School of American Archaeology was established in Santa Fe, New Mexico in 1909, a physical center was provided for the American initiative. Its creation was the high point of a proactive strategy toward American work by the Institute, in particular reflecting the policies of Kelsey, who had been elected president in 1907. Institute sponsorship and the initiative of Edgar L. Hewett had created an innovative and successful program of American research that, for a time, was the equal of the governmental and academic archaeological programs, which had previously had the field to themselves.

Conclusion

The ultimate failure of the Institute's American program, as envisioned by Hewett, was in large part a result of failure to capitalize on its initial success. Rather than consolidate his relationships with the existing participants in the program, Hewett promoted further expansion, including fieldwork in the American Midwest and Guatemala.[7] While this expanded the network of affiliated societies involved in fieldwork, it made it more difficult to maintain relationships with all the parties involved. Hewett's desire to keep each of the projects under his personal supervision exacerbated the situation. Mistrust of his motivations and accusations of broken promises prevented many of the original objectives from being attained.

The affiliated societies were also inherently unstable. Fluctuating membership and a tendency toward factionalism made them unreliable partners. Despite the successful Puye campaign of 1907, for instance, the Southwest Society declined to support a second season. Hewett's aggressive courting of the society had attracted the animosity of Palmer, leading to a divisive battle within the managing board (Lummis to Martindale, 30 November 1908,

Lummis Arizona Papers). While Lummis was ultimately successful in forcing the resignation of Palmer and the other rebels, which included the original patron of the project, Mary Foy, the episode spelled an end to his agenda for Southwest research. Thereafter he directed his energies toward the completion of the Southwest Museum facility, the ground for which was broken at a site north of downtown Los Angeles in November 1912, and toward personal advocacy of Hewett's projects within the councils of the Institute.

The nature of the goals of research based on the "western idea" also militated against long-term success. For local audiences, the short-term goals of fieldwork were far more important than the development of a stable research program. Once these were achieved, interest waned. Beyond the establishment of "claims" and the acquisition of artifacts for local exhibition, little effort was invested in analysis and publication. The lack of follow-through greatly diminished the impact of the work on subsequent scholarship, and was anathema to members of the developing professional class of archaeologists in eastern institutions. Hewett responded to increasing criticism from the American Committee by engineering the takeover of that committee by interests friendly to the American work (Hinsley 1986, 225), but this also led to the gradual isolation of the School under his direction from the mainstream of American archaeology. Where it remained influential was in the training of young archaeologists, although after 1912 few serious students remained involved in the program.

American work remained part of the agenda of the Institute only so long as the personalities involved continued to exercise influence. After the completion of Francis Kelsey's term as president, the program lost ground. With the growth of professional organizations such as the American Anthropological Association and Section H of the American Association for the Advancement of Science, American archaeology developed in a distinct context of its own. As the 20th century wore on and the archaeological disciplines continued to professionalize, the issues of cultural legitimacy, which had linked the Institute to American work, became increasingly less compelling. As Hewett and Lummis became preoccupied with local matters, the programs that they had developed ceased to attract national attention.

It is ironic that the American work of the Institute after the turn of the century owed its success to a mechanism that had evolved for the support of Classical archaeology. It is also ironic that its greatest impact occurred only after segments of the public were convinced of its cultural value, qualities which 19th-century scholarship had insisted were inherent in only the Classical civilizations. The combination of the "western idea" and the affiliate structure of the Institute led to a remarkable, if brief, fluorescence of a popular archaeology in the American West. Largely forgotten, these efforts are perhaps best summed up in the words of one of their principle advocates: "What you need, what the science of man needs now, is not so much more students, nor more scientific societies run by Latin professors nor even more devoted souls toiling and starving to investigate—but an audience" (Lummis in Fiske and Lummis 1975, 71).

That audience—the middle classes of the new towns of the Western United States—was ultimately what drove the American work, and their interests produced a distinctly American mode of archaeology, which is a key component of the social history of the discipline.

REFERENCES

Primary Sources

American Institute of Archaeology (AIA) Archives, Boston University, 656 Beacon Street, Boston.

Bureau of American Ethnology (BAE) Papers, National Anthropological Archive, Smithsonian Institution, Washington, D.C.

Cummings, Byron. Papers, Arizona Historical Society, Tucson. Department of Anthropology Papers, University of California, Berkeley, Bancroft Library.

Hewett, Edgar Lee. Papers, Museum of New Mexico, Fray Angelico Chavez History Library.

Kelsey, Francis W. Papers, Bentley Historical Library, University of Michigan.

Lummis, Charles Fletcher. Papers, Special Collections, University of Arizona, Tucson.

Lummis, Charles Fletcher. Papers, Southwest Museum, Los Angeles.

Secondary Sources

Allen, R. 1990. "The History of the University Museum's Southwestern Pottery Collection." In *Beauty from the Earth: Pueblo Indian Pottery From the University Museum of Archaeology and Anthropology*, edited by J.J. Brody, 61–88. Philadelphia.

Archaeological Institute of America. 1880. *First Annual Report of the Executive Committee, with Accompanying Papers, 1879–80*. Cambridge, Mass.

———. 1889. *Tenth Annual Report: 1888–89*. Cambridge, Mass.

———. 1890. *Eleventh Annual Report: 1889–90*. Cambridge, Mass.

Dyson, S.L. 1989. "The Role of Ideology and Institutions in Shaping Classical Archaeology in the Nineteenth and Twentieth Centuries." In *Tracing Archaeology's Past: The Historiography of Archaeology*, edited by A.L. Christenson, 127–35. Carbondale, Ill.

Fiske, T.L., and K. Lummis. 1975. *Charles F. Lummis: The Man and His West.* Norman, Okla.
Gifford, C.A., and E.A. Morris. 1985. "Digging for Credit: Early Archaeological Field Schools in the American Southwest." *American Antiquity* 50:395–411.
Gordon, D. 1972. *Crusader in Corduroy.* Los Angeles.
Hewett, E.L. 1900–1901. *Syllabus of Lectures on the Pre-Historic Archaeology of New Mexico.* Las Vegas.
Hinsley, C.M., Jr. 1987. *Savages and Scientists: The Smithsonian Institution and the Development of American Anthropology, 1846–1910.* Washington, D.C.
———. 1984. "Wanted: One Good Man to Discover Central American History." *Harvard Magazine* 87:64B–64H.
———. 1986. "Edgar Lee Hewett and the School of American Archaeology in Santa Fe, 1906–1912." In *American Archaeology Past And Future*, edited by D.J. Meltzer, D.D. Fowler, and J.A. Sabloff, 217–36. Washington, D.C.
———. 1996. "Digging for Identity: Reflections on the Cultural Background of Collecting." *The American Indian Quarterly* 20:180–96.
Hobbs, H.R. 1946. "The Story of the Archaeological Society, 1. Prologue: The Awakening of Interest." *El Palacio* 53:79–88.
Lange, C.H., and C.L. Riley. 1996. *Bandelier: The Life and Times of Adolf Bandelier.* Salt Lake City.
Lee, R.F. 1970. *The Antiquities Act of 1906.* Washington, D.C.
Lummis, C.F. 1905. "Catching Our Archaeology Alive." *The Southwest Society of the Archaeological Institute of America*, Second Bulletin, 3–15.
———. 1910. "Sixth Annual Report." *The Southwest Society of the Archaeological Institute of America*, Fifth Bulletin.
———. 1929. *Flowers of Our Lost Romance.* Boston.
Marchand, S. 1996. *Down from Olympus: Archaeology and Philhellenism in Germany, 1750–1970.* Princeton.
Mark, J. 1980. *Four Anthropologists: An American Science in its Early Years.* New York.
Morley, S.G. 1910. "The South House, Puye." *The Southwest Society of the American Institute of Archaeology,* Sixth Bulletin.
Norton, C.E. 1880. "To the Members of the Archaeological Institute of America." *First Annual Report of the Executive Committee, with Accompanying Papers, 1879–80*, 13–26. Cambridge, Mass.
Palmer, F.M. 1905a. "Beginning the Southwest Museum." *Southwest Society of the Archaeological Institute of America*, Second Bulletin, 16–27.
———. 1905b. "A Land of Mystery." *Out West* 23:525–38.
———. 1907. "The First Arizona Expedition." *Southwest Society of the Archaeological Institute of America*, Third Bulletin, 41–8.
Peet, S. 1878. "The Field We Occupy." *The American Antiquarian* 1:45–7.
Rothman, H. 1989. *Preserving Different Pasts: The American National Monuments.* Urbana, Ill.
Sheftel, P.S. 1979. "The AIA 1879–1979: A Centennial Review." *AJA* 83:3–17.
Snead, J.E. 1999. "Science, Commerce, and Control: Patronage and the Development of Anthropological Archaeology in the Americas." *American Anthropologist* 101:256–71.

Trennert, R.A. 1987. "Fairs, Expositions, and the Changing Image of Southwestern Indians, 1876–1904." *New Mexico Historical Review* 62:127–50.

Trigger, B.G. 1986. "Prehistoric Archaeology and American Society." In *American Archaeology Past and Future*, edited by D.J. Meltzer, D.D. Fowler, and J.A. Sabloff, 187–215. Washington, D.C.

White, J.W. 1901. "Twenty-Second Annual Report of the Council of the Archaeological Institute of America." *AJA* 2nd series 5 (supplement):1–12.

Wilcox, D. 1987. "Frank Midvale's Investigation of La Ciudad." *Arizona State University Office of Cultural Resource Management Anthropological Field Studies* 19.

NOTES

[1] The argument in this chapter is based on that developed in ch. 3 of my *Ruins and Rivals: The Making of Southwest Archaeology* (Tucson 2001). Support for the research on which this paper is based has been derived from a variety of sources, most recently the American Philosophical Society. The assistance of a large body of archivists and librarians has been essential. Some of these include Kim Walters, of the Southwest Museum in Los Angeles; Priscilla Murray, who arranged access to the AIA Archives at Boston University; Orlando Romero, of the Fray Angelico Chavez History Library at the Museum of New Mexico; and the Special Collections staff at the University of Arizona library. Special thanks go to Monica Smith, whose advice at a critical juncture proved most useful.

[2] This process paralleled that of the development of local natural history societies in the United States (Benson 1988).

[3] Hewett visited the American School of Classical Studies in Rome in 1908 (Fletcher to Cummings, 11 April 1908, Cummings Papers).

[4] The Harvard students were Alfred V. Kidder, Sylvanus Morley, and John Fletcher. Because of the subsequent prominence of Kidder and Morley in American archaeology, the 1907 fieldwork has attained an almost mythical status within the discipline.

[5] Morley, in particular, was developing into a protégé of Bowditch, and was soon to receive the Central American fellowship (Brunhouse 1971).

[6] Hinsley (1986) provides an extensive discussion of the events surrounding the founding of the School of American Archaeology.

[7] Undated report of the Director of American Archaeology to the AIA American Committee for the first half of 1908 (Hewett Papers).

— 8 —

The Dream that Failed:
The AIA's Department of Canada (1908–1915)[1]

James Russell

During the last 30 years the Archaeological Institute of America has enjoyed modest growth in Canada, but its activities have been limited to a relatively small number of local societies, for the most part in major centers such as Montreal, Toronto, Winnipeg, and Vancouver. In the hope of enlarging the number of societies and undertaking fundraising among Canadian members, a Canadian affiliate of the AIA came into being in 1994.[2] At the time, this initiative seemed to be a novel idea, but in fact a remarkably similar Canadian venture known as the Archaeological Institute of America–Department of Canada, with its own corporate organization, had been launched with great success nearly 90 years before. In this paper, which is based largely on information from the AIA Archives at Boston University, I review the remarkable growth of the Department of Canada and its precipitate decline.[3]

When the AIA and the American Philological Association (APA) assembled in Toronto for their 10th joint Annual Meeting on the last four days of 1908, the event marked the first time that the two organizations had ventured outside the United States for their annual conference. For the AIA, the Toronto meeting was memorable, both for the lavish hospitality extended by the President and faculty of the University and members of the newly formed Toronto society, and for a program that AIA President Francis Willey Kelsey (1858–1927) said "was far the strongest that has ever been presented

Fig. 8.1. Francis W. Kelsey, president of the Archaeological Institute of America, 1907–1912. (Courtesy of the Kelsey Museum Archives, University of Michigan)

at such a meeting, as regards the average standing among the contributors and the weight and interest of the subjects."[4]

For Kelsey himself (fig. 8.1), then completing his first year as president, the Toronto meeting must have been especially gratifying, for he had placed a high priority on establishing a strong AIA presence in Canada. What precisely inspired Kelsey to undertake this mission remains unclear, but it is certain that once he had embarked on it, he pursued it with all his energy and enthusiasm. The campaign commenced in the spring of 1908 when Harry Langford Wilson (1867–1913), professor of Roman archaeology and Latin epigraphy at Johns Hopkins, and a Canadian himself, was sent out by the Institute to visit several cities of central Canada to organize local societies.[5] Through careful planning in advance and the support of leading members of the community in each city, he was able on 4 May to report to the General Secretary of the AIA that enough members had enrolled to ensure the imminent formation of societies in four cities: Toronto, Kingston, Ottawa, and Montreal. The AIA Council subsequently recognized all four societies during the Toronto meeting. President Kelsey's own interest in the Canadian initiative is reflected in his willingness to undertake a lecture tour of the new societies earlier in the same month. His visit to Ottawa on 3 December 1908, where he gave a lecture on the recently discovered Boscoreale Treasure, entitled "A Roman Farmhouse and its Buried Treasure," marked the inauguration of that society (fig. 8.2).[6]

During the months following the Toronto meeting the momentum was maintained, so that by the end of 1909, three additional societies had come into being, two in the Maritime provinces, at Halifax and St. John, and one in western Canada, at Winnipeg, with a fourth new society in Hamilton in the process of formation. Thus, in two years the AIA in Canada had established eight new societies, with a cumulative membership already over 500.

> ## ARCHAEOLOGICAL INSTITUTE OF AMERICA
> ### DEPARTMENT OF CANADA.
>
> #### OTTAWA SOCIETY.
>
> Towards the formation of a local Society or branch of the Canadian Department of the Archaeological Institute of America, whose aims and objects have already been set forth---or may be gleaned from the enclosed leaflets---the following Ladies and Gentlemen of Ottawa City have signified their intention of being Life or Annual Members. From these a Provisional Executive Committee has been chosen to prepare for organization, and for the forthcoming lectures by President Kelsey, of Michigan University, and by Dr. Hogarth, of the British Museum, London, etc.
>
> #### PROVISIONAL EXECUTIVE:
>
> RT. HON. SIR CHARLES FITZPATRICK.
> J. S. EWART, K.C.
> E. R. CAMERON, K.C.
> H. M. AMI.
> GEO. F. HENDERSON, K.C.
> PROFESSOR ADAM SHORTT.
> DR. J. F. WHITE.
> DR. W. D. LESUEUR.
>
> #### LIFE AND ANNUAL MEMBERS:
>
> Cameron, E. R.
> Ewart, J. S.
> Fitzpatrick, Sir Charles.
> Lesueur, W. D.
> Henderson, Geo. F.
> Bonar, Dr. James.
> Glashan, Dr. J. C.
> Duhamel, His Grace Archbishop.
> White, Dr. J. F.
> Boville, Thos. Cooper.
> Scott, Duncan Campbell.
> Ross, Philip D.
> Harriss, Mrs. Charles A. E.
> Ahearn, Mrs. Thomas
> Ami, Mrs. H. M.
> King, Dr. W. F.
> Fleming, R. F.
> Machado, Jose A.
> Bryce, Dr. P. H.
> Dunbar, R. J.
> Fleming, Sir Sandford
> Nelson, Frank.
> Ross, Crawford.
> Brock, Prof. R. W.
> Davies, Sir Louis
> Hardie, William.
> Meiklejohn, A. J.
> Doughty, Dr. G. A.
> Maclennan, Hon. Justice.
> Low, Dr. A. P.
> McCarthy, Hamilton.
> Kydd, Geo.
> Ami, H. M.
> Shortt, Prof. Adam.
> White, James.
> Jackson, J. A.
> Cory, W. W.
> Pedley, Frank.
> Orde, J. F.
>
> #### OTHER CANADIAN SOCIETIES.
>
> Local Societies have recently been organized in Toronto, Hamilton, Kingston and Montreal.
>
> #### PRESIDENT KELSEY'S LECTURE.
>
> Enclosed herewith please find cards of invitation to attend Professor F. W. Kelsey's Illustrated Lecture, on " **A Roman Farmhouse and its Buried Treasures**," on Thursday evening, December 3rd, at 8 p.m., in the Assembly Hall of the Normal School.
>
> Through the kindness and courtesy of His Excellency Earl Grey, this Lecture is given under His distinguished Patronage.
>
> These Cards are sent to intending Members for their own use, and for distribution to such friends as they would like to invite to the President's Lecture on this interesting subject.
>
> Intending Members are requested to make the meeting a success. Presentation of Cards at the door not necessary.
>
> A full attendance of Members and their friends expected.
>
> H. M. AMI,
> Secretary, pro tem.

Fig. 8.2. Prospectus announcing the formation of the Ottawa society of the Archaeological Institute of America and the inaugural lecture, 3 December 1908 (AIA Archives).

Yet the growth of the AIA in Canada was far from over. The succeeding two years saw further expansion in western Canada, with three more societies established in the prairies at Regina, Calgary, and Edmonton, respectively; each chapter achieved a membership of around 50. This was a remarkable accomplishment for what were then little more than frontier communities, each with a population of around 30,000, the vast majority of inhabitants being recent immigrants. Meanwhile two more societies were formed in the Pacific coast cities of Vancouver and Victoria. Finally, after much effort, a society was also formed in Quebec City with a predominantly anglophone membership. By 1912, the Department of Canada reached its zenith, boasting a total of 14 societies, 760 members, and $5,522 in receipts. This membership figure represents as much as 22% of the Institute's total membership of 3,100 at the time. This achievement compares favorably to the current AIA-Canada: with only six local societies, totaling 383 members, it accounts for about 4% of the AIA's present membership of fewer than 9,500.[7]

That this remarkable growth was accomplished in the space of only four years was a tribute to the efforts of various individuals; first and foremost, President Kelsey himself, who initiated the policy, and whose enthusiasm for the AIA's expansion into Canada remained undiminished through the entire five years of his presidency; second, a group of distinguished Canadian academics, both within Canada itself and at American universities, whose services Kelsey enlisted as emissaries in the early months, first to organize local societies and later to foster their growth through AIA lecture tours throughout Canada. Prominent among these was Harry L. Wilson of Johns Hopkins, already mentioned, and Frederick William Shipley (1871–1945), professor of Latin at Washington University, St. Louis, both future presidents of the AIA,[8] and Henry Rushton Fairclough (1862–1938), professor of Latin at Stanford, who took a special interest in fostering the two Canadian societies of the Pacific Northwest.[9] The third major force in promoting the AIA in Canada was an energetic Montrealer, Adoniram Judson Eaton (b. 1850), professor of classics at McGill University, who served as secretary of the AIA's Department of Canada from 1909 till its suspension in 1915.[10] Eaton also played a vigorous role in organizing new societies and boosting the membership of existing societies, astutely employing his considerable rhetorical skills to flatter local pride. This is well illustrated in his visit to Hamilton where his words of encouragement to the local membership, hitherto a mere branch of the Toronto society, were reported by the *Hamilton Spectator*: "The organization of the Hamilton members into an independent Society not only removes any stigma of being an adjunct of the Toronto Society, but also entitles the local society to representation on the Council of the Institute."[11]

Space does not permit a detailed analysis of the composition of the

Canadian membership, though it is clear from the reports received from friends and colleagues in various Canadian centers commenting on the membership lists of the local Canadian societies of around 1912 that a demographic and prosopographical analysis of the AIA in Canada would yield much interesting information on the social and cultural history of the nation at the beginning of this century.[12] The Canadian societies display a number of common features that they doubtless shared with the American societies of the day. First, with the exception of the occasional school-mistress, female academic, or, in rare instances, the wife of an influential citizen, the membership was exclusively male. Second, with rare exceptions the membership was drawn from the favored classes of society, well-to-do politicians, businessmen, retired army officers, and leading members of the clergy, and the medical, legal, and academic professions.[13] Several provincial premiers, lieutenant governors, and civic mayors may be noted, a number of federal senators, and even a future prime minister—Richard Bedford Bennett (1870–1947), the Canadian equivalent of President Herbert Hoover, who was already showing signs of leadership as president of the Calgary society of the AIA in 1912. Membership in the AIA was a mark of distinction, as is evident from the many entries in the 1912 edition of Morgan's *Canadian Men and Women of the Time*, which included AIA membership alongside such social groups as private and country club memberships.

Doubtless the social cachet of belonging to a society that attracted the movers and shakers in the community was an important factor in promoting membership in the local AIA, but there must have been other factors in an age of competing claims on the limited pool of people with cultural aspirations. Even in 1912 archaeology needed no Indiana Jones to attract a public fascinated by the glamour of a discipline that had produced a succession of sensational discoveries in regions of the Old World long favored by the educated classes of the New World, which were still predominantly European in outlook. The Bronze Age civilizations of the Aegean, recently enhanced by the revelation of Minoan Crete, and the now-efficient technology of the stereopticon or "magic lantern" provided a potent mix that could draw audiences in the hundreds. It was not for nothing that Kelsey was eager to engage the services of younger Bronze Age archaeologists of the caliber of David George Hogarth (1862–1927), Arthur Evans's successor as director of the Ashmolean Museum, and John Linton Myres (1864–1954),[14] another of Evans's close Oxford friends, to tour the newly formed Canadian societies. Both accepted

Kelsey's invitation and undertook tours in 1909, each lecturing on subjects that were to enhance their scholarly reputations in later years.[15]

In a few Canadian centers, such as Montreal, already a city with well over a million inhabitants, or Toronto, by far the largest city of English Canada, or even Ottawa, with a disproportionately large middle class employed in various departments of government, the formation of an AIA society might have happened independently. In other cities there already existed a flourishing cultural society with broad interests devoted to mutual enlightenment. The AIA appeared in these centers just at the time when members of societies like the Association of Literature, Science and Art in Hamilton, and the Art, Historical and Scientific Association of Vancouver were beginning to feel the need for more specialized societies to cater for their narrower interests.[16] In Toronto, on the other hand, the AIA must also have benefited greatly from the excitement generated by the campaign to establish a museum to house the remarkable collection being assembled by the charismatic Charles Trick Currelly (1876–1957), who had acquired his archaeological training as a staff member of the Egyptian Exploration Fund under Flinders Petrie in 1902. He was to become the first director of the Royal Ontario Museum, opened in 1914 by the Duke of Connaught, the Governor General of Canada (1911–1916)[17] and the Honorary Patron of the AIA's Department of Canada.[18] Currelly himself went on to do yeoman service as an AIA lecturer in Canada and the United States.[19] In Vancouver the leadership of another resident scholar, Charles Hill-Tout (1858–1944), one of the pioneers in the archaeology of the Pacific Northwest, gave an intellectual focus to the burgeoning AIA society of that city.[20] He also became a regular lecturer for the AIA and presented papers at the Annual Meeting at a time when Americanists were still welcomed on the program.[21] For most communities, however, and especially on the prairies, in what were still settlements hardly removed from their pioneer beginnings, the local AIA and similar societies must have played a vital role in nurturing the intellectual and cultural life of the small group of educated people trying to retain contact with civilized living in what must have seemed at times a thoroughly hostile environment.

With the AIA now so strongly established in Canada, it was inevitable that there would be pressure from some members that the Department of Canada play a more independent role within the Institute. Such a demand in itself was not inconsistent with Kelsey's original plan in encouraging the growth of the AIA in Canada. Indeed, the notion that the Canadian societies might eventually form a distinct Department of Canada had already been stated from the outset in a provisional document circulated at the 1908 AIA Council meeting in Toronto. This was little more than a prospectus, however, giving the new body its identity and defining its purpose "to promote archaeological study and research in the Dominion of Canada in all fields represented by the work of the Institute. At the present time these fields are Greek, Roman and Oriental Archaeology, the Art of the Renaissance, and the primitive civilization of the American continent." In matters of organizational substance it was clearly laid down that the Canadian societies should, in accordance with the regulations of the Institute, bear the same relation to the Institute as the societies already in existence in the United States. On the other hand, the same document, while authorizing the establishment of a committee for the Department of Canada, declined to prescribe its future role, leaving it entirely to the new committee to formulate proposals on the subject. In effect, therefore, the Canadian societies would continue to function, like their American counterparts, collecting fees from their members and remitting the total sum each year directly to the central office in Washington, D.C., as was the practice at the time.[22] The central office, in turn, would continue to organize three or four Institute lectures per annum for each society and underwrite the cost of each tour. This arrangement left little scope for the office-bearers of the nascent Department of Canada to exercise much authority or even influence over the local Canadian societies. It was equally clear that if the relationship between the Department of Canada and the Institute proper were to change, the initiative for doing so would rest with the officers of the Department. They were not slow to exercise their right.

For most of its history, the Department of Canada was administered from Montreal by the powerful duo of William Peterson (1856–1921), the department's president and a distinguished classical scholar and Principal of McGill University, and Judson Eaton, the energetic and determined secretary of the organization and a professor of Greek.[23] They took their cue from Kelsey's own annual report to the Institute of 1908–1909, in which he declared, "To cope with the problems confronting the Affiliated societies in Canada successfully requires not only an intimate knowledge of existing conditions, but also freedom of initiative. . . . During the present year, undoubtedly a system will be devised which will enable the officers of the

Department of Canada to work to greater advantage, and will encourage them to deal with their own problems more independently." The result was a resolution adopted by the Council of the Department of Canada in Ottawa in February 1910, which was subsequently endorsed nearly two years later at the Annual Meeting of December 1911 by the Council of the AIA. This effectively recognized the Department of Canada's status as an independent unit in affiliation with the parent AIA in the United States, with authority to administer the lecture program in Canada and to collect membership dues from the local Canadian societies. It also recognized the Department's right to retain for its own purposes any surplus remaining after transmitting an annual contribution to the Institute for the services it provided to the Canadian membership.

The long delay of nearly two years between the initial resolution and its final endorsement reflects a continuing and increasingly bitter disagreement between the two principals responsible for implementing the arrangement, Judson Eaton and Mitchell Carroll (1870–1925), general secretary of the Institute at the central office of the AIA in Washington, D.C.[24] The positions of the two men were irreconcilable, and personal rancor only exacerbated the dispute. In a confidential memo to Kelsey dated 25 March 1912, Carroll maintained that "the Department of Canada should be merely a geographic expression and we should foster in the different cities the Affiliated (i.e., Canadian) societies on the same basis as in the United States." Eaton, on the other hand, aimed to satisfy national pride by establishing one single centralized "large society in Canada with branches in the different cities and that all communication with the Institute be conducted only through the Secretary of the Department. He also wishes a separate fiscus for the Department." It is clear, however, that Eaton's imperialistic design for the Department of Canada encountered an unenthusiastic reception from societies in other parts of Canada, who resented the two-tiered system of direction from Montreal and Washington respectively.

Carroll was not slow to exploit this disaffection in fomenting disunity within the Department. In 1912, during the last months of Kelsey's presidency, relations between Eaton and Carroll continued to deteriorate, as each in his correspondence with Kelsey blamed the other for the problems besetting the Canadian organization. In a series of confidential notes to Kelsey, Carroll painted a dismal picture of the Department of Canada, declining memberships in the older societies, failure of the new societies to maintain the minimum membership for accreditation, falling revenues, lax communications between the secretary in Montreal and the societies, inadequate arrangements for lecturers on tour, and widespread complaints from members not receiving publications. Blame for this he laid squarely on Eaton himself, under whom, if he was permitted to follow the present course, "only schism can result." Unfortunately, the AIA Archives contain little to give us Eaton's side of the case, but they do contain one telling letter to Kelsey in which he protested the unfairness of having been criticized for his failure to make adequate arrangements for a lecture tour, when in fact "the itinerary of the tour had been taken out of my hands," presumably by Carroll, the general secretary. He deplored the "infinite harm from dual control in the lecture system and clashing of orders" when Carroll interfered in what he regarded as his responsibility.

Through all these difficulties, Kelsey remained confident in the wisdom of his Canadian initiative, and, with only a month left in office, in a report to Eaton on his recent lecture tour of western Canada, he extolled the warmth and enthusiasm of the reception he had received, dispelling any misgivings he had previously felt about his encouragement of new societies in that part of the country. "Now," he wrote, "I see no reason why, in Canada as in the United States, the societies located in these thriving cities should not develop with the country and become increasingly fruitful as centers of cultural activities, contributing increasingly to the general uplift."

In the years immediately following Kelsey's presidency, the Department of Canada maintained a full program of lectures for its constituent societies, though it was evident from the sharp falloff in membership that enthusiasm was waning in some of the smaller centers. Moreover, despite Carroll's cajoling, the Canadian societies were proving increasingly remiss in forwarding their annual contributions to the central office. Nevertheless, the commitment of the AIA to the Canadian enterprise remained strong, since Kelsey was succeeded, first by Harry L. Wilson, one of the original group of Canadians who had assisted him in establishing the first Canadian societies at the beginning of his presidency, and, on his death after only a few months in office, by another of Kelsey's Canadian group, F.W. Shipley, who was elected at the Annual Meeting in Montreal in January 1914 and presided over the AIA for the next four years. It is a sad irony that the demise of the AIA's Department of Canada occurred early in his presidency, brought about not from internal schism, as Mitchell Carroll had predicted, but from events far more devastating. The outbreak of World War I on 4 August 1914 produced a tremendous outpouring of patriotic fervor throughout English Canada, and the call to arms was answered in many communities almost to a man. In Edmonton, for example, out of the exclusively male list of 40 members of the AIA around 1912, as many as 17 (43%) enlisted in the Canadian Expeditionary Force in 1914 for service overseas.[25] With a hemorrhage of young men on that scale, many doomed never to return, it is little wonder that most of the Canadian societies of the AIA found it impossible to continue operations. The situation was recognized formally in the following year when, on the recommendation of Secretary Judson Eaton, the officers of the Institute declared the Department of Canada "temporarily" suspended from 30 June 1915.[26] A number of the larger societies, such as Montreal, Toronto, Vancouver, and Winnipeg, continued to meet during the War, maintaining truncated lecture programs, which included another tour of Western Canada by the indefatigable Kelsey in 1917.[27]

With the return of peace, the prospect of holding the joint Annual Meeting of the AIA/APA of December 1919 again in Toronto, 11 years after the successful Toronto meeting of 1908 that had witnessed the birth of the Department of Canada, perhaps rekindled hope for its revival, but this was not to be. On 3 December, with just over three weeks to go before the meeting began, the Chairman of the local organizing committee in Toronto, Professor Norman Wentworth DeWitt (1876–1958), cabled the presidents of both the AIA and APA advising them of a severe outbreak of smallpox in Toronto;[28] there was no sign of its abating, and the public health authorities were urging that all public gatherings be cancelled. Americans would be required to produce certificates of vaccination on entering Canada, and the same would be required as a condition of readmission to the United States. In an age without email or fax machines, the crisis was handled by the executives of both organizations with remarkable alacrity; within 24 hours they had accepted DeWitt's advice to cancel the Toronto meeting; within 48 hours a hotel had been booked with arrangements to hold the meeting in Pittsburgh on the same dates as originally planned for Toronto; within 72 hours notification letters were in the mail to members of both the AIA and APA.[29]

To judge from the subsequent history of the AIA in Canada, the cancellation of the Toronto meeting of 1919 may be seen as the cruel omen of a long winter. By the time that the two organizations again held their joint meeting in Toronto in the midst of the Great Depression in December 1934, the Toronto society was the sole survivor of the once flourishing AIA presence in Canada. Over half a century would elapse from the demise of the Department of Canada in 1915 until the AIA's fortunes north of the 49th Parallel began to revive with the gradual reappearance during the late 1960s and 1970s of long-defunct societies, beginning with Vancouver in 1967 and the Montreal, Ottawa, and Winnipeg societies during the following decade, and the welcome appearance of a new society in the Niagara Peninsula.

REFERENCES

Archaeological Institute of America (AIA). 1995–1996. *Bulletin of the Archaeological Institute of America* 87 (July 1995–June 1996):99–100.

Briggs, W.W., Jr., ed. 1994. *Biographical Dictionary of North American Classicists*. Westport, Conn.

Carroll, M. 1907a *The Attica of Pausanias*. Boston and New York.

———. 1907b. *Women: In All Ages and in All Countries*. Philadelphia and London.

Currelly, C.T. 1956. *I Brought the Ages Home*. Toronto.

Davis, H.W.C., and J.R.H. Weaver, eds. 1927. "Sir William Peterson." In *The Dictionary of National Biography, 1912–1921*, 433–4. London.

de Grummond, N.T., ed. 1996. *An Encyclopedia of the History of Classical Archaeology*, 2 vols. Westport, Conn.

Fairclough, H.R., trans. 1916, 1918. *Virgil*. 2 vols. Loeb Classical Library. New York and London.

———, trans. 1926. *Horace: Satires, Epistles and Ars Poetica*. Loeb Classical Library. New York and London.

Hunt, A.I. 1987. "Mutual Enlightenment in Early Vancouver." Ph.D. thesis, University of British Columbia.

Morgan, H.J., ed. 1912. *Canadian Men and Women of the Time*, 2nd ed. Toronto.

Shipley, F.W., trans. 1924. *C. Velleius Paterculus: Compendium of Roman History. Res Gestae divi Augusti*. Loeb Classical Library. New York and London.

Weaver, J.H.R., ed. 1937. "David George Hogarth." In *The Dictionary of National Biography, 1922–1930*, 421–3. London.

Williams, E.T., and H.M. Palmer, eds. 1971. "Sir John Linton Myres." In *The Dictionary of National Biography, 1951–1960*, 762–3. London.

Wilson, H.L. 1898. *The Metaphor in the Epic Poems of P. Papinius Statius*. Baltimore.

———. 1903. *D. Iuni Iuvenalis Saturarum libri v*. New York and Boston.

NOTES

[1] I am grateful to Dr. Susan Heuck Allen for organizing the 1997 Colloquium, from which this chapter resulted, and inviting my participation. I also wish to thank Professor Elizabeth A. Fisher, The George Washington University, Washington, D.C. and colleagues at the University of British Columbia, Professors Charles W. Humphries, Robert A.J. McDonald, and Robert B. Todd, for their helpful advice and comments; and Robin Meador-Woodruff, Kelsey Museum of Archaeology, University of Michigan for her help in supplying the photograph of Francis W. Kelsey (fig. 8.1) from the Archives of the Museum.

[2] The affiliated Canadian organization, known popularly as AIA-Canada, was incorporated as a Canadian society in 1994 with the title Archaeological Institute of America - Institut Archéologique d'Amérique and registered as a "charitable organization" under the Income Tax Act in 1994. It has a governing board of three officers (President, Secretary, and Treasurer) and a Council consisting of the Presidents of the six local Canadian societies of the AIA and of the two societies currently in the process of formation (Edmonton and Hamilton). The principal function of the organization to date has been to raise funds to enhance the lecture program in Canada and to provide travel assistance to Canadian graduate students giving papers at the AIA Annual Meeting. Fees from Canadian members are channeled through a Canadian bank account to the headquarters of the AIA in Boston, which continues to administer the various programs and services provided to Canadian members.

[3] Except where otherwise indicated, all material pertaining to the Department of Canada is contained in boxes 14 (formation of the organization in 1908–09) and 17 (events of 1910–1912). I wish to thank Mr. Mark J. Meister, former Executive Director of the AIA, and the AIA Archives Committee for permission to quote and paraphrase material from the AIA Archives; and also Nasim Momen, Director of the Stone Science Library and her staff, for their kind assistance during my visits to the Archives in their former location.

[4] As professor of Latin language and literature at the University of Michigan from 1889 until his death, Kelsey built up a large collection of papyri and other antiquities and established the Classics Department as a major center of papyrological research. His scholarly activities covered a broad spectrum of philological and archaeological interests, a fact reflected in his election in successive years as president of the APA (1906–1907) and of the AIA (1908–1912). The Francis W. Kelsey Museum of Ancient and Medieval Archaeology of the University of Michigan is named in his honor.

For information on individuals mentioned in this paper, see Briggs (1994) for Kelsey, Fairclough, Shipley, and de Witt; Morgan (1912) for Currelly, De Witt, Eaton, Fairclough, Hill-Tout, Peterson, Shipley, Wilson; de Grummond (1996) for Hogarth, Kelsey, and Myres; and the *Dictionary of National Biography*, Leslie Stephen and Stephen Lee, eds. London (1885–1993) for Hogarth and Myres.

[5] Wilson, a native of Wilton, Ontario, was a graduate of Queen's University, Kingston (B.A., 1887; M.A., 1888). He pursued advanced research at the Johns Hopkins University (Ph.D. 1896) and the University of Bonn. He joined the faculty at Johns Hopkins in 1902 where he remained until his death. A specialist in Silver Latin poetry, he was the author

of *The Metaphor in the Epic Poems of P. Papinius Statius.* Baltimore (1898) and *D. Iuni Iuvenalis Saturaram libri v.* New York and Boston (1903).

[6] An amusing note that must sound familiar to scholars on the lecture circuit who give slide presentations appears in Kelsey's letter of 11 December 1908 to the Secretary of the Ottawa society thanking him for his hospitality during his Ottawa visit. He adds, "As sometimes happens, the last slide used at Ottawa was left in the stereopticon. Would you be so kind as to call the operator and ask him to pack the slide carefully and send it to me by mail?"

[7] These statistics are taken from the most recent published information in AIA (1995–1996, 99–100). The total consists of 496 individuals already registered as members of AIA-Canada and a further 19 listed with the American membership whose names had not yet been transferred to AIA-Canada when the figures were compiled.

[8] Shipley was born at Cheltenham, Ontario, and graduated with the gold medal in Classics from the University of Toronto in 1892. On completion of his Ph.D. at the University of Chicago in 1901, he joined the faculty of Washington University as Professor of Latin where he remained until retirement in 1941. He is best known today for his translation of Velleius Paterculus and the Monumentum Ancyrum in the Loeb Classical Library. *C. Velleius Paterculus: Compendium of Roman History. Res Gestae divi Augusti* with an English translation by F.W. Shipley. New York and London (1924).

[9] Fairclough was a native of Barrie, Ontario, and, like Shipley, was a graduate of the University of Toronto (B.A., 1883; M.A. 1886). He completed his Doctorate at Johns Hopkins University in 1896 and served on the faculty at Stanford as professor of Latin for his entire career (1901–27). Regarded as the leading Vergilian critic of his day, Fairclough remains a familiar name through his Loeb translations of the works of Vergil and Horace. *Virgil, with an English Translation by H.R. Fairclough.* 2 vols, New York and London (1916–1918) and *Satires, Epistles and Ars Poetica of Horace, with an English Translation by H.R. Fairclough.* New York and London (1926).

[10] Eaton, a native of Annapolis, Nova Scotia, was educated at Acadia University (B.A. 1873; M.A. 1877), Harvard University (B.A. 1876), and Yale and Leipzig Universities (D.Phil. 1885). He joined the faculty at McGill in 1886 and remained there until retiring early in 1911, partly to devote his attention to the AIA's Department of Canada.

[11] I owe this information to Professor Emeritus Alexander G. Mc Kay. See also the following note.

[12] I am extremely grateful to the following friends and colleagues who responded so promptly and enthusiastically to my enquiries, Prof. Emeritus Edmund Grindlay Berry (Winnipeg), Prof. Emeritus Robert J. Buck (Edmonton), Prof. Emeritus Charles William J. Eliot (Halifax and St. John, N.B.), W.T. Lane (Vancouver), Prof. Emeritus Alexander G. McKay (Hamilton), Prof. Peter L. Smith (Victoria), and Mrs. Margaret Walker (Calgary). Unfortunately, it has proved impracticable within the confines of this short paper to do justice, except for a few specific illustrations, to the wealth of information received. I hope in the near future to undertake, with the collaboration of these and other colleagues in centers as yet undocumented, a detailed study of all fourteen of the AIA societies established in Canada during this period.

[13] It should be noted, however, that the professional composition of individual societies varied greatly. Businessmen and merchants appear more frequently in the membership lists of industrial and commercial centers such as Hamilton and St. John. By contrast, university and administrative centers, such as Halifax, Kingston and Toronto, show a preponderance of academics and lawyers. At Kingston, for example, as many as 23 of the 37 male members of the local society in 1909 were on the faculty of Queen's University; the remainder whose professions can be identified were four members of the clergy, including two bishops, four lawyers, three businessmen and one army major. One of the two females listed was a Queen's faculty member.

[14] Hogarth had already acquired vast field experience, having traveled with Professor Sir William M. Ramsay (1851–1939) in Asia Minor, excavated at various sites in Egypt, including Naukratis, and at Phylakopi on Melos before joining Sir Arthur Evans (1851–1941) at Knossos in 1900. He was to continue as Curator at the Ashmolean till his death. Myres was at the time Professor of Greek at Liverpool but would shortly (in 1910) move to Oxford to assume the newly created Wykeham Professorship in Ancient History, which he held till retirement in 1939. He was an imaginative scholar who combined a sound grasp of the literary texts with a command of historical geography and archaeology. He held the first Sather Lectureship at the University of California, Berkeley in 1914 and was reappointed in 1927. He was knighted in 1943.

[15] Hogarth's lecture was entitled "Hittite Discoveries in Relation to Early Greek History," Myres's "Cyprus and the Prehistoric Age of the Mediterranean." Hogarth also undertook a second AIA lecture tour in 1921.

[16] For an excellent study of the latter and the development of specialized societies in Vancouver, see Hunt (1987).

[17] The Duke of Connaught, Prince Arthur William Patrick Albert (1850–1942), was the third son (seventh child) of Queen Victoria.

[18] Currelly, a native of Huron County, Ontario, trained first for the Methodist ministry at the University of Toronto (B.A. 1898, M.A. 1901), but found his true métier as a collector while working with Petrie in Egypt. His career as a collector and Director of the Royal Ontario Museum is engagingly recounted in his autobiography (Currelly 1956).

[19] For an amusing account of how he took advantage of his lecture tour of the American and Canadian societies on the Pacific coast to acquire aboriginal artifacts in Santa Fe and Victoria for the Royal Ontario Museum (*ibid.* 203–8).

[20] Hill-Tout, a native of Devon, England, emigrated to Canada in 1884, eventually settling in British Columbia in 1890. Here he was able to apply a long-standing interest in anthropology to the native peoples of the Lower Mainland whose languages, customs, and archaeology absorbed his scholarly attention for the rest of his life. His many publications are fundamental to the archaeology of coastal British Columbia and earned his election as F.R.S.C. (Fellow of the Royal Society of Canada). He was a vice president of the AIA-Department of Canada.

[21] E.g., at Pittsburgh, December 1911, where he delivered a paper "Neolithic Man in British Columbia" (abstract in *AJA* 16 [1912] 102–3).

[22] Although a fixed percentage of fees collected by each society was designated for the

Institute, these funds were not remitted until the end of the year, and only if the local society did not require the money to cover its own expenses. This was hardly an arrangement conducive to the stable and predictable budgeting necessary for the central office of the Institute to fulfill its responsibilities to the membership. It was only in 1923 that the AIA abandoned this system in favor of the present practice, by which the Institute collects membership fees and provides a *per capita* rebate to the individual societies.

[23] Peterson, a native of Edinburgh and a graduate of Edinburgh University (M.A. 1875), pursued further studies at Göttingen and Oxford (M.A. 1883). He enjoyed a considerable reputation for his work in Latin prose authors, especially Cicero, but his greatest achievements were as a university administrator, first as the first Principal of University College, Dundee, and subsequently of McGill University. He was knighted in 1915. See further, *Dictionary of National Biography, Supplement, 1912–1921*, Oxford (1927), 433–4.

[24] Carroll (Ph.D. Johns Hopkins, 1895) was professor of classical philology at the George Washington University in Washington, D.C. Throughout his career he taught classical archaeology, specializing in Greek topography. He was the author of a work on Pausanias and edited the first volume on Greek women of a 10-volume series (Carroll 1907).

[25] I am indebted to Professor Emeritus Robert J. Buck for this information. See also n. 12 above.

[26] The last annual report of the Department of Canada, covering the fiscal year ending 30 June 1915, provides a stark illustration of the sorry condition of the Canadian societies. Four, including Edmonton, had already suspended operations by that date, and of the remainder, only six actually reported revenues from fees. The total sum of $1494.25 for 1915 represents a decline of 73% in fees collected from the income recorded in 1912 (see above).

[27] The War itself was even reflected in the lecture program. The AIA's Norton Lecturer for 1917–1918, Professor Victor Horta (1861–1947), director of the Royal Academy of Fine Arts, Brussels, whose tour included various societies in the western United States and Canada, lectured on "Cathedrals and Civic buildings of Belgium and Northern France as Affected by the War."

[28] DeWitt was born in Tweedside, Ontario, and educated at Victoria College, University of Toronto (B.A. 1899) and the University of Chicago (M.A., Ph.D. 1906). Except for short-term appointments in the United States, he spent his entire career as professor of Latin at Victoria College, Toronto (1908–45). He was a distinguished Vergilian scholar who also conducted important research in Epicurus. He served as president of the APA in 1946–1947 and played a leading role in organizing the joint meetings of the APA and AIA held in Toronto in 1934 and 1950.

[29] For the correspondence on the abortive Toronto meeting, see AIA Archives box 21.7.

— 9 —

The Archaeological Institute of America between the Wars

Stephen L. Dyson

This essay is about an epoch of challenge, even crisis, in the history of the Archaeological Institute of America. It is an era in which the AIA attempted to redefine itself in relation to a changing American educational and cultural scene. Populists clashed with traditionalists in a struggle that highlighted tensions of region and class in the world of American scholarship and brought into conflict some of the most powerful archaeological personalities of the age. Ironically, while the traditionalists momentarily triumphed, after a short interval the AIA was started on the road to revival by a new president who appeared on the surface to be a Harvard traditionalist but who saw the need for change and adopted many of the techniques of the populists.

The AIA was founded by a group of Boston intellectuals in 1879 with a mission that was an odd and complex combination of idealism and ambition (Bennett 1890; Norton 1909–1910; Dort 1954; Dimaggio 1982; Dyson 1998, 33–42). It was to educate the American public about the newly emerging discipline of archaeology, promote fieldwork, and help found archaeological research institutions. It was also to help to advance Charles Eliot Norton's mission of improving American society and culture through the study of the great art of the past (Emerson 1912; Vanderbilt 1959; Duffy 1996). That first, visionary generation succeeded in its goals beyond any reasonable expectations. By 1914 AIA chapters had been founded across the nation, linked by an ambitious lecture program that had no parallel anywhere else in the world (Dyson 1998, 42–6, 49–53). Research schools established under the aegis of the AIA flourished in Athens and Rome (Lord 1947, 1–49; Valentine and Valentine 1973; Dyson 1998, 53–60, 109–19; Winterer, this volume). AIA-sponsored expeditions were conducting research in both the Old World and the New (Butler 1921; Dyson 1998, 68–75). American classical archaeologists, who had overwhelmingly received their advanced education in Germany, were now returning to found graduate programs in their native land (Briggs 1995). American field projects were beginning to earn the respect of the Europeans and achieve Norton's goal of a distinctive and original American contribution to classical archaeological scholarship (Dyson 1998, 82–7).

Early American classical archaeology was also a complex blend of elitism and egalitarianism and that was mirrored in the AIA. Harvard professors figured prominently in the early annals of American classical archaeology, but Western Reserve College in Cleveland, Ohio with Harold North Fowler (1859–1955) and Samuel Ball Platner (1863–1921) played a more important role in those early decades than did Yale or Columbia (Fowler 1921; Sanborn 1956). The most powerful and successful president of the AIA after Norton was Francis W. Kelsey (1858–1927) of the University of Michigan, who held office from 1908 to 1912 (Riggs 1927). By the end of the 19th century, America had developed a unique group of quality women's colleges, and their students helped America lead the way in breaking the gender barrier at the Athens and Rome schools. Intrepid field researchers like Harriet Boyd Hawes (1871–1945) and Hetty Goldman (1881–1972) showed that women were as adept at field archaeology as the men (Allsebrook 1992; Bolger 1994; Dyson 1998, 87–95; Allen, Introduction, this volume).

Such a period of youth, innovation, and openness was not destined to last. One might use the tragic fate of Herbert Fletcher de Cou (1868–1911), shot to death in the ruins of Cyrene, an action which brought to an end the last major AIA research expedition in the Mediterranean, to personify the end of this golden age of the AIA (Kelsey 1910–1911; Dyson 1998, 76–82). The reality was more complex, however. The AIA was in many ways the victim of its own successes, and also its early application of the principles of federalism and delegation so important to success in America. This became especially clear in the years after World War I.

By the post-World War I period, major universities like Princeton and

Johns Hopkins had created programs in classical archaeology which assumed most of the responsibility for advanced education in the discipline (Lavin 1983; Williams 1984; Dyson 1998, 95–102, 163–8, 185–200). Overseas research institutions, especially the American School of Classical Studies at Athens, took over the excavation agenda which the founders, like Norton, had seen as a central mission for the AIA. Corinth rather than Cyrene represented the future of American classical archaeology (Lord 1947; Dyson 1998, 85–7).

Archaeologists working in areas other than Greece and Rome increasingly sought their own identity outside the AIA. From the beginning a tension had existed between those who saw the AIA as an organization focused on the Mediterranean and those who had a more wide-ranging vision of what AIA archaeology should be. In the 1920s and the 1930s the non-classical archaeologists went their own way with little effort on the part of the Mediterranean-oriented AIA leadership to keep them in the fold. The process started with the founding of the College Art Association in 1913 and ended with the establishment of the Society for American Archaeology in 1935 (Griffin 1985; Dyson 1998, 200–7; Snead, this volume). It was ironic that the last of the schools founded under the auspices of the AIA was the School for American Research in Santa Fe, which opened in 1919 (Hinsley 1986; Snead, this volume). At its inauguration Francis Kelsey could still celebrate the old values of AIA archaeological universalism, but these were words from the past and for the past. Chartres and Pecos were no longer sites discussed in papers at the Annual Meeting or in the pages of the *American Journal of Archaeology (AJA)* (Dyson 1998, 201–2). Classical archaeologists were increasingly cut off from the larger archaeological community. They were drawn ever closer to the philologists who were themselves increasingly moving from the universal *Wissenschaft* of 19th-century Germany to the Oxbridge model of a language-literary studies with little connection with material culture (Allen, Introduction, this volume).

Two widely different yet oddly interconnected cultural and educational agendas played themselves out in relation to what was the remaining core AIA constituency. It was becoming increasingly clear that the classics either archaeological or literary could no longer assume to enjoy a central, privileged place in American education and culture. Pragmatists threatened to marginalize the Greek and Roman past (Dyson 1998, 158–60). One reaction on the part of the classics community was to package antiquity in increasingly popular forms, to develop new media and to cultivate new audiences. Not accidentally, it was during this inter-war era that summer programs were established at both the American Academy in Rome and the American School of Classical Studies at Athens. The central purpose of those new programs was to revitalize the teaching of classics, especially in the secondary schools (Oldfather 1936; Dyson 1998, 207–10).

The AIA had from almost its very beginnings used the lecture program and the local chapter as an instrument of genteel popular education in the tradition of Chautauqua and the Lowell Institute. Francis Kelsey combined belief in a dynamic Mediterranean research mission (more for Michigan than for the AIA) with the strong conviction that the future of the AIA was going to be based as much on the local archaeological interests of members in the Midwest and Far West as on the European orientation of the east coast establishment (Snead, this volume). This also meant that the AIA had to maintain some interest in and concern for archaeology in areas other than the Mediterranean. Other leaders of the period such as Mitchell Carroll (1870–1925), long time secretary of the AIA, and David Moore Robinson (1880–1958) of Johns Hopkins shared this split vision (Dyson 1998, 202–3).

Yet even the lecture program had limits on its outreach, and in many areas the local chapters reflected too greatly the interests and concerns of the academics. The populists felt the AIA needed to do more to reach the educated, nonprofessional interested in archaeology. One result of this perceived need to enhance the popular base of the AIA was the decision to publish *Art and Archaeology*. In December of 1912 the Council of the AIA authorized the officers "to transform the BULLETIN into a non-technical illustrated monthly magazine as rapidly as was consistent with financial stability and the maintenance of high editorial and artistic standards" (*Art and Archaeology* July 1914, 2). The first issue appeared in 1914. Since this interesting initiative on the part of the AIA has largely been forgotten, the history of *Art and Archaeology,* the ancestor of *Archaeology,* deserves attention here (Dyson 1998, 203–7; Katz 1998, 366).

In an era before photographically illustrated magazines aimed at a general, educated public had become common, *Art and Archaeology* published lively, intelligent articles on the full range of world archaeology. The first issue of July 1914 featured articles on "Masterpieces of Aboriginal American Art-Stucco Work," "The School of Classical Studies of the American Academy in Rome," "The Visitation at Pistoia by Luca Della Robbia," and "Modern

Masterpieces of Classical Architecture-The Lincoln Memorial." It was in many respects an updating of Charles Eliot Norton's mission of archaeology as an instrument of general education and the elevation of public taste.

Art and Archaeology got off to a good start and flourished in the 1920s. It was, however, from the beginning caught up in controversy and in AIA politics. The first editor was David Moore Robinson of Johns Hopkins, a dynamic but always controversial figure, who did believe strongly in the need for classical outreach (Robinson 1917; Dyson 1998, 101–2, 193–5, 203–4). He was ousted as editor in 1918 and then sniped at his successors from the outside (Dyson 1998, 204). Important also in the establishment of the magazine was Mitchell Carroll, general secretary of the AIA, and leader of the powerful Washington society (Kelsey 1926).

Art and Archaeology was from the beginning closely associated with the Washington society, which regarded itself as an independent fiefdom within the AIA. In 1921, when financial and political concerns threatened the AIA's support for the magazine, the Washington society actually assumed financial responsibility for the magazine. Carroll remained a strong, controversial figure whose dynamic activities on behalf of the Washington-based AIA headquarters, *Art and Archaeology*, and the Washington society, which he had been instrumental in founding, did not sit well with the northeast classical archaeology establishment.

This conservative faction was led by James Egbert (1859–1948) and William Bell Dinsmoor (1886–1973), both long associated with Columbia. Egbert belonged to that school of conservative classicists, who saw the discipline as a bulwark against the philistines, and thought that it could best fulfill that mission by affirming traditional scholarly values (Dyson 1998, 158–60). Dinsmoor, whose academic star was just rising at this period, represented the most conservative, positivistic values in classical archaeology (Dyson 1998, 172–173, 204–206). Homer Thompson, in his obituary of Dinsmoor, admitted that he was an austere New Englander out of place even in New York (Thompson 1974). Rhys Carpenter (1889–1980), in a note that accompanied a gift copy to Dinsmoor of his *Aesthetic Basis of Greek Art*, observed in an amused fashion "I am sending you my little prayer book on Greek aesthetic. In looking it over, I cannot see that you can possibly like it or commend it, so perhaps you will let me know what you most dislike about it" (Carpenter to Dinsmoor, n.d., AIA Archives, box 20).

By 1921 the conservatives felt satisfied that they had distanced themselves from Mitchell Carroll, who left the secretaryship in 1918, and *Art and Archaeology*, which was now the responsibility of the Washington society. However, they faced the embarrassing situation that more and more general members wanted to maintain their subscriptions to *Art and Archaeology* rather than get *AJA*, which was now the sole official publication of AIA. Even the professionals had serious problems with the *AJA* under the editorship of William Nickerson Bates (1867–1949) of the University of Pennsylvania, accusing him of everything from extreme cronyism in accepting and rejecting articles to producing a journal with a uniformly dull cover design (Luce 1949). The AIA was faced with a substantial loss of membership and revenue, as nonacademics threatened to align themselves with the Washington society rather than the national organization to get their *Art and Archaeology*.

The plot thickened when Ralph Magoffin (1874–1942) was elected president of the AIA in 1921, a position he held until 1931 (Dyson 1998, 206–7). As a middle westerner associated with Johns Hopkins and then New York University, he was outside of the Ivy League elite represented by Egbert, Dinsmoor, and others (Luce 1942). He understood clearly that the AIA had to reach out to a popular audience. He had served as associate editor of *Art and Archaeology* and appreciated the important role it played in creating popular support for archaeology. Early in his presidency he expressed support for the goals of the magazine and worked to broker compromises that would meet the wish of many members to associate the magazine more closely with the AIA. While Magoffin had respectable academic credentials, including a Ph.D. from Johns Hopkins, and publicly stated his support for the research mission of the AIA, he also was a popularizer, producing general audience archaeological books like *The Romance of Archaeology* (Magoffin and Davis 1929). He proved successful in increasing the support base for the AIA. From 1917 to 1930 membership rose from 3,215 to 3,460.

The positions advocated by Magoffin and personified by *Art and Archaeology*, however, did not go unchallenged. As other branches of the archaeological profession that had formerly operated under the AIA umbrella went their own way, power increasingly concentrated in a core of classical archaeologists, whose center of operations was the major university and museums of the northeast. Their rallying point was the *American Journal of Archaeology*, whose scholarly virtues were seen as a counterweight to the vulgar popularism of *Art and Archaeology*.

Attacks on Magoffin began almost immediately, led initially by his predecessor Egbert, who accused him among other things of trying to popularize even *AJA*. Another leader of this faction was William Dinsmoor of Columbia. The list of dissenters included such northeast elite stalwarts as George Henry Chase (1875–1952) and Stephen Lucas (1887–1962) of Harvard, Mary Hamilton Swindler (1884–1967) of Bryn Mawr, Rufus Morey (1877–1955), Emerson Howland Swift (1889–1975) and Baldwin Smith (1888–1956) of Princeton, and Gisela Richter (1882–1972), Edward Robinson (1858–1931), and Edward Newell (1886–1941) of New York (Dyson 1998, 204–7). The only middle westerner among these traditionalists was Louis Lord (1875–1957) of Oberlin College, a Kelsey protégé.

Their chief expressed concern was what they perceived as the failure of the AIA to maintain its research profile. They noted pointedly that in Charles Eliot Norton's day, 81% of the AIA budget went to research, while under Magoffin the Institute expended only 12% of its budget on research, mainly through AIA-associated institutions. Less clear was the position of the critics as to what the research mission of the AIA should be at a time when the American School of Classical Studies at Athens had taken over so many of the archaeological activities of the AIA.

As the 1920s passed, the eastern conservatives increasingly sharpened their attacks on *Art and Archaeology* and on Ralph Magoffin. In 1931 the anti-Magoffin faction presented a petition to the "Trustees, Officers and Executive Committees of the Archaeological Institute of America and its Affiliated Societies" asking for the resignation of President Magoffin. Their attack focused on his failure to promote AIA research, his general fiscal management of the AIA, and his excessive support of "propaganda and popularization," an attitude which had not only undermined the reputation of the AIA, but "had exposed his writing to the criticism that 'it conveys a wholly wrong impression of what archaeology is.'" The damaging quote was from a review of one of Magoffin's popular books in the British journal in *Antiquity* (Crawford 1930, 503). The petition, which was signed by 48 scholars, mainly from the northeastern establishment, was not a pleasant document (Dinsmoor and Elderkin to the Trustees, Officers, and Executive Committee of the AIA and its Affiliated Societies, 1931, AIA Archives, box 29).

As so often happened in the history of the AIA, regional differences soon emerged in the Magoffin controversy. When his northeastern opponents turned to the powerful Chicago society of the AIA for support, they were rebuffed. The Chicagoans were sympathetic to the financial concerns, but they felt that the forced replacement of the president would be too disruptive for the organization. As for the ideal goals of AIA, the Chicagoans straddled the two camps. They "believed that full support should be given the *American Journal of Archaeology*." On the other hand, they favored "a certain amount of popularization. To make the Institute a purely research organization is not practicable" (carbon copy, without names, n.d., AIA Archives, box 29).

Magoffin responded vigorously to the charges against him. He placed his actions squarely in the tradition of Francis Kelsey, another president who had felt that the AIA should broaden its base of support. He stated emphatically that "it is my opinion that back of the exceptions which are now being taken to the national administration there is little else than an attempt on the part of some of the adherents of a 'small Institute idea' to bring a return to the Institute of thirty years or so ago" (AIA Archives, box 29). He provided detailed refutations of the various charges made against him.

The onset of the Great Depression, however, had strengthened the hand of the anti-Magoffin conservatives, who advocated a limit on AIA activities in times of financial crisis. The attacks on the president continued. He survived no-confidence motions brought against him, but clearly his spirit was broken. He refused to run for reelection, claiming that he did not want the length of his presidency to exceed the 10 years of founder Charles Eliot Norton. In 1931 turned over the office to his rival, Louis Lord.

Especially hard hit by the Depression was *Art and Archaeology*. While all programs of AIA were affected by the financial collapse, those that depended on a more volatile popular base were more dramatically affected. Elite universities were not going to cancel their subscriptions to the *AJA*, but in hard times, the purchase of *Art and Archaeology* seemed less necessary to its lay readers. The magazine struggled, cutting the number of issues and running deficits, while advertising revenues largely disappeared.

Art and Archaeology, which was in its death agonies when Magoffin left office, now faced a hostile central administration at the AIA. In 1933, the AIA annual report contained this denunciation of the magazine: "President Lord presented the view of a faction of the Institute which feels it better without *Art and Archaeology*. Professor Dinsmoor endorsed the view on the two grounds that the Institute does not wish to be represented at all by a magazine of popular character," and then to use his own words "*Art and Archaeology* has ceased to be what the Institute expected. It has become largely an art magazine. To keep up the interests of the Institute, it should be limited to archaeology." In 1934 the editors admitted defeat, and *Art and Archaeology* ceased publication.

Lord inherited an AIA deeply divided and unsure of its mission. It was also an organization that faced major financial problems as membership declined and giving was hindered by the fiscal realities of the Depression years. This financial situation was not helped by the sense of loss, even betrayal, felt by lay members over the death of *Art and Archaeology*. Local societies felt strongly that their members still needed a more general access publication than *AJA*. There was a short-lived experiment with distributing the British journal *Antiquity* to members, but the arrangement proved too cumbersome. Ironically it was under William Dinsmoor, who served as president from 1937 to 1945, that pressures for some popular AIA publication reached the point that the organization had to revisit the issue. Local societies were polled, and their responses showed the correctness of Magoffin's insights. As one society secretary put it succinctly "the publications are not reaching the right people. Most of our members cannot read the *AJA*. . . . In summary, all our differences stem from the fact that the Institute is trying to make one series of lectures and one publication appeal to both laymen and archaeologists" (Dorothy Kent Hill to William Dinsmoor, June 1945, AIA Archives, box 36).

A growing crisis in general support threatened the whole organization. By 1935, one year after the demise of *Art and Archaeology,* AIA membership had shrunk to 1,489, just more than half that of 1930. With the route of populist expansion rejected, President Lord had little choice but to cut costs. *Art and Archaeology* was gone, and even the activities of the lecture program were seriously curtailed. Ironically, at that moment the need for extreme financial austerity came into conflict with the position of archaeologists like Dinsmoor that the AIA should be more deeply involved in research. After a long hiatus in direct support of fieldwork, the AIA began making modest contributions to Hetty Goldman's excavation at Tarsus.

Lord argued that with its grave financial problems the AIA could not even afford this small, worthy investment in field research. Hetty Goldman reacted with fury to the prospect of the loss of funds, and rallied support in the Ivy League archaeological establishment. Lord resisted, but Goldman's supporters bided their time until he departed for a trip to Europe. A hasty council, "representative" of the AIA, was assembled in Boston to discuss the

Goldman subsidy issue. The members included Paul Sachs (1878–1965), an uncle of Goldman, and several of her Harvard mentors. Lord was overruled and Goldman received her funds (Dyson 1998, 94–5; 207).

These internal struggles did not totally isolate AIA from dramatic political changes in Europe. Members of the AIA were especially shaken by the rise of Nazism in Germany and its impact on the intellectual and scholarly world. Members of the American archaeological community who were members of organizations like the German Archaeological Institute faced especially serious ethical dilemmas. Since its origins, American classical archaeology had closely identified with German scholarly values. On the other hand, refugee German scholars like Karl Lehmann-Hartleben (1894–1960) kept them informed about what was happening to those values under the Nazis. In late 1938 both Benjamin Meritt (1899–1989) and C.R. Morey resigned in protest from the German Archaeological Institute. For both practical and ideological reasons, not all took that stand. When Morey requested that T. Leslie Shear (1880–1945), who directed the Agora excavations of the American School of Classical Studies, join them in the resignation, Shear responded that he "felt that such an action on my part as you propose would be unwise from the point of view of the School. This is especially true at the present time when the dictatorial regime in Greece is distinctly pro-German in its attitude" (Shear to Morey, 17 December 1938, AIA Archives, box 31).

William Dinsmoor hesitated about taking an official position as president of the AIA. However, a visit to Germany for the Sixth International Archaeological Congress in August 1939 and the grim events of late 1939 and early 1940 convinced him that action was needed. In a stinging letter to the president of the German Archaeological Institute, Dinsmoor submitted his resignation (10 May 1940, AIA Archives, box 31). In the letter he recalled that his membership went back to 1914 and that he had long tried to keep an open position on the involvement of the German archaeological community in the Nazi excesses. Now he felt that he had no choice but to leave the organization. His letter closed with the blunt statement: "I regard my membership for more than twenty years in the German Archaeological Institute as a blot on my record, and in order to expunge what would be disgraceful to prolong, I herewith tender my resignation from the German Archaeological Institute."

The AIA limped into the period of World War II and beyond with declining membership and in an increasingly parlous financial condition. Then in 1946 Sterling Dow (1903–1995) of Harvard assumed the presidency. Dow had some of the facade of Dinsmoor, but more of the soul of Norton (Vermeule 1995). He realized that major steps had to be taken to stop the slide in AIA membership and finances. Among the innovations that some colleagues felt was needed was the creation of a more popular publication than *AJA*. Dow read the letters, reports, and surveys going back to before the war that argued for and against such an initiative. He rummaged through old boxes filled with back copies of *Art and Archaeology*. He read them and admitted that the magazine was much better than he had been led to expect. Dow launched a series of initiatives that led to the creation of *Archaeology* and the return of the AIA to its old vitality based on a combination of scholarly and popular activities (Dyson 1998, 220–2). Charles Eliot Norton would have been pleased.

REFERENCES

Allsebrook, M. 1992. *Born to Rebel: The Life of Harriet Boyd Hawes*. Oxford.

Bennett, C.E. 1890. "The Work and Aims of the Archaeological Institute of America." *Report of the First Annual Meeting of the Wisconsin Society Archaeological Institute of America*, 15–24.

Bolger, D. 1994. "Ladies of the Expedition: Harriet Boyd Hawes and Edith Hall in Mediterranean Archaeology." In *Women in Archaeology*, edited by C. Classen, 41–50. Philadelphia.

Briggs, W.W., Jr. 1995. "Basil L. Gildersleeve: The Formative Influence." In *German Influences on Education in the United States to 1917*, edited by H. Geitz, J. Heideking, and J. Herbst, 245–56. Cambridge.

Butler, H.C. 1921. "The Investigations at Assos." *Art and Archaeology* 12:17–26.

———. 1922. *Sardis, 1, the Excavation 1910–1914*. Leiden.

Dimaggio, P. 1982. "Cultural Entrepreneurship in Nineteenth Century Boston: The Creation of an Organizational Base for High Culture in America." *Media, Culture, and Society* 4:33–50.

Donohue, A. 1985. "One Hundred Years of the *American Journal of Archaeology*." *AJA* 89:3–30.

Dort, A.V. 1954. "The Archaeological Institute of America Early Days." *Archaeology* 7 (4):195–201.

Dow, S. 1980. "A Century of Humane Archaeology." *Archaeology* 33 (3):42–52.

Duffy, T.P. 1996. "The Gender of Letters: Charles Eliot Norton and the Decline of the American Intellectual Tradition." *The New England Quarterly* 69:91–109.

Dyson, S.L. 1998. *Ancient Marbles to American Shores: Classical Archaeology in the United States*. Philadelphia.
Emerson, E.W. 1912. "Charles Eliot Norton: The Man and the Scholar." *Bulletin of the Archaeological Institute of America* 3:83–128.
Fowler, H.N. 1908. "Charles Eliot Norton." *AJA* NS 12:395–7.
———. 1921. "Samuel Ball Platner." *Bulletin of the Archaeological Institute of America* 12:151–3.
Griffin, J. 1985. "The Formation of the Society for American Archaeology." *American Antiquity* 50:261–71.
Gulick, C.B. 1956. "Harold North Fowler, 1859–1955." *Annual Report of the American School of Classical Studies* 16–17.
Harland, J.P. 1963. "Stephen Bleecker Luce, 1887–1962." *Annual Report of the American School of Classical Studies*.
Hinsley, C. 1986. "Edgar Lee Hewett and the School of American Research in Santa Fe, 1906–1912." In *American Archaeology Past and Future*, edited by D.J. Meltzer, D.D. Fowler, and J.A. Sabloff, 217–33. Washington, D.C.
Katz, P.P. 1998. "The Archaeological Institute of America and Outreach: Fifty Years of *Archaeology* Magazine." *AJA* 102:366.
Kelsey, F.W. 1926. "Mitchell Carroll." *Art and Archaeology* 21:103–12.
Lavin, A.M. 1983. *The Eye of the Tiger*. Princeton.
Luce, S. 1942. "Ralph Van Deman Magoffin." *AJA* 46:412.
———. 1949. "William Nickerson Bates." *AJA* 53:388.
Magoffin, R., and E.C. Davis. 1929. *The Romance of Archaeology*. Garden City, N.Y.
Morey, C.R. 1925. "Allan Marquand: Founder of the Department of Art and Archaeology." *Art and Archaeology* 20:105–8, 136.
Mylonas, G. 1951. *Studies Presented to David Moore Robinson*. St. Louis, MO.
Norton, C.E. 1909–1910. "The Work of the Archaeological Institute of America." *Bulletin of the Archaeological Institute of America* 1:251–66.
Oldfather, W.A. 1936. "In Memoriam Grant Showerman of Wisconsin and Rome." *American Scholar* 5:367–72.
Patterson, T.C. 1986. "The Last Sixty Years: Toward a Social History of Americanist Archaeology." *American Anthropologist* 88:7–26.
Riggs, A.S. 1927. "Francis Willey Kelsey." *Art and Archaeology* 23:272, 284.
Robinson, D.M. 1917. "Reproductions of Classical Art." *Art and Archaeology* 5:221–34.
Sanborn, C.A. 1956. "Harold North Fowler." *AJA* 60:285.
Sanders, H. 1927. "Francis Willey Kelsey." *CP* 22:308–10.
Sheftel, P. 1979. "The Archaeological Institute of America 1879–1979: A Centennial Review." *AJA* 83:3–17.
Thompson, H. 1974. "William Bell Dinsmoor 1886–1973." *Yearbook of the American Philosophical Society* 156–63.
Vanderbilt, K. 1959. *Charles Eliot Norton*. Cambridge, Mass.
Vermeule, E. 1995. "Sterling Dow, 1903–1995." *AJA* 99:729–30.
Williams, E.R. 1984. *The Archaeological Collections of the Johns Hopkins University*. Baltimore.

— 10 —

The Great Divides: The AIA and Professional Responsibility in Archaeology[1]

Clemency Coggins

In a memorable paper entitled "The Great Tradition versus the Great Divide," English archaeologist Colin Renfrew addressed the Centennial meeting of the Archaeological Institute of America in Boston, December, 1979, outlining the founding principles of the AIA with their emphasis on the promotion of archaeological investigation in the United States as well as in foreign countries; a stance belied by the disdain for New World archaeology harbored by most of the Institute's founders (Renfrew 1980, 290–1).[2] In Renfrew's definition "The Great Tradition, then, is concerned with investigation and publication relating to the early civilizations of the Classical world" (Renfrew 1980, 290). He goes on to quote the *First Annual Report of the Executive Committee* (1880): "The study of American archaeology relates, indeed, to the monuments of a race that never attained a high degree of civilization . . . whose intelligence was for the most part of a low order . . . [prehistoric] American archaeology offers . . . nothing to compare with the historic archaeology of civilized man in Africa, Asia and Europe" (291). This majority view was vehemently opposed by a few founding members, and herein lay the Great Divide, and I would suggest the ambivalent origins of future policies of professional responsibility in the AIA.

This divide is only one example of the inherent "duality," or contradictions, characteristic of the AIA. At the turn of the century this divide was simplistically seen as deriving from a systematic scientific perspective in opposition to a more humanistic and philological one, and six decades later English scientist C.P. Snow (1905–1980) still spoke of such a division between the "two cultures" (Snow 1964; Coggins 1998, 56). From its late 19th-century beginnings, anthropology, a new discipline that subsumed New World archaeology in the United States, associated itself with the methodologically scientific and less historical side of this equation, while the classicists generally identified themselves as humanists. If the "scientific" perspective involved the objective study of cultures that were "other," such neutrality contrasted with the passionate identification of humanists with the ancient achievements of their own western heritage. The AIA was intended somehow to unite these approaches in the practice of archaeology, a goal only approaching success at the AIA's centennial. A second paper, by James Wiseman, approached the disciplinary divide constructively, proposing a broader definition of archaeology. "Archaeology . . . touches upon almost all the natural and social sciences, as well as the humanities. It may be this breadth of intellectual concern, almost presumptuous in its scope, that has been a greater impediment to the recognition of archaeology as a legitimate professional discipline than has the obsolete university organizational structure" (1980, 279–285). In pursuit of an inclusive reconfiguration of archaeology, Wiseman had introduced a new interdepartmental archaeology program at Boston University in 1979.

The Institute came to embody additional divides, however. An important one, inherent in the division noted above, has been the understanding of archaeology as it is perceived by museum curators and collectors in distinction to field archaeologists. This may involve academic disciplines of art history and of philology versus various more "scientific" pursuits of classical archaeology and anthropology. This divide has had serious repercussions in the successful comprehensive pursuit of archaeology, in that it often involves money. "Archaeology is an expensive enterprise that requires extensive nonprofessional patronage" (Dyson 1998, xi). Indeed, in the AIA's first Annual Report, Norton saw that "to perform even a small part of this work, large sums of money are required" (AIA1880, 8). Usually dependent on the collections of field archaeologists or of private collectors, museum curators and art historians have little need to plan and finance large archaeological excavations themselves. They analyze what they have, and tend to be interested in the object for itself, often more than for its broader historical and contextual significance. Thus, although government and foundation funding is now available for excavation with explicit cultural and scientific rationales, individual collectors may still sponsor excavations while continuing to collect objects that represent the invalidation of the very work they would support—while curators and art historians foster these contradictory pursuits in their focus on the qualitative. Thus the relative availability of funding for archaeology reifies the divide; limited funding for the more expensive scientific excavation contrasts with the smaller-scale use of private moneys that perpetuate the narrower humanistic goals of museums and collectors. Nevertheless, dedicated supporters of archaeological preservation are found on every side.

Related to this last disciplinary divide is another which is one of the most important in the AIA. This is the divide between the professional and nonprofessional membership of the many local societies in the United States and Canada. While nonprofessional interests and involvement may equal that of professionals, most of these members do not hold advanced academic degrees in archaeology and are less aware of the tensions among different intellectual and methodological approaches. This divide is exemplified by the majority attendance of professionals at the Annual Meeting, where they read learned papers of the type published in the Institute's scholarly journal, the *American Journal of Archaeology*. This professional focus contrasts with the Institute's extensive public lecture program through the many North American societies, and the popular publication of excavations worldwide in the Institute's magazine, *Archaeology*. The membrane between these two kinds of membership is highly permeable, but it still exists. All of these divides were present at the founding of the AIA and continue today. They are basic to the development of policies of professional responsibility in the Institute, and they explain why the author of this article has been involved in these AIA matters for over 20 years.

As an Americanist, an art historian, and an archaeologist (but not a field archaeologist) my work has bridged many of the divides enumerated above, although, as an Americanist, I was an outsider in the AIA. First, in my experience, the division between the aesthetics of collectors and the emphasis on knowledge provided by field archaeology became glaringly evident to me 30 years ago in Guatemala and Mexico as the appetite of the antiquities market overwhelmed the unstudied remains of Maya civilization. Recognition of this ongoing destruction coincided with the drafting of the UNESCO Convention on the Means of Prohibiting and Preventing the Illicit Import,

Export and Transfer of Ownership of Cultural Property in 1970, and with my own efforts for the ratification of this UNESCO Convention in the United States; these were supported and amplified by AIA endorsement in the last decade before implementation by Congress (Coggins 1969, 1998). These efforts by the AIA, in conjunction with other professional organizations, were essential to the eventual passage of the Cultural Property law in 1983. Any success the author may have had in bridging divides within the AIA, as Chairman of the Subcommittee on the Preservation of Archaeological Resources, then of the Committee for Professional Responsibilities, derived from an embrace of both art historical and scientific archaeology, and of both humanistic and anthropological goals. It also derived from the fact that the efforts of a New World art historian, if noticed by most professional members of the AIA, were not generally viewed as having relevance or potential effect on classical archaeology. In fact, it is the view of the author, that it was through the fitful and often tenuous relationship of the AIA to American archaeology that the Institute became involved in many of the ethical and legislative activities that are now so important in the organization.

From the Beginning

The dedicated Hellenism of Charles Eliot Norton, founder of the AIA and president from 1879 to 1889, is often explained as emblematic of his Boston Brahmin status. "Classical art was central to the aesthetic values of the American cultural elite" (Dyson 1998, ix), and as creator of the aesthetic discipline of art history at Harvard, where Norton's courses, not surprisingly, stopped at 1600 C.E. (Sheftel 1979, 4)—presumably to include the Renaissance rebirth of Classicism. Among the founders of the AIA, however, were several men who espoused American Archaeology: historian Francis Parkman (1823–1893) who insisted, futilely, on its primacy, (Sheftel 1979, 5) and promoted the "acquisition of knowledge [over] the acquisition of objects" (Dyson 1998, 42); Stephen Salisbury (1835–1905) of the American Antiquarian Society, Worcester, who sponsored archaeological excavations in Yucatan, Mexico (Coggins 1992, 9–10); Harvard scientist Alexander Agassiz (1835–1910), who mounted expeditions in this hemisphere; Frederic Ward Putnam (1839–1915), curator (director) of the Peabody Museum of Archaeology and Ethnology, Harvard, who excavated prehistoric New

England and Midwestern sites; and Americanist anthropologist Lewis H. Morgan (1818–1881). Morgan was famous for his work in the American Southwest and for his book *Ancient Society* (1877) in which, following various European models, he described the evolution of prehistoric societies in terms of sequential stages of savagery, barbarism, and civilization—a developmental trajectory that placed American aborigines (in barbarism) well below the civilized (classical) ancient world in accomplishment (Hinsley 1981, 133–8). In the newly established AIA these theories would serve principally to illustrate what the Greeks had overcome and how, ultimately, they had come to excel. With this rationale of cultural evolution, the AIA sponsored and published work in Southwestern American archaeology and ethnology for almost 30 years,[3] culminating in the 1907 foundation in Santa Fe, New Mexico, of the School of American Archaeology (later the School of American Research) that joined the AIA schools in Athens, Rome, and Jerusalem (Snead, this volume). While Americanist work actually absorbed much of the early Institute funding, the interest and focus of the membership was primarily on the first AIA excavations at Assos, a Greek site in Turkey (Allen, ch. 3, this volume).[4]

It was, however, in the American field that the first resolution on the preservation of cultural property was formulated, at the 20th anniversary of the Institute and the first general meeting, in 1899 (*AJA* 3:149). This resolution urged "the United States government . . . to care for the preservation of monuments of the earlier inhabitants of this country," although this was immediately preceded by another resolution, so that in retrospect the pair seems to symbolize the duality still inherent in the AIA today; theoretically compatible, these are the concern for the scientific preservation and study of ancient civilizations versus the acquisition and conservation of their remains. The first resolution urged the United States government "to modify existing regulations affecting importation of objects of archaeological interest." This was a protest against recent changes in import regulations that had resulted in impeding the growth and exchange of museum collections, as explained in a paper "Some Points of Museum Policy" by Sara Yorke Stevenson (1847–1921) of Philadelphia (153–5). Stevenson predicted "scientific materials" will be exhausted in 25 years, and the U.S. Government must not frustrate those who "would supply the needs of public museums." This first resolution concerned museum collections of Old World objects (e.g., Egyptian), while the second resolution addressed New World monuments;

together they represented the professional concerns of the young organization; separately they described its diverging foci.[5]

National Responsibilities

In 1904, five years later, the AIA, in conjunction with other scholarly organizations and institutions, was involved in its first major lobbying effort in Washington. This was for passage of a law to protect the remains of American Indian antiquity, and in that year the AIA formed the Committee on the Preservation of the Ruins of American Antiquity to lobby for it, such as the one formed by the American Anthropological Association.[6] Working closely with Frederic Putnam, director of the Peabody Museum at Harvard, the AIA, under Thomas Day Seymour (1848–1907), (president, 1903–1907), was concerned with drafting and lobbying for the bill. The crisis situation that had led to these efforts sounds sadly familiar. On 5 January 1905, an article in the *Chicago Times-Herald* was headlined "Fear Doom of Relics. Nation is Asked to Act. Bill before Congress. Aimed at Pothunter." This described the looting of sites as a recognized industry in the Southwest where "in several cities there are large establishments filled with that sort of plunder. . . . Several big dealers send out expeditions regularly to replenish their supplies, and carloads are sent east, [and] to Europe." The article suggests professional archaeologists need not plan on future work in the devastated region (AIA Archives, box 12.3). In this crusade the Reverend Henry Mason Baum (b. 1848), eccentric and impassioned editor of *Records of the Past,* informed his readers: "Today, our own country stands alone among civilized nations of the world without legislation for the protection of its priceless monuments. . . . Years ago a spirit of vandalism seized the tourist. . . . This led to excavating for commercial purposes. Now, even the Indians are digging for pottery," and Baum goes on to attack what he saw as the irresponsible excavations of the Smithsonian Institution.[7] Baum, who worked tirelessly for the proposed law, was angry at the opposition of the Smithsonian, alone among cultural and academic institutions,[8] because the Institution apparently wanted control of all excavations on public lands.[9] This position was eventually abandoned, and the Secretary of the Interior was designated to grant excavation permits and oversee the transmission of collections to public museums. In 1906 the American Antiquity Act was finally passed, after almost a decade of rejection and reformulations. This law has been described as "the most basic piece of federal legislation affecting archaeology" (McGimsey 1972, 111). In the same year the AIA was incorporated by an act of Congress "for the purpose of promoting archaeological studies by investigation and research in the United States and foreign countries" ("AIA News and Notes," *AJA* 10:174–6).[10]

Civilization Threatened

Twelve years later, in 1918, at the end of World War I, in a third recorded cultural property resolution, the AIA joined 17 U.S. institutions in resolving to protect "historic monuments and objects of art of all periods in Nearer Asia."[11] The next year the AIA supported League of Nations initiatives to preserve antiquities in the new states of the former Ottoman empire (*Bulletin* 9 [1918] 89; AIA Archives, box 21.6)—threatened regions wherein lay the interests of many AIA members. Twenty-two years passed before, in 1942, another grave crisis, the devastation threatened by World War II in Africa and Europe, involved many professional members of the AIA, especially William Dinsmoor (1886–1973), president from 1939 to 1945, in war efforts related to their expertise (*Bulletin* 33 [1942] 5). President Dinsmoor, who chaired the American Council of Learned Societies Committee on the Protection of Cultural Treasures in War Areas, worked throughout the war creating hundreds of sets of maps to alert bombing missions to the location of artistic and historic monuments in war areas, so they might be avoided (*Bulletins* 33–37 [1942–1946]). After the war, Dinsmoor described the large role the AIA had played in the protection of archaeological and artistic monuments, adding that "before the present war, the armies of the United States had never had occasion to assume any definite interest or responsibility with regard to the historic monuments and cultural institutions in areas in which they might be engaged" (*Bulletin* 36 [1945] 4–8).

International Reponsibilities

After the horror of World War II, a new international consciousness and optimism led to the creation of the United Nations, and UNESCO, the United Nations Educational, Scientific and Cultural Organization. An AIA delegate to a UNESCO conference in 1947 reported briefly it was not clear what role the AIA might play (*Bulletin* 38 [1949] 59), but six years later a member attended another UNESCO conference on international cooperation

(*Bulletin* 44 [1953] 24), and in 1956 the AIA was represented on the UNESCO National Commission (*Bulletin* 47 [1956] 14). Perhaps the most important international cultural property initiative after the war was the drafting of the 1954 Hague Convention on the Protection of Cultural Property in the Event of Armed Conflict. "This was the first comprehensive international agreement for the protection of cultural property" (Greenfield 1996, 187), and it served as a precedent for the later UNESCO Draft Convention of 1970. The United States has never signed the Hague Convention, however, and Jeannette Greenfield (1996, 187) remarks on how unenforceable it has recently proven to be, even among signatories, in the wartime destruction of the cultural heritage of Dubrovnik, Croatia.

Postwar international concerns for the peacetime protection of cultural property cystallized in 1970 with the UNESCO Cultural Property Convention, which the United States was actively involved in drafting (Bator 1982; Coggins 1998). Malcolm Wiener, then AIA General Counsel, explained the convention at the Executive Committee meeting in March 1970 (*Bulletin* 61 [1970] 49), and at the December Annual Meeting the AIA Council passed a resolution in support of the UNESCO Draft Convention, as did the American Schools of Oriental Research, the American Oriental Society, the College Art Association, and the American Association for the Advancement of Science. Preceding the passage of this resolution Rodney Young (1907–1974), (AIA president from 1969 to 1972), observed that "the Convention might not be approved by the U.S. government [and further that] most U.S. museums which have the great influence on the circulation of archaeological objects are independent, and thus would not be bound by it."[12] However, nine institutions soon passed resolutions in support of the Convention.[13] There was comment in the ensuing discussion about the responsibilities of the source countries for "both repressing illegal and encouraging legal excavation and export of antiquities." (*Bulletin* 62 [1971] 43) Young described the resolution, passed by 104 attending members (8 against, 7 abstentions), as "a pioneering gesture by the Institute" (*Bulletin* 62 [1971] 43, 9)

The resolution:

> The Archaeological Institute of America condemns the destruction of the material and historical records of the past by plundering of archaeological sites both in the United States and abroad and by the illicit export and import of antiquities.

The Archaeological Institute of America supports whole-heartedly the UNESCO Draft Convention on the Means of Prohibiting and Preventing the Illicit Import, Export and Transfer of Ownership of Cultural Property, and urges ratification of the Draft Convention by the United States Government at the earliest practicable moment. It further urges its members individually and therough the local societies of the Institute to make their support of the Draft Convention felt by communications to the appropriate governmental authorities.

The Archaeological Institute of America calls upon its members, as well as educational institutions (universities and museums) in the United States and Canada, to refrain from purchasing and accepting donations of antiquities exported from their countries of origin in contravention to the terms of the UNESCO Draft Convention.

The Archaeological Institute of America urges that, in accordance with the provisions of the UNESCO Draft Convention, concerned countries take practical steps to facilitate the legitimate export, import and exchange of archaeological materials and antiquities. The Archaeological Institute of America applauds the efforts of local authorities, both in the United States and abroad, to prevent the despoliation of archaeological sites and the illicit export and import of antiquities and archaeological materials, and pledges its support in such efforts.

One key point in this resolution would pose problems for many members of the Institute: this was the injunction to "refrain from purchasing and accepting donations of antiquities exported from their countries of origin in contravention to the terms of the UNESCO Convention" (*Bulletin* 62 [1971] 34). This admirable statement of principle, which may have seemed self-evident to many professional members, had a profound effect on the attitudes and practices of many others—initiating a movement for change that is still proceeding very slowly, almost 30 years later. In 1970, this resolution placed many actively acquiring museum curators and collectors, who remained members of the AIA, in a position of violating the resolution, or of disregarding it as rhetorical. The resolution was, of course, unenforceable, but it has continued to exert a moral pressure among the membership, and to serve as an example outside the organization. In view of this resolution and later developments, it is noteworthy that at the 1969 Council meeting President Rodney

Young had "announced an important and generous gift, the largest in the history of the Institute (some $78,000) to be known as the von Bothmer Publication Fund and used for publications in the fields of Greek, Etruscan and Roman antiquity, first preference going to the *Corpus Vasorum Antiquorum* fascicles." A resolution of thanks was voted as was the election of Bernard N. (1912–1993), Dietrich, and Maria Elizabeth von Bothmer to the status of Benefactors of the Institute (*Bulletin* 61 [1971] 43–4). Three years later benefactor Dietrich von Bothmer was not elected a Trustee of the Institute in the wake of his acquisition, as curator of classical art, of the "Euphronios Krater" for the Metropolitan Museum of Art (*Bulletin* 64 [1973] 54). With this acquisition, the serious consequences of one of the great divides in AIA professional membership were brought home to the organization, since von Bothmer and the Metropolitan Museum were apparently violating the UNESCO Convention and the recently adopted principles of the AIA.

In October 1972, General Counsel Malcolm Wiener informed the Executive Committee of the progress of the UNESCO implementing legislation through Congress, and noted the support of many academic museums. In January 1973, the UNESCO Convention was finally ratified by the U.S. Senate, and in December 1973, at the Council meeting, the AIA adopted an updated version of the 1970 resolution, plus a second highly significant resolution that followed from it:

> Recognizing that museums, whatever their speciality, have a communality of interests and concerns, which comes into particularly sharp focus in matters of ethics and professional behavior, and that they are the custodian of man's material heritage and of the part of his natural heritage which he has collected for study and transmission to future generations;
>
> Be it resolved that the Archaeological Institute of America cooperate fully with the United States Government and foreign countries in their endeavors to preserve cultural property and its documentation and to prevent illicit traffic in such cultural property.
>
> The Archaeological Institute of America believes that Museums can henceforth best implement such cooperation by refusing to acquire through purchase, gift, or bequest cultural property exported subsequent to December 30, 1973, in violation of the laws obtaining in the countries of origin.

We further believe that the governing bodies, directors and curators of Museums should, in determining the propriety of acquiring cultural property, support and be guided by the policies of the UNESCO Convention on the Means of Prohibiting and preventing the Illicit Export, Import and Transfer of Ownership of Cultural Property and the implementing provisions adopted by the signatory states.

It is recommended that all nations establish effective laws and develop proper control over export so that illicit traffic may be stopped at its sources. However, wherever possible, within the limits of national law, consideration should be given to legitimate and honorable means for the acquisition of cultural property. It is hoped that nations will release for acquisition, long term loan, or exchange, cultural property of significance for the advancement of knowledge and for the benefit of all peoples.

In order to augment and clarify further the intent of this resolution and determine methods of accomplishing its aims, the governing body of a museum should promulgate an appropriate acquisition policy statement commensurate with its by-laws and operational procedures, taking into consideration the International Council of Museums' recommendations on "Ethics of Acquisition" (*Bulletin* 65 [1973–1974] 30).

President Homer Thompson then moved and council adopted the following resolution: "That the Annual Meeting should not serve for the announcement or initial scholarly presentation of objects in conflict with the Resolution on antiquities adopted by the Archaeological Institute of America's Council in December, 1970."

These resolutions cannot be viewed as entirely rhetorical, although one might dismiss the exhortation of countries of origin. The resolutions were passed, but the votes are not recorded. Here museums are directly and specifically enjoined to adapt their acquisition policies to these principles—although this was unenforceable. The final resolution was, however, enforceable and constitutes the first clear directive in the Institute's history for changing the professional behavior of members. Papers submitted for presentation at the Annual Meeting were not henceforth to serve as the "initial scholarly presentation of objects in conflict with" the 1970 resolution; this same policy also applied to publication in the *American Journal of*

Archaeology (Kleiner 1990, 525–7). The purpose was to deny to recently imported objects without provenience[14] the scholarly validation, and thus the enhanced market value, resulting from legitimization by Institute-sanctioned papers. This was a major departure, but it placed the ultimate responsibility for compliance on the committee charged with soliciting and accepting papers. This was very difficult to enforce since "initial scholarly presentation" was open to interpretation.

In March 1973 the formation of a Committee for the Preservation of Archaeological Resources was proposed in Executive Committee, where cultural property issues were occupying more and more time. Also considered at that meeting were museum accession and deaccession policies; the despoliation of American archaeological sites; the UNESCO World Heritage Convention; strengthening the 1970 AIA UNESCO Resolution, with sanctions for noncompliance; and appealing to the Metropolitan Museum to return coins belonging to the American Numismatic Society (*Bulletin* 64 [1973] 54–5). At the 1973 Council meeting the Committee for the Preservation of Archaeological Resources was formally constituted with President Thompson as chairman (*Bulletin* 65 [1973–1974] 29). The next spring, in April 1974, Trustee William Kelly Simpson proposed the AIA adopt the College Art Association Code for the professional practice of art history (*Bulletin* 65 [1973–1974] 26). This was probably the first proposal for an AIA code of ethics.

In 1974, under Frederick Matson, incoming president (1975–1976), the AIA joined the Society for American Archaeology in a major campaign to pass the "Moss-Bennett" bill, a law that would require the scientific excavation of U.S. archaeological sites threatened by development or destruction involving any federal funds. As a result of this law, a registry of professional archaeologists working in the United States was proposed. In Executive Committee James Wiseman moved the creation of an interorganizational committee to accredit government-sponsored archaeological research in the U.S., and for the development of a code of archaeological standards and ethics. On the international front the committee decided not to move on the Turkish invasion of Cyprus until the situation was settled (*Bulletin* 66 [1974–1975] 4, 25–6), while in the meeting of the Committee for the Preservation of Archaeological Resources, Chairman Thompson noted an "appreciable change in attitude among museum officials and collectors" (*Bulletin* 66 [1974–1975] 36).

United States implementing legislation for the UNESCO convention was still not passed in 1976, and in an Executive Committee meeting President Matson solicited an official AIA letter of support for the legislation. It was moved and voted that the AIA national office take steps to involve local societies in an effort to pass the legislation. In March, Homer Thompson, chair of the Committee for Preservation of Archaeological Resources, had attended a UNESCO meeting in Paris on the international exchange of cultural property (*Bulletin* 67 [1975–1976] 6). On the national front, the Registry of Professional Archaeologists (1974), a result of the passage of the Archaeological and Historic Data Preservation Act, had become the Society of Professional Archaeologists (SOPA) in 1975. A year later the AIA joined SOPA, with a representative on the board (*Bulletin* 68 [1976–1977] 4).

The Committee for Professional Responsibilities

It is evident that, with the creation of the Committee for the Preservation of Archaeological Resources, the AIA became more involved in cultural property issues and, in March 1977, a major revision of the AIA committee structure was proposed in which a Committee for Professional Responsibilities would be one of four standing committees. This new standing committee would reorganize the various concerns of the old Committee for the Preservation of Archaeological Resources into subcommittees on UNESCO, Law of the Sea, and SOPA, among areas of special concern in 1977 (*Bulletin* 68 [1976–1977] 3, 5). Oscar White Muscarella, associate curator in Near Eastern art at the Metropolitan Museum of Art, was the first chairman of the new Committee for Professional Reponsibilities, whereas the author chaired the Subcommittee for the Preservation of Archaeological Resources. In June the AIA sent a letter of support for the UNESCO implementing legislation to Congress and the Executive Committee noted that because the American Association of Dealers in Ancient, Oriental and Primitive Art was lobbying against the legislation, the AIA should lobby for it. In 1978 and 1979, with the UNESCO legislation still not passed, the Subcommittee for the Preservation of Archaeological Resources became active in lobbying. Two new subcommittees of the Committee for Professional Responsibilities were also created. These were on Membership and Academic Affairs, which dealt with AIA internal affairs, and the second, on the Code of Ethics, which produced drafts of a code for comment. Discussion of the proposed code centered on how detailed it should be, and whether it should apply to all members, or if there should be a separate, more stringent, professional one, and finally whether or not there should be sanctions (*Bulletin* 70 [1978–1979] 7, 37).

While work on a Code of Ethics progressed, the Subcommittee for the Protection of Archaeological Resources, along with many other organizations, continued to lobby Congress, but the UNESCO legislation was defeated again because of art dealer and private museum lobbying (*Bulletin* 71 [1979–1980] 10, 26, 37). Little had changed two years later when this Subcommittee organized a legislative workshop at the Annual Meeting in San Francisco, which was noteworthy for attendance by the Native American press. The next year a legislative update session in Philadelphia immediately preceded the successful passage of the UNESCO implementing legislation, signed by U.S. President Ronald Reagan on 12 January 1983, 10 years after it was introduced in Congress (*Bulletin* 73 [1981–1982] 11, 13). Several different Congressmen and Senators had sponsored it in those years, and the AIA and other cultural institutions had tirelessly supported it. Since the UNESCO legislation provided for a Presidential Cultural Property Advisory Committee with representatives from the various "interests": archaeology, museum, art market, and the public, the AIA determined to nominate possible members for consideration. Meanwhile, Trustee John Slocum (1914–1997) was appointed to the U.S. Commission on UNESCO. In 1983, in the spirit of its lobbying role the AIA explored opposition to an amendment to the National Stolen Property Act that would annul the "McLain Decision"—a 1979 judicial decision that had accepted Mexico's claim to ownership of all its cultural property, thus rendering its importation into the United States subject to the National Stolen Property Act (*Bulletin* 74 [1982–1983] 7, 13, 32). The McLain decision was a significant deterrent to the importation of illegally exported cultural property from Mexico, and possibly a precedent for seizing such materials from countries with laws like Mexico's.

The AIA positions on professional ethics led to discussion and to two motions that were passed in Executive Committee. The discussion considered (again) whether a museum that does not endorse the AIA's 1970 and 1973 resolutions should be eligible to host receptions at the Annual Meeting. The first motion revisited the policy prohibiting the initial scholarly presentation of undocumented artifacts in papers at the Annual Meeting, stipulating that this injunction should be printed on the abstract forms and the submitting author requested to acknowledge it, thus putting the responsibility on the author instead of the organizing committee. The second moved that members of AIA tours be informed of the antiquities laws of the countries visited (*Bulletin* 74 [1982–1983] 13, 31–2).

Once the U.S. UNESCO legislation was finally passed, the Institute continued to be involved through the presence of AIA members on the Cultural Property Advisory Committee, which was to deliberate on the requests of countries applying to the United States for import controls on illegally exported cultural property, as specified in the new U.S. Cultural Property law. Three AIA members were on the original committee: Patricia R. Anawalt, John Slocum, and the author. In the next years, other continuing professional concerns of the Committee for Professional Responsibilities involved the ongoing debate over whether to have separate general and professional codes of ethics and, in Congress, work on historic shipwreck legislation (*Bulletins* 76–79 [1984–1985 to 1987–1988]). After the AIA's decision in 1984 to produce a Code of Ethics for all members first, professional members were urged to join SOPA and adopt their code (*Bulletin* 77 [1985–1986] 85–6; 78 [1986–1987] 42–3). Several drafts of a brief general code were produced and a final version was passed by Council in December 1990 (*Bulletin* 82 [1990–1991] 37).

> The Archaeological Institute of America is dedicated to the greater understanding of archaeology, to the protection and preservation of the world's archaeological resources and the information they contain, and to the encouragement and support of archaeological research and publication.
>
> In accordance with these principles, members of the AIA should:
> (1) Seek to ensure that the exploration of archaeological sites be conducted according to the highest standards under the direct supervision of qualified personnel, and that the results of such research be made public;
> (2) Refuse to participate in the illegal trade in antiquities derived from excavation in any country after December 30, 1970 when the AIA Council endorsed the UNESCO Convention on Cultural Property, and refrain from activities that enhance the commercial value of such objects;
> (The Council approved the following revision of the second provision 29 December 1997):

(2) Refuse to participate in the trade in undocumented antiquities and refrain from activities that enhance the commercial value of such objects. Undocumented antiquities are those which are not documented as belonging to a public or private collection before December 30, 1970, when the AIA Council endorsed the UNESCO Convention on Cultural Property, or which have not been excavated and exported from the country of origin in accordance with the laws of that country.

(3) Inform appropriate authorities of threats to, or plunder of archaeological sites, and illegal import or export of archaeological material.

This general code brought to the fore the long-standing divisions in the Institute. These were apparent in two matters considered in the Committee for Professional Responsibilities: first, the AIA's long-standing association with the *Corpus Vasorum Antiquorum,* which, by publishing many classical vases of unknown provenience in collections around the world, thus provides the initial scholarly presentation of such collections; and second, the reluctance of the Institute to involve collectors and many private museums in the organization. Trustee Richard Warren Levy stated that "the policy of the AIA toward collectors was self-defeating, most specifically regarding Trustees and museums" since collectors who adopt the new Code of Ethics might become Trustees and thus learn about the goals and principles of the Institute as well as supporting it financially, while ethical museums always should be seen as potential members of the organization (*Bulletin* 83 [1991–1992] 37–8). These two issues are basically the same ones articulated by Sara Stevenson who, in 1899, saw the need for collections to fill the museums for both aesthetic and educational purposes, while in 1879, Francis Parkman had believed such objects must represent knowledge in historical context before any inherent qualities as trophies of Classical civilization. It is the belief that these views can coexist benignly that animates the changing perceptions held by archaeologists and museum curators today.

In 1991 and 1992 the Gulf War and Yugoslavian conflicts aroused concerns about the preservation of the antiquities in the Middle East and Balkans, and the Committee for Professional Responsibilities was charged with composing a generic AIA statement on "the destruction of ancient monuments, antiquities, and cultural institutions during war and peacetime" (*Bulletin* 83 [1991–1992] 61–2). In addition, a new international convention, called Unidroit, designed to meet some of the objections of art-importing countries to the restrictions of the UNESCO Cultural Property Convention, had become a new subject for the Committee for Professional Responsibilities, and a subcommittee was formed to monitor it; a third topic involved the general AIA Code of Ethics, which was in force and printed in the membership brochure, while work continued on refining the 1979 draft code of Professional Ethics for professional members of the AIA (*Bulletin* 83 [1991–1992] 22–3)—which saw final form only in December 1998.

The Vice President for Professional Responsibilities

Perhaps most important in 1991 for the Committee for Professional Responsibilities and the AIA was the approval of the new regulations (or constitution) of the Institute. The final version was approved by the Council in December 1991, after eight years of discussion and revision. This version mandated four vice presidents: a First Vice President, who was successor to the President, and three more who report to the President: for Societies, for Publications, and for Professional Responsibilities. The last was to be an Academic Trustee, member of the Executive Committee, and Chairman of the Committee for Professional Responsibilities (*Bulletin* 83 [1991–1992] 116). This new executive structure has been in place for the last 10 years, during which three have served as Vice Presidents for Professional Responsibilities: Karen D. Vitelli, Claire L. Lyons, and, as of December 1998, Ricardo J. Elia. As was true when the Committee for Professional Responsibilities became a standing committee in 1977, the professional activity of the Institute in such matters increased again with the creation of a dedicated vice president, whose major areas of concern are still in the preservation of archaeological resources, professional employment, and professional standards and accountability. In 1994, the Committee for Professional Responsibilities, under Vice President Karen D. Vitelli, produced both an AIA Directory of Professionals in Archaeology and a Code of Professional Standards (*Bulletin* 86 [1994–1995] 2–3, 54).

After the Second World War, the AIA embraced an international view of cultural property that had become necessary because of the wartime destruction of archaeological resources in regions of classical civilization and others. These concerns inevitably led to an analogous concern for destruction in peacetime, with particular attention to the loss of archaeological sites through looting and development, and thus to international means of preserving cultural patrimonies in general. These goals were, and are, incompatible with the existence of a continuing market in "new" antiquities, and to the collecting and curating of objects traceable to the recent, clandestine destruction of a country's cultural patrimony. Herein still lies one of the "Great Divides" in the membership of the AIA—between the collector, whether individual or institutional, and most archaeologists.

The AIA, a private organization with more than 9,000 dedicated members, professional and amateur, has consistently, if episodically, expressed its concern for the conservation of archaeological sites everywhere, as well as for the preservation of archaeological collections—positions that have led to conflicting definitions and views of short- versus long-term goals generated by the "Great Divides"—but these differences, once couched in disciplinary terms involving quantitative versus qualitative methodologies, and Western versus non-Western foci, are today joined in response to the escalating loss of every heritage.

REFERENCES

Archaeological Institute of America (AIA). 1880. *First Annual Report of the Executive Committee, with Accompanying Papers, 1879–1880.* Cambridge, Mass.

Bator, P. 1982. *The International Trade in Art.* Chicago.

Coggins, C.C. 1969. "Illicit Traffic of Pre-Columbian Antiquities." *Art Journal* 29:94.

———. 1992. "Dredging the Cenote." In *Artifacts from the Cenote of Sacrifice, Chichen Itza, Yucatan, Mexico,* edited by C. Coggins, 9–29. Memoirs of the Peabody Museum of Archaeology and Ethnology 10 (3). Cambridge, Mass.

———. 1998. "United States Cultural Property Legislation: Observations of a Combatant." *International Journal of Cultural Property* 7:1, 52–67.

Dyson, R.H., Jr. 1980. "Report of the President: Further Comment on the Great Divide." *Bulletin of the Archaeological Institute of America* 71 (1979–1980):3–5.

Dyson, S.L. 1998. *Ancient Marbles to American Shores: Classical Archaeology in the United States.* Philadelphia.

Elia, R. 1998. "American Museums and the Collection of Archaeological Objects." Paper presented at the Centennial Annual Meeting of the Archaeological Institute of America, Washington, D.C.

Greenfield, J. 1996. *The Return of Cultural Treasures,* 2nd ed. Cambridge.

Hinsley, C.M. 1994. *The Smithsonian and the American Indian: Making a Moral Anthropology in Victorian America.* Washington, D.C.

Kleiner, F.S. 1990. "On the Publication of Recent Acquisitions of Antiquities." *AJA* 94:525–7.

McGimsey, C.R. 1972. *Public Archaeology.* New York.

Morgan, L.H. 1878. *Ancient Society.* New York.

Renfrew, C. 1980. "The Great Tradition versus the Great Divide: Archaeology as Anthropology." *AJA* 84:287–98.

Sheftel, P.S. 1979. "The AIA 1879–1979: A Centennial Review." *AJA* 83:3–17.

Snow, C.P. 1964. *The Two Cultures and the Scientific Revolution.* Cambridge.

Wiseman, J. 1980. "Archaeology in the Future: An Evolving Discipline." *AJA* 84:279–85.

———. 1998. "Reforming Academia." *Archaeology* 51 (5):27–30.

NOTES

[1] This idiosyncratic overview of AIA professional concern with cultural property has relied on the AIA *Annual Reports, Bulletins, American Journal of Archaeology* (*AJA*), and the AIA Archives (AIA Archives, box #.folder#) moved to the AIA headquarters at 656 Beacon Street, Boston, Massachusetts in the summer of 1998. Most quotations before 1950 may be found in the AIA Archives. In the more than a century of archival material, *Annual Reports,* and *Bulletins* consulted, different kinds of information were included, emphasized, or saved at different periods, so this discussion must be considered more a general impression than an exhaustive study. I am grateful for the help provided by the headquarters staff, especially former Executive Director Mark Meister, and to Boston University colleagues Ricardo Elia for background information and James Wiseman for his perspective on the history of the AIA.

[2] Most scholars who have investigated the early years of the AIA have been struck by this contradiction in founding attitudes; see Sheftel 1979, 3; Dyson 1980, 3–4; Dyson 1998, ch. 1; Allen, Introduction, this volume.

[3] The third article published in the *First Annual Report of the Executive Committee* of the AIA was Americanist L.H. Morgan's "A Study of the Houses of American Aborigines with a Scheme of Exploration of the Ruins in New Mexico and Elsewhere"(AIA 1880, 29–80).

[4] In the AIA *Bulletin,* William B. Dinsmoor (1886–1973), outgoing president (1939–1945), observed that the Institute had once favored the Santa Fe School above all others financially, but that in 1945 there were few Americanists in the Institute, and Norton had been devoted to Hellenic and Latin cultures, considering "Navajos, Mayas, and Incas beyond the pale." He suggested Americanists might profit from contact with older civilizations, and looked to expand AIA activities in Turkey and Egypt (*Bulletin* 37 [1946] 13–14).

[5] In the Presidential Colloquium at the centennial Annual Meeting, Ricardo Elia, incoming Vice President for Professional Responsibilities, also noted these two resolutions that treated "protection of archaeological sites from looting on the one hand, and collection of foreign antiquities on the other" (Elia 1998, 2).

[6.] Seymour to Francis W. Kelsey (1858–1927), 15 January 1904 (AIA Archives, box 12.4). Unidentified handwritten notes of a meeting of the Committee on the Preservation of the

Ruins of American Antiquity to discuss the Americanist resolution, with a list of members present; 31 January 1905 (AIA Archives, box 11.3).

[7] *Records of the Past* III, 4 April 1904, 100–2; offprint sent to Kelsey (AIA Archives, box 11.3).

[8] H.M. Baum to Richard Rathbun (1852–1918), secretary of the Smithsonian Institution, 28 April 1904 (AIA Archives, box 11.3).

[9] Proof of an article by H.M. Baum, "Pending Legislation for the Protection of Antiquities on the Public Domain" sent to AIA General Secretary Francis Kelsey (AIA Archives, box 12.3).

[10] Copy of the Congressional document of incorporation (AIA Archives, box 12.12).

[11] AIA General Secretary G.M. Whicher (1860–1937) to W.H. Buckler (1867–1952), 11 March 1919 and 1 December 1919 (AIA Archives, box 21.6).

[12] The only museums directly affected by the UNESCO Convention would be government institutions, of which there are relatively few in the United States, compared to private ones.

[13] Nine institutions with museums had, or were soon to, endorse the principles of the 1970 Draft Convention by adopting new acquisition policies reflective of its principles—virtually all universities affiliated: University Museum, University of Pennsylvania; Harvard University museums, including Busch Reisinger, Dumbarton Oaks, Fogg, Houghton Library, Semitic, and Peabody; the Field Museum of Natural History, Chicago; University Museum, Southern Illinois University, Carbondale; Thomas Burke Memorial Washington State Museum, University of Washington, Seattle; Arizona State Museum, Tucson; Utah Museum of Natural History, Salt Lake City; Peabody Museum, Salem, Massachusetts (*Bulletin* 62 [1971] 32).

[14] The author uses "provenience" to refer to the original context of an object, since "provenance" usually refers to its history of ownership.

— II —

Computer Technology and the Archaeological Institute of America

Harrison Eiteljorg II

Computers have slowly taken over many jobs in both the academic and business worlds, and archaeology provides no exception to the rule. Computers have become more and more common in the field, classroom, and research lab. However, computer use has progressed in some unexpected ways. The rise of the Internet and especially the World Wide Web has made certain resources—often not the most scholarly—easily accessible. Email has become nearly ubiquitous, and other relatively simple tools—especially word processing—have helped ease some of the burdens of rather routine scholarly work. The potentially most significant changes brought to archaeology by computer technology, however, come from the use of more sophisticated tools for fieldwork and analysis.

The most important of those more sophisticated tools—database management programs (DBMS), geographic information systems (GIS), and computer-assisted design programs (CAD)—bring unprecedented power to the field archaeologist, as well as those working on corpora and post-excavation analytic projects. With these programs data can be better recorded, better stored, better analyzed, better utilized, and better combined with data from other projects in later years. Despite the power of this technology, these sophisticated computer applications have worked their way into the archaeological mainstream very slowly. There are, indeed, many computer users and many specialists who know how to use these tools effectively. However, the use of the tools is by no means widespread, and younger scholars are not routinely learning how to use them.[1] Whereas the early use of the technology was predictably limited to those who, for one reason or another, decided that computers brought serious benefits, it seems possible that archaeological computing will remain a specialty rather than a common tool used and understood generally. That has real perils for the field. Nearly any scholar can learn to draft, read, and critique a site plan; draw, understand, and evaluate a pot profile; make, comprehend, and assess information in tabular format; or draw, use, and appraise a map; however, the same is not true for data in digital form. To create, use, or evaluate digital data, one must have considerable experience with specific kinds of software and an awareness of the ways data should be organized by different kinds of software. As a result, only a selection of archaeologists is currently able to generate, use, or evaluate data in digital form. Others—many archaeologists at the moment—are unable to direct computer specialists in their work (much less apply sophisticated computer tools themselves), cannot effectively access digital data, have no criteria with which to evaluate digital data, and often cannot even choose the type of software needed for a particular job.

This is a dangerous trend that indicates a need to change attitudes about computers and computing. The ability to use the sophisticated programs available to scholars must become more widespread, meaning, of course, that these tools must be worked into the curriculum. Those who continue to treat computing as a separate area of specialization will risk denying themselves and their students access to substantial quantities of information, the capacity to evaluate that information, and the ability to direct their computer specialists in the field.

Despite these signs of problems with computer usage, the AIA has not attempted to take a direct role in solving them. The Institute has provided a venue for computer presentations at its Annual Meeting (see below, p. 199) and a forum for discussion of technology issues via the AIA list (see below, p. 193), but there have been neither theoretical nor practical initiatives concerning the use of computer technology from the Institute. Therefore, this article contains no further discussion of the use of computer technologies by scholars; the remainder of the article will include only discussions on the use of computer technologies by the Institute and the activities of the Institute's Committee on Computer Applications and Electronic Data.

Use of computers within the Institute has not generally been problematic; the tools in use are not so complex or difficult that staff members require extensive training. Indeed, the Institute brought computers into its work without fuss or fanfare starting in the 1980s, but not until 1990 was there a computer committee of any sort. The early uses of computers in the office, mostly for typical office tasks such as word processing, did not seem to require careful oversight from the Governing Board. The membership database, maintained on a computer by an outside vendor, was an exception. Getting information from the vendor to the local society officers who needed it was a significant problem, and regular complaints from local societies about access to membership information seemed to require action. As a result, the first computer committee was formed in the fall of 1990 as an ad hoc committee intended principally to assist with making the membership database more useful to the local societies and, in the process, to the office staff.

The ad hoc committee was supplanted the next year by a standing committee, the Committee on Computer Applications and Electronic Data. The chairman of the ad hoc committee, the author, became chairman of the new standing committee, and its first meeting was held at the 1991 Annual Meeting in Chicago. It was an open meeting, not limited to those who had been appointed to the committee, and the committee meetings have remained open to nonmembers. The committee remains very active today.

The second committee, as the name was meant to imply, was formed to deal with archaeological computing as well as the ongoing issue of providing access to membership information for local societies. The committee, though, concerned itself primarily with archaeological computing, leaving the issue of the membership database mostly to the chairman.

Membership Database

The ad hoc committee's attempt to deal with the problems of the AIA membership database, though the first true job of the committee, was its least successful effort. Local society officers had long been bothered by slow, inadequate access to membership information; they were frustrated by being unable to obtain current addresses and membership lists for local mailings. They believed, rightly, that a good computer system should alleviate the problems. Some on the ad hoc committee thought that an individual could be hired to create a system that would meet the AIA's unusual needs (the Institute has complex reporting requirements for *Archaeology* magazine subscribers, members or not). Others preferred a corporate vendor. In the end, a corporate vendor was hired to create a database system for membership, a contract was signed, and software was developed. Over the course of time, however, the software never performed as required, and the effort was abandoned when the vendor filed for protection under bankruptcy statutes. The committee realized that the office staff had to know what they wanted and why; an outside committee could not be the driving force for introducing automation. Once the office staff had committed to the process, the staff could decide how the system should work and evaluate its competence better than a board-level committee. Consequently, the committee removed itself from office automation work but remained as a potential resource for that work. Its focus, however, switched to matters involving archaeological computing at that time, the same time that the committee became a standing committee.

In 1997, a new membership database system was found and evaluated by office staff and others (not including members of the committee). The new program was expected to perform the required functions without additional, specialized software. The Institute began using the new system in 1998, but it proved to be inadequate. Unfortunately, the Institute did not maintain a parallel system until the new system could be tested and demonstrated to be functioning correctly. As a result, new memberships and renewals were lost, and many people were seriously inconvenienced. Local societies complained loudly to the central office that membership records were incorrect, and those complaints were all too accurate. Financial record-keeping was also compromised. The ultimate effect on the AIA cannot be assessed at this time, but it was a serious blow to membership, and it required countless hours of work to monitor and attempt to correct the situation.

Other institutions certainly have had problems with membership databases, and the combination of membership and magazine subscriptions for members into a single system added some unique requirements. Nonetheless, the failure to anticipate the kinds of problems that could arise and to guard against them, specifically by running old and new membership systems in parallel until the new one had been thoroughly tested, might have been understandable in 1985 but not in 1998.

After a lengthy examination of the needs of the Institute and the possibilities offered by various vendors, another fulfillment contractor and membership database was selected in 2000. An outside consultant was hired to assist in the process. This system will be maintained by an outside contractor at the outset but will eventually be operated in the AIA offices by AIA staff so that the

Institute will not again be so dependent on an outside contractor for its membership information. The system was brought up slowly, and every effort was made to be sure that it was functioning correctly before the prior system was discarded. As of this writing, the new system seems to be working properly.

Archaeological Computing

The Committee on Computer Applications and Electronic Data had greater success in facilitating the use of computer technology by encouraging discussion and the exchange of information. The committee also assisted with the creation of a project for long-term curation of digital information that may ultimately prove very important for the discipline. There were four specific initiatives of note. In addition, the committee helped to change the AIA Code of Professional Standards.

The AIA List

Internet discussion lists[2] were relatively new when the AIA List was begun in February of 1992; most were rather broad in subject matter. In addition most were unmoderated, allowing free-flowing conversation but also allowing a very high ratio of chaff to wheat. Members of the committee, having experience with such lists, decided very emphatically that the AIA List would be a moderated list in order to lower the ratio of chaff to wheat transmitted. The list remains a moderated one, with all messages passing through the list moderator (the author) or his assistant for review. In practice, very few messages intended for the list are turned away, but the messages that come to the list in error, such as requests for help unsubscribing, personal messages inadvertently sent to the list, and the like, are usually caught and dealt with by the moderator or his assistant.[3]

During the first years of the list operation, the moderator operated the list as a volunteer. Beginning in 1996, however, the AIA reimbursed the Center for the Study of Architecture for the costs of moderating the list. Bryn Mawr College has provided the computing services from the inception of the list, with only one period of disruption when the College computing system had a serious problem.

The list was always sent as digests of messages; that is, messages were grouped together rather than being sent one at a time, and very soon after the list was begun the moderator developed a system to group messages by topic. The topic was included in the message subject line so that readers could eliminate a message on the basis of the header and without bothering to open it. That practice has continued to the present, with slight improvements. To the best of the author's knowledge, this procedure is a unique way to group and categorize material in a discussion list.

Since the list has been moderated, the flow of messages is not so fast as in unmoderated lists. As a result, there has been less free-flowing conversation on the AIA list but more announcements and notices of interest. In 1997 there were nearly 600 digests sent out over the course of the year, representing approximately 1,200 to 1,500 individual messages. In 1998 there were about 700 digests sent, and in 1999 about 600 were sent. That decline in 1999 may represent a decline in the number of messages, but a cursory examination of the records suggests that the decline is the result of more messages sent in larger digests.

Some members have objected to the absence of more spontaneous conversations, but others seem to appreciate the fact that the list contains news items and none of the off-topic streams of messages often found elsewhere. One member went so far as to send a message to the moderator: "Through this list, I have been able to expand and develop my professional contacts, participate in conferences that I would never have known about otherwise, and to add 4 significant publications to my corpus of work since 1995—all of which made a very real impact on my promotion from associate to full professor last year. And just this past week, I have been accepted to participate in a conference with potential for publication, again as a result of your list. I am indeed grateful and indebted to you!"[4]

Membership reached 200 within less than a year and, at this writing, is about 1,100 (compared to about 9,200 members of the AIA and about 200,000 subscribers to *Archaeology* magazine). Membership ebbs and flows with the seasons, growing over 1,100 during the academic year and shrinking below that number during the summer. Subscribers are not restricted to professional archaeologists or to members of the AIA, and they come from all over the world. The list is a service to the professional community, as intended, and it has not been used explicitly to encourage membership.

The Archaeological Data Archive Project

At the 1992 meeting of the committee the members returned to one of the questions that had been posed for the committee's first meeting: should the

AIA endeavor to store computer data from excavations. By and large, the committee members thought that a centralized archive for computerized archaeological data was a good idea, and they thought that archiving digital data should be done by the AIA. The members felt that having large quantities of data in one place could provide enormous benefits to the archaeological community. Nonetheless, the members of the committee did not think the AIA would support such an idea financially. The author, who was then chairman of the committee, volunteered to take on the task through the Center for the Study of Architecture (CSA), and a series of proposals was circulated among the members during the spring of 1993. During the course of the debate about those proposals, the emphasis shifted somewhat so that archival storage and care became the core, with access to large quantities of data moving into the background.

The proposals culminated in the creation of the Archaeological Data Archive Project (ADAP) as a project of CSA. The ADAP was endorsed by the AIA at the May 1993 meeting of the Executive Committee. The ADAP was endorsed by the American Anthropological Association (AAA) in 1995; the Society for American Archaeology (SAA) has supported the project by publishing information about it in the SAA *Bulletin*, but the SAA does not endorse non-SAA projects. No other professional archaeological society has initiated such a project; the ADAP remains the only U.S. digital archaeological archive that is not based at a university.

After the project had begun, discussions were held about the possibility of turning the ADAP over to the AIA, but an ad hoc committee of the AIA, formed to consider the possibility, rejected taking on the responsibility for the archive. Thus, the Archaeological Data Archive Project remains a CSA project, unrelated to the AIA.[5]

The AIA Web Site

There was agitation for an AIA Web site in 1995, but no funding was available until 1996, after hard debate in the Finance Committee. An outside contractor was hired to do some of the work, and the author assisted and finished the production when costs rose and the vendor was unable to finish on time. By the time the AIA Web site had been launched, the Society for American Archaeology site had been up for some time, but most other archaeological organizations were just beginning to have a presence on the Web.

The AIA Web site was hosted on the CSA server through Bryn Mawr

College from 1996 until the spring of 1998. Its initial address was so complex that many objected (http://csaws.brynmawr.edu:443/aia.html); that address was simplified to csa.brynmawr.edu/aia.html. The address changed again in 1998, to www.archaeological.org, when the site moved to a commercial server, and this new URL was registered by the AIA so that there need be no more changes in the future.

Maintenance of the Web site initially had been done by the author but shifted to the AIA office, in particular Wendy O'Brien, then Assistant Director of Administration. When the site moved to the commercial service provider in 1998, all site maintenance became the responsibility of the Boston office of the Institute.

In the spring of 1999 the central office began a complete reworking of the site, but the Committee on Computer Applications and Electronic Data was not consulted or even made aware of the project. The author had been reappointed chairman (having been succeeded as chairman first by Susan Lukesh, Associate Provost at Hofstra University, and then by Timothy Gregory, Ohio State University) and discovered the new work just before taking office; Timothy Gregory was also unaware of the work. Correspondence between the central office and the committee chairman ensued, and although the Executive Director agreed that the committee should oversee the Web site project, work on the Web site did not stop, and the committee remained outside the process. A new, reworked site was fully operating in the fall of 1999, without consultation with the committee, despite the correspondence earlier in the year. As a consequence, the chairman resigned. This episode reflects the tension that sometimes exists between AIA committees and the Institute's office staff when lines of communication and authority are not clear. (A similar disconnect between the committee and the central office occurred when the Executive Director did not inform the computer committee about proposed work on a Web version of the *Archaeological Fieldwork Opportunities Bulletin*.)

The Web site provides membership services as well as a variety of other services to scholars and interested amateurs. Among other things, there are individual pages concerning membership categories and costs, publications, local societies, the Annual Meeting, and fellowships. In order to test for reactions to electronic publication issues, experiments in presentation of images in color, especially of pottery and site photographs, were undertaken on the AIA Web site; scholars were asked to comment. Another innovation was the posting of a list of volunteers willing to speak to school groups, with groupings by location and area(s) of expertise.

Many local societies have their own Web pages, and those can be reached through the AIA site; of course, the AIA Web site is generally accessible from local society sites as well.

Another addition to the site was a page with listings of Web sites concerning archaeology and capsule reviews of those sites. The sites are also grouped according to whether they are primarily sites with lists of other Web resources or sites with material about specific archaeological projects or issues. From 1998 to the middle of 1999 AIA Trustee Nancy Bernard was responsible for creating and maintaining that particular Web page, but she has not been able to continue the work, and maintenance of the page has stopped.

Some statistics were created for the period from 9 March 1998 through 16 April 1998 (in anticipation of an AIA Board of Trustees meeting). During that period, one or another page on the AIA site was accessed about 230 times each day. Of special interest is the fact that the page listing archaeological Web sites was accessed about 14 times per day at the beginning of the period and nearly 60 times per day by the end of the period. The dramatic increase followed the appearance of a *New York Times* article mentioning that particular AIA Web page; the increased usage is a testimony to the power of the press even in electronic matters.

During the month of May 1999, the site was accessed more than 300 times per day. No particular page on the site seemed to account for an unusual share of the access requests. (The May 1999 figures were provided to the committee to help its members consider the future of the Web site.) The increase in usage from 1998 to 1999 may be ascribed to the passage of time. More people were using the Web for information in 1999, and more people had learned about the AIA site. Continued growth in usage should be expected. (Regular statistics for Web usage were not generated during that period; so more direct comparisons of specific months in succeeding years cannot be made.)

Three other Web sites have also been mounted by the Institute. *Archaeology* magazine opened its site in 1996 about the time that the Institute's site was mounted, and an *AJA* site began late in 1995. The magazine site includes information on the magazine itself, the main focus of the site, but it also includes breaking archaeological news and tries to attract people to the field of archaeology, not just to the magazine. It has been very well received and is an impressive way to reach out to a larger public. Most of the original work on the *Archaeology* magazine Web site was done by Andrew Slayman, a staff writer. Staff member Amélie Walker is now in charge of the site; the URL is www.archaeology.org/. *Archaeology* magazine also operated a Web site for its children's magazine, *Archaeology's Dig,* until that magazine was sold in 2001.

The first *AJA* site included recent tables of contents, lists of books received, the *AJA*'s Style Guidelines for Book Reviews, a statement on editorial policy, Notes for Contributors, and standard abbreviations. The site was created by Susan Alcock and John Cherry, who were then the Book Review Editors of the *AJA*. The current *AJA* site was completely redesigned after the new editor-in-chief of the *AJA*, R. Bruce Hitchner, (University of Dayton) came into office. It was launched in 2000. The site is now much more complex and includes tables of contents for current issues, past issues (back to 1991 at the time of this writing), and the issue scheduled for release next. In addition, there are full-text versions of current articles available for viewing or for purchase in the format known as PDF. There are also, for some articles, supplements to the published work available only at the Web site. Subscriptions to an electronic version of the journal (again, in PDF format) can even be purchased via the *AJA* site.

It is noteworthy that the desired and desirable goal of putting back issues of the *AJA* online has been stymied by a recent court decision in the case of *The New York Times* v. Tasini. This decision presents unfortunate roadblocks to the electronic publication of old compilations, such as journals, and its ramifications are not yet clear.

It is interesting to note that the Web sites for the Institute (www.archaeological.org), the magazine (www.archaeology.org), and the journal (www.ajaonline.org) use unrelated URLs and do not consistently refer to one another. Whereas one would expect the AIA home page to be the starting point for all AIA Web materials, the other two sites operate independently.

The AIA's home page contains no link to either the *Archaeology* magazine home page or the *AJA* home page. The *Archaeology* magazine home page has two links to the AIA home page, but the links are less obvious than other links on the page (a result of specific choices in the display of the page). There is a similar link to the *AJA* Web site. The *AJA* home page has links to both the AIA home page and the *Archaeology* magazine home page, but the links are so far below the real content of the page that a typical reader might never see them. These independently-operated Web sites reflect the AIA's difficulty in running such disparate (and physically separate) operations as though all are part of a single enterprise. They are of course, but one might not know it from the Web sites.

Technology Showcase and Workshops at the Annual Meeting
Workshops and meetings concerning issues in computing occurred at the AIA/APA Annual Meetings in the late 1980s and early 1990s. The author held workshops in 1987, 1989, and each year thereafter until 1998, bringing his own equipment to demonstrate computer programs. Meetings concerning word processing and databases were held under the auspices of the APA. Then in 1994, through a fortunate confluence of needs of the AIA and the APA, it was possible to set up a computer booth in the exhibition area at the Annual Meeting. That first group of workstations was small and relatively unimpressive, but it was clear from the beginning that the members of the organizations appreciated the presence of the computers (some simply to keep up with email while away from home and office), and the desire for more formal programs was born.

In 1995 and thereafter formal computer demonstration areas were set aside in the exhibit area and termed the "Technology Showcase." Macintosh and Windows machines, with display systems for larger audiences, were set up and networked. The committee planned these demonstrations with James O'Donnell and Maria C. Pantelia of the APA and with the conference manager, Shelley Griffin, to determine where the computers would be placed and what programs would be included. The enthusiastic cooperation of the APA was crucial, and APA member Linda Wright and her colleague Bill Mar provided the skill and time to set up the systems. Their work was shown to be crucial when they could not attend the 1997 meeting, and the systems were much less robust. The 1998 Technology Showcase functioned well, and there were several demonstrations. At the same time, however, more speakers wanted computers available for sessions, and the number of computers available in the Technology Showcase seemed unnecessary, especially since they were so often used for email. It was decided that the 1999 meetings should include a regular session room with a computer and projector. This is, in fact, what the committee had been intending to encourage—the integration of computing into the regular sessions.

Individual workshops were held in the demonstration area. In addition, the committee organized workshops for scholars using computer technology in new and interesting ways. Those scholars were able to demonstrate their work and to discuss the processes with the audience.

AIA Code of Professional Standards

In addition to the undertakings listed above, the Committee on Computer Applications and Electronic Data urged a change in the AIA Code of Professional Standards. That change added an explicit reference to the ethical responsibilities for maintaining digital data. The Code of Professional Standards was altered in 1997 so that section I, 4 now reads, "Archaeologists should anticipate and provide for adequate and accessible long-term storage and curatorial facilities for all archaeological materials, records, and archives, including machine-readable data which require specialized archival care and maintenance."

The simple change in the wording of the code marks a very serious issue—the issue that guided the committee to assist in the founding of the Archaeological Data Archive Project. Computer data are inherently fragile. Their tendency to decay can be rather easily counteracted, but the problem of obsolescence resulting from changes in the underlying hardware and software presents a grave danger to all computer users. The problem has still not been widely recognized, but without effective planning there can be significant losses of digital materials.

Virtual Pompeii

The project known as *Virtual Pompeii*, one of the largest early AIA computing projects, was conducted without the involvement of the Committee on Computer Applications and Electronic Data. It was a project that was brought to the board of the Institute by the Development Committee. The director of the project was a member of the staff of the Studio for Creative Inquiry at Carnegie Mellon University who had experience with virtual reality systems and had previously worked on a project involving an Egyptian structure. He persuaded the AIA to support the project financially, with the expectation that the results could be used to promote archaeology and that costs could be recouped by renting the system to museums. A profit was anticipated in the long run.

The intent was to create a virtual reality experience based on a small part of Pompeii (the Triangular Forum and the adjacent theater) at the time of the eruption of Vesuvius in A.D. 79. A portion of the project was available for demonstration at the computer trade show called Siggraph (Special Interest Group for Graphics) in August of 1995. A similar, but still incomplete, demonstration was then displayed at the M.H. de Young Memorial Museum in San Francisco at the end of 1995. Various attempts to complete the project ensued, but unfortunately the presentation was never finished or turned over to the Institute in usable form. As a result the Institute was obliged to seek redress according to the terms of the original contract.

The Committee's Agenda for the Future

A portion of the discussion that culminated in the creation of the Archaeological Data Archive Project concerned the issue of standards in archaeological data recording. Over the years, some members of the committee have argued for strong standards, others for more general ones, still others for documentation standards rather than data recording standards. The committee is now involved in debates about standards for digital data recording. This will be important work in the next few years.

The committee has also begun, in conjunction with CSA, a project to record general information about archaeological projects in the Mediterranean basin. That information is now available on the Web (http://csanet.org/archproj), and it will permit scholars and interested non-professionals to find basic information about excavations, surveys, rescue operations, and so on.

Electronic Publication

One of the issues that came up in the first meeting of the Committee on Computer Applications and Electronic Data was electronic publication, and that issue was the topic for a well-attended, committee-sponsored panel discussion at the 1998 Annual Meeting. Since that time, many changes have occurred, and the AIA has made important moves toward electronic publication. All manuscripts are treated as electronic documents and formatted so that they can be printed in volume, printed one at a time, put into an electronic format appropriate for use on the Web, or formatted for sale as PDF files. As a result, all documents now passing through the AIA's Publications Department are, to the extent possible, ready for a future that has yet to be defined. Electronic publications other than the *AJA* have not yet been attempted, but the AIA is prepared.

In the meantime, various aspects of electronic publication have advanced, but problems remain. The PDF format has become widely accepted as a good way to publish electronically, though it has its drawbacks, and online sales of PDF documents have shown that it is possible to sell and deliver documents over the Web. In general, however, people do not like to read long documents on computer screens, and authors are reluctant to have manuscripts published only electronically (often because tenure and advancement may depend on print publications).[6] Therefore, the AIA, like most scholarly organizations, must await future developments while trying to be ready for whatever those developments are.

The Future of Computing at the AIA

As we look to the future of computers and the AIA, some things seem rather obvious. For instance, the AIA Web site will continue to grow, and the *Archaeology* magazine site will also continue to evolve. The current editor-in-chief of the *AJA* has already made significant changes to the AJA Web site, and more are expected. The Internet discussion list will probably last for some time, but the nature of the moderated list may make the AIA List change in ways not yet clear. The use of computers to deal with membership will also continue to evolve. It is ironic that the most basic business function of computers for the Institute—maintaining a membership list—has been the most difficult to solve.

AIA activities regarding the ways archaeologists use computer technology in their work are less clear.[7] The Institute has not chosen to participate in data archiving, but it is beginning to work on issues of data standards, issues that will be crucial for the discipline and for effective access to digital data. Electronic publication may have great potential to change the way scholars work, but the Institute, like other, similar organizations, has yet to define its role in this area. Nonetheless, the Institute is well positioned to move into electronic publication and will doubtless do so in the near future, bringing major changes to the field. The Institute seems prepared to take a leadership position in this area, but there will need to be closer cooperation between the AIA committee volunteers, members, and AIA staff if the promise is to become reality.

REFERENCES

Eiteljorg, H., II. 1999. "Requiring Students to Use Computers—The Time Has Come." *CSA Newsletter* 12 (2) Fall. (http://www.csanet.org/newsletter/fall99/nlf9908.html).

Lock, G., and K. Brown. 2000. "Is there such a thing as 'Computer Archaeology'?" In *On the Theory and Practice of Archaeological Computing*, edited by A. Taschen and P. Daly, 133–54. Oxford University Committee for Archaeology, Monograph 51. Oxford.

NOTES

[1] E.g., several surveys provide data on this situation: Eiteljorg 1999; Lock and Brown 2000.

[2] In moderated lists, messages are first checked and then distributed. In unmoderated lists, all messages are automatically redistributed, whether they are relevant to the business of the list or not.

[3] Commercial messages are also rejected, and the initial announcement of the list included a statement that the moderator would also intercept rude, intemperate, or profane messages. When that policy was announced, there was considerable displeasure, as some saw the policy as an attempt to censor messages to the list. The moderator therefore agreed that a sender who insisted that the offensive portions of his/her message were understood and intentional would be permitted to post the message. Fortunately, it has not been necessary to make such decisions, since rude, intemperate, or profane messages have not been received.

[4] Quoted with permission from an unsolicited email message sent to the author by Professor Linda Ellis on 27 April 1998.

[5] The ultimate success of the ADAP remains in doubt at the time of this writing. Operating in an institution without the standing of a professional organization such as the AIA, the archive has struggled to gain credibility. In addition, the quantity of digital data ready for deposit remains small; so the utility of an archive is limited and will remain limited until the archive reaches a critical mass. The one clear success as an archival venture of this sort – the Archaeology Data Service in England – enjoys the advantages of a larger governmental archiving initiative (the Arts and Humanities Data Service), governmental requirements for data archiving, and significant government funding.

[6] When the author of one AIA monograph was offered the opportunity of publishing his monograph's data tables electronically, which would have saved some costs of publication and made the finished product both less expensive and more useful, the author rejected the notion. He was willing to have the data tables published both in print and electronic forms but not in electronic form only.

[7] As in so many areas, the AIA is sorely dependent upon volunteers to define its role in computing. The committee has been active and has accomplished a good many things, but growth is always limited by the availability of volunteer time. Thus, the AIA's continuing role in this area is yet to be decided, but it will likely be determined by those who are willing to invest their time and efforts in the process.

— APPENDIX I —

Past Presidents of the Archaeological Institute of America and Editors-in-Chief of the *American Journal of Archaeology* (1879–2002)

Susan Heuck Allen and Kim M. Hebert*

Past Presidents of the Archaeological Institute of America

Charles Eliot Norton	1879–1889
Seth Low	1890–1896
John Williams White	1897–1902
Thomas Day Seymour	1903–1907
Francis Willey Kelsey	1908–1912
Harry Langford Wilson	1913
F.W. Shipley	1913–1917
James Childester Egbert	1918–1921
Ralph Van Deman Magoffin	1922–1930
Louis Eleazar Lord	1931–1936
William Bell Dinsmoor	1937–1945
Sterling Dow	1946–1948
Hugh Hencken	1949–1951
Kenneth J. Conant	1952
Henry T. Rowell	1953–1956
George E. Mylonas	1957–1960
Jotham Johnson	1961–1964

Margaret Thompson	1965–1968
Rodney S. Young	1969–1972
James B. Pritchard	1973–1974
Frederick R. Matson	1975–1976
Robert H. Dyson, Jr.	1977–1980
Machteld J. Mellink	1981–1984
James R. Wiseman	1985–1988
Martha Sharp Joukowsky	1989–1992
James Russell	1993–1994
Stephen L. Dyson	1995–1998
Nancy C. Wilkie	1999–present

Editors-in-Chief of the *American Journal of Archaeology*

Arthur L. Frothingham, Jr.	1885–1896
John Henry Wright	1897–1906
Harold North Fowler	1907–1916
James N. Paton	1917–1919
William Nickerson Bates	1920–1923
George W. Elderkin	1924–1930
Mary Hamilton Swindler	1931–1945
John Franklin Daniel	1946–1948
C. Bradford Welles	1949
Glanville Downey	1949–1951
Ashton Sanborn	1952–1953
Richard Stillwell	1954–1973
Jerome J. Pollitt	1974–1977
Brunilde Ridgway	1978–1985
Fred S. Kleiner	1985–1998
John Bennet	January–June, 1998
R. Bruce Hitchner	July, 1998–present

*Much of this material was assembled using Phoebe Sheftel's 1979 article, "The Archaeological Institute of America 1879–1979: A Centennial Review" *AJA* 83:3–17.

— APPENDIX 2 —

Award and Fellowship Winners of the Archaeological Institute of America (1965–2002)

Susan Heuck Allen and Kim M. Hebert

Awards and Prizes of the Archaeological Institute of America

Gold Medal Award for Distinguished Archaeological Achievement

Carl W. Blegen	1965
Hetty Goldman	1966
William B. Dinsmoor, Jr.	1967
Rhys Carpenter	1968
Oscar Theodore Broneer	1969
George E. Mylonas	1970
Robert John Braidwood	1971
Homer A. Thompson	1972
Gordon R. Willey	1973
Margarete Bieber	1974
Eugene Vanderpool	1975
Edith Porada	1976
Lucy Shoe Meritt	1977
George M.A. Hanfmann	1978
Dows Dunham	1979
John Langdon Caskey	1980

William Andrew McDonald	1981
Peter H. Von Blanckenhagen	1982
James Bennet Pritchard	1983
Margaret Thompson	1984
Saul S. Weinberg	1985
George R. Bass	1986
Dorothy Burr Thompson	1987
John Desmond Clark	1988
Brunilde Sismondo Ridgway	1988
Virginia R. Grace	1989
John W. Hayes	1990
Machteld J. Mellink	1991
Evelyn Byrd Harrison	1992
Charles Kaufman Williams, II	1993
Emeline Richardson	1994
R. Ross Holloway	1995
Wilhelmina F. Jashemski	1996
Clemency Chase Coggins	1997
Anna Marguerite McCann	1998
Patty Jo Watson	1999
Emmett L. Bennett, Jr.	2001
Robert McCormick Adams	2002
Philip Betancourt	2003

Centennial Award

Willard Frank Libby	27 December 1979

Pomerance Award for Scientific Contributions in Archaeology

Marie Farnsworth	1980
Frederick R. Matson	1981
Cyril Stanley Smith	1982
J. Lawrence Angel	1983
Herbert E. Wright, Jr	1984
Charles A. Reed	1985
Elizabeth K. Ralph	1986
George L. Cowgill	1987
George (Rip) Rapp, Jr.	1988

Harold T. Edgerton	1989
Robert H. Brill	1990
Karl W. Butzer	1991
(No award given)	1992
Hans E. Suess	1993
Michael G.L. Baillie	1993
Bernd Becker	1993
Bernd Kromer	1993
Gordon W. Pearson	1993
Jon R. Pilcher	1993
Minze Stuiver	1993
Robert Maddin	1994
James Muhly	1994
Tamara Stech	1994
Norman Herz	1995
W. David Kingery	1996
Martin J. Aitken	1997
Nikolaas J. van der Merwe	1998
Edward V. Sayre	1999
Curt W. Beck	2001
Garman Harbottle	2002

James R. Wiseman Book Award

1989 Anna Marguerite McCann, *The Roman Port and Fishery of Cosa: A Center of Ancient Trade.*

1990 Oscar White Muscarella, *Bronze and Iron: Ancient Near Eastern Artifacts in the Metropolitan Museum of Art.*

1991 Bruce Graham Trigger, *A History of Archaeological Thought*; Frances Dodds van Keuren, *The Frieze from the Hera I Temple at Foca del Sele.*

1992 Robert Chapman, *Emerging Complexity: The Later Prehistory of South-East Spain, Iberia, and the West Mediterranean.*

1993 Sarah P. Morris, *Daidalos and the Origins of Greek Art*; John Malcolm Russell, *Sennacherib's Palace without Rival at Nineveh.*

1994 Patricia Anawalt and Frances Berdan, *Codex Mendoza.*

1995 Andrew Wallace-Hadrill, *Houses and Society in Pompeii and Herculaneum.*

1996 P.R.S. Moorey, *Ancient Mesopotamian Materials and Industries: The Archaeological Evidence.*
1997 Carol C. Mattusch, *Classical Bronzes: The Art and Craft of Greek and Roman Statuary.*
1998 Janet DeLaine, *The Baths of Caracalla: A Study in the Design, Construction, and Economics of Large-Scale Building Projects in Imperial Rome.*
1999 Joseph Coleman Carter, *The Chora of Metaponto: The Necropoleis.*
2001 Graeme Barker, David Gilbertson, Barri Jones, and David Mattingly, *Farming the Desert: The UNESCO Libyan Valley Archaeological Survey.* Vol. 1, *Synthesis.*
2002 Lynn E. Roller, *In Search of God the Mother: The Cult of Anatolian Cybele.*

*Martha and Artemis Joukowsky Distinguished Service Award**

1989 Norma Kershaw, James Ottaway, Jr., and Leon Pomerance (awarded posthumously)
1990 Lloyd E. Cotsen
1991 Charles S. LaFollette
1992 Judith Feinberg Brilliant
1994 Anna Benjamin
1996 Leonard V. Quigley
1997 Raymond L. Den Adel
1999 James R. Wiseman
2001 Ira Haupt, II
2002 Frank Wezniak

*The name was changed from the Distinguished Service Award to the Martha and Artemis Joukowsky Distinguished Service Award at the December 1997 Annual Meeting.

Kershaw Outstanding Local Society Prize

1996 San Diego Society
1997 Los Angeles Society
1998 Finger Lakes and Niagara Peninsula Societies
1999 Long Island Society
2001 Winnipeg Society
2002 Cleveland Society

Undergraduate Teaching Award
    1996   Frederick A. Cooper
    1997   Curtis N. Runnels
    1998   Susan E. Alcock
    1999   Patrick A. Thomas
    2001   Kevin Glowacki
    2002   P. Nick Kardulias

Conservation and Heritage Management Award
    1998   Department of Conservation and Materials Science, Institute of Archaeology, University of London
    1999   Lawrence J. Majewski
    2001   Museum of London
    2002   Wet Organic Archaeological Materials Working Group

Outstanding Public Service Award
    1998   Walter V. Robinson, Boston Globe
    2002   Nancy Bookidis and Charles K. Williams, II

Honorary Fellow for Life
    Charles S. La Follette
    Abraham J. Multer
    Joseph Veach Noble
    H. Alexander Smith
    Malcolm Wiener
    Gladys Davidson Weinberg

Fellowships of the Archaeological Institute of America

Olivia James Traveling Fellowship
    1962   William B. Dinsmoor, Jr., American School of Classical Studies at Athens (ASCSA)
    1963   Charles R. Beye, Stanford University
    1964   Elizabeth Milburn and Irene Winter
    1965   Pierre Mackay

1966 Irwin Merker
1967 Donald R. Laing, Jr., Western Reserve University
1968 Thomas Jacobson
1969 David Gordon Mitten
1970 Sharon Gobbs and Eugene Borza
1971 Jeffrey Klein and Steven Diamant
1972 Stella Grobel Miller, ASCSA, Richard Stites Mason, ASCSA, and John Oleson, American Academy in Rome
1973 Dean L. Moe, Harvard University, and Nancy J. Skon, University of Pennsylvania
1974 Albert Leonard, Jr., University of Chicago, Patricia Getz Preziosi, Yale University, and Jeremy Rutter, University of Pennsylvania
1975 Eric R. Hostetter, Harvard University
1976 Michael Max Eisman, Temple University, and Trudy S. Kawami, Columbia University
1977 Ira S. Mark, New York University, Institute of Fine Arts, and Patricia M. Bikai, University of Pennsylvania
1978 Susan I. Rotroff, Mount Allison University and Irene F. Bald, ASCSA
1979 Robert Barry Koehl, University of Pennsylvania and Margaret Miles, Princeton University
1980 Donald R. Keller, Sarah P. Morris, and Helayna I. Thickpenny (Kathleen S. Wright declined)
1981 Barbara Jeanne Hayden, University of Pennsylvania, David Gilman Romano, University of Pennsylvania, and Lynn Patricia Stowell, University of Michigan, (Nancy Leinwand, Bryn Mawr College, declined)
1982 Joan Aruz, New York University, Institute of Fine Arts, and Paola Visona, University of Michigan
1983 William M. Murray, University of South Florida, and Elizabeth Williams-Forte, University of California, Berkeley
1984 Polymnia Muhly and Leslie Ike
1985 Elizabeth Simpson and Michael Hoff
1986 Laura Gadberry, New York University, Institute of

Fine Arts, (Christopher C. Parslow, Duke University, declined)
1987 Eric Cline, University of Pennsylvania
1988 Elizabeth P. McGowan, New York University, Institute of Fine Arts, and Nicolle E. Hirschfeld, Texas A&M University
1989 Yasemin Arnold, Cornell University
1990 Jean Alison Adams, Princeton University
1991 Donald Charles Haggis, University of Minnesota
1992 Margaret Susan Mook, University of Missouri
1993 Elizabeth Anne Meyer, Yale University
1994 Ann L. Foster, University of Pennsylvania
1995 Elizabeth Key Fowden, Princeton University
1996 David Lawrence Conlin, Brown University
1997 John Robert Leonard, State University of New York at Buffalo
1998 Catherine M. Keesling, Georgetown University
1999 Heather E. Grossman, University of Pennsylvania
2000 Christopher H. Roosevelt, Cornell University

Harriet and Leon Pomerance Fellowship Recipients
1973 Robert Bridges, Bryn Mawr College
1974 Bax Richard Barton, University of Edinburgh. Supplement to: James D. Muhly, University of Pennsylvania and Karen J. Polinger, Yale University
1975 Livingston Vance Watrous, University of Pennsylvania. Supplement to: Robert R. Stieglitz, Brandeis University
1976 Jeffrey Scott Soles, Cambridge, Mass. Supplement to: Kenneth C. Gutwein, New York University
1977 Halford W. Haskell, University of North Carolina
1978 Faith C.D. Hentschel, Yale University
1979 Thomas G. Palaima, ASCSA
1980 David S. Reese, St. John's College
1981 Emily B. Miller, California State University at Fullerton
1982 Martha V. Demas, University of Cincinnati
1983 Barbara B. Kling, University of Pennsylvania

1984 Miriam E. Caskey, University of Cincinnati
1985 Judith Weinstein Balthazar, University of Pennsylvania
1986 Lucinda McCallum, University of Pennsylvania
1987 Priscilla Keswami, University of Michigan
1988 Pamela Russell, University of Pennsylvania
1989 Susan Heuck Allen, Brown University
1990 Leslie Preston Day, Wabash College
1991 Cheryl Ward Haldane, Texas A&M University
1992 Ruth Ellen Palmer, Rutgers University
1993 Maureen Anne Basedow, University of Tübingen
1994 Christine Shriner, Indiana University
1995 Nicolle Elise Hirschfeld, University of Texas at Austin
1996 Kellee A. Bernard, University of Pennsylvania
1997 Robert Angus K. Smith, Bryn Mawr College
1998 Francis A. De Mita, Jr., University of Michigan
1999 Amy Eloise Raymond, University of Toronto
2000 Jan Arvanitakis, University of Toronto

Anna C. and Oliver C. Colburn Fellowship Recipients
1990 Kim S. Shelton, University of Pennsylvania
1991 Aileen Ajootian, McMaster University
1992 Thomas Francis Tartaron, Boston University
1993 Lisa Virginia Benson, University of Missouri, Columbia
1994 Patricia A. Butz, University of Southern California
1996 Sarah A. Taft, Rutgers University
1998 Sarah T. Brooks, New York University, Institute of Fine Arts
2000 Heather F. Sharpe, University of Phoenix

Helen M. Woodruff Fellowship Recipients
1991 Charles Brian Rose, University of Cincinnati
1993 Katherine E. Welch, New York University, Institute of Fine Arts
1994 Leah Johnson, University of California, Berkeley

1995 Christopher Hallett, University of Washington, Seattle
1996 Francesca Santoro L'hoir, Macalester College
1997 Sheila Dillon, Independent Scholar
1998 Margaret Laird, Princeton University
1999 Anne Marie Yasin, University of Chicago
2000 John Curtis Franklin

Kenan T. Erim Award Recipients
1993 Katherine Welch, New York University, Institute of Fine Arts
1994 Sheila Dillon, New York University, Institute of Fine Arts
1995 Julie Van Voorhis, New York University, Institute of Fine Arts
1996 Andrew King-Yin Leung, University of Pennsylvania
1997 Lisa Renee Brody, New York University, Institute of Fine Arts
1998 Laura Herbert, New York University, Institute of Fine Arts
1999 Bahadir Yildirim, New York University, Institute of Fine Arts
2000 Michelle L. Berenfeld, New York University, Institute of Fine Arts

Woodruff Traveling Fellowship
1997 Margaret Louise Woodhull, University of Texas, Austin
1998 Melanie Grunow, University of Michigan
1999 Kimberly Bowes, Princeton University
2000 Kathryn J. McDonnell, University of North Carolina
2001 Thomas J. Morton, University of Pennsylvania

Archaeology of Portugal Fellowship
1999 Robert R. Stielitz, Rutgers University
2000 Michael MacKinnon, Boston University

— APPENDIX 3 —

Part 1. Current Local Societies of the Archaeological Institute of America in Order of Their Charters of Foundation

Susan Heuck Allen and Kim M. Hebert

1879	Boston, MA
1884	Baltimore, MD
	New York, NY
1889	Chicago, IL
	Detroit, MI
	Madison (formerly Wisconsin), WI
	Philadelphia, PA (formerly Pennsylvania)
1895	Cleveland, OH
1902	Washington, D.C.
1903	Pittsburgh, PA
1904	Denver, CO (formerly Colorado)
1904	Los Angeles County, CA
1905	Cincinnati, OH
1906	Rochester, NY
	St. Louis, MO
	San Francisco, CA
	Walla Walla, WA
	Kansas (formerly Kansas City) KS

1908	Narragansett (formerly Rhode Island and later Providence)
	Toronto, Canada*
1909	Western New York (Buffalo)
1910	Minnesota (formerly Minneapolis/St. Paul)
1911	Hartford, CT
1912	Richmond, VA
1916	Santa Fe, NM
1920	Springfield, OH
1923	Oberlin-Wooster, OH
1929	Oxford, OH
1930	Lynchburg, VA
1937	New Haven, CT
	Princeton, NJ (formerly New Jersey)
1947	Atlanta, GA
1948	Iowa City (formerly Iowa), IA
	Western Massachusetts
	Mississippi-Memphis (formerly Mississippi)
	North Carolina (Chapel Hill)
	Spokane, WA
1950	Greensboro, NC
1952	Toledo, OH
1953	Central Illinois (Urbana)
	Central Missouri (Columbia)
	Kentucky (Lexington/Louisville)
1954	Worcester, MA
1956	Central Indiana (Indianapolis/Bloomington)
	Seattle, WA
	Tallahassee, FL
1958	Ann Arbor, MI
	Columbus, OH
1961	San Diego, CA
	Stanford, CA
1962	Central Texas (formerly Austin)
1963	Central Michigan (East Lansing)
	Santa Barbara, CA
1964	Eugene, OR
	New Orleans, LA

Appendix 3

1965	Appleton, WI
	Charlottesville, VA
	Dallas-Ft. Worth, TX (formerly Dallas)
	Nashville, TN
	Staten Island, NY
1966	Albany, NY
	Athens, GA
	Boulder, CO
	Central Pennsylvania (University Park)
	Vancouver, Canada*
1967	Houston, TX
	Milwaukee, WI
	Montreal, Canada*
1968	Long Island, NY (formerly North Shore)
	Lubbock, TX
	Niagara Peninsula, Canada*
	Rockford, IL
1969	Northern New Jersey (Madison)
1970	Finger Lakes (Ithaca), NY
1971	South Pennsylvania (Chambersburg)
1972	Kent-Akron, OH
1973	East Tennessee (Knoxville)
1976	Tucson, AZ
1977	Westchester, NY
	Ottawa-Hull, Canada*
1978	Winnipeg, Canada*
1984	North Coast (Santa Rosa/Sacramento), CA
1985	Gainesville, FL
1986	Valparaiso, IN
1989	Tampa Bay
1991	Orange County, CA
	Ohio Valley (Parkersburg, WV)
1994	Joaquin Valley (Fresno), CA
1995	Lincoln-Omaha, NE
	Salem, OR
	Williamsburg, VA
1996	Hawaii (Honolulu)

	South Florida (Miami/Ft. Lauderdale)
1997	Athens, Greece
	Central Florida (Orlando)
	Oklahoma City, OK
	Portland, OR
1998	Southern Nevada (Las Vegas)
	Central Arizona (Phoenix)
1999	Western Carolina (Brevard-Asheville)
	South Carolina (Charleston)
	Western Illinois (Monmouth)
2001	North Alabama

Societies in formation at time of publication: Brazos Valley, TX; Northern Arizona; Edmonton, Canada*; Hamilton, Canada*

*At the height of the Department of Canada around 1912, there were as many as 14 local societies in the following cities, listed in order of foundation: Kingston (1908), Montreal (1908), Ottawa (1908), Quebec City (1910), Calgary (1911), Edmonton (1911), Hamilton (1911), Regina (1911), Vancouver (1911), and Victoria (1911) (see Russell, this volume). The present six Canadian societies and the two societies at Edmonton and Hamilton currently in the process of formation belong to AIA-Canada.

— APPENDIX 3 —

Part 2. Inclusive List of AIA Local Societies with Name Changes and Dates of Foundation and Dissolution[1]

Wendy O'Brien

Akron	1927–1936
Albany	1967
Albuquerque	1929–1936
Allentown	1929–1940
Ann Arbor	1958
Appleton	1965
Athens	1966
Atlanta	1947
Auburn	1928–1939
Austin[2]	1977
Baltimore	1884
Bethlehem	1925–1945
Boston	1879
Boulder	1966
Bronx	1925–1936
Brooklyn	1929–1936
Buffalo	1909–1943
Burlington, Ontario	1978–1984
Calgary	1912–1918

Cedar Rapids	1926–1934
Central Illinois	1954
Central Indiana	1956
Central Michigan	1964
Central Missouri	1953
Central Pennsylvania	1966
Central Texas[3]	1962–1977
Charlottesville	1965
Chicago	1889
Cincinnati[4]	1892–1899; 1905–1913; 1923
Cleveland	1895
Colorado	1904–1913
Colorado Springs	1913–1936
Columbus	1958
Dallas-Fort Worth[5]	1965
Denver	1913–1936; 1992
Des Moines	1926–1938
Detroit	1889
East Tennessee	1974
Edmonton	1912–1914
Essex Fells	1928–1936
Eugene	1964
Finger Lakes	1972
Gainsville	1983
Grand Forks	1964–1988
Greensboro	1950
Halifax	1909–1918
Hamilton	1913–1918
Hartford	1911
Hawaii	1995
Houston	1967
Huntington	1930–1936
Independence	1922[?]–1925
Indiana	1915–1920
Iowa	1902–1941
Iowa City[6]	1949
Kansas	1957

Kansas City	1906–1936
Kansas State	1910–1915
Kent-Akron[7]	1972
Kentucky	1953
Kingston	1908–1911; 1913–1914
Lake Cayuga	1923–1936
Lancaster	1967–1980
Lehigh Valley	1946–1980
Lincoln	1929–1936
Lincoln-Omaha	1995
Long Island[8]	1988
Los Angeles[9]	1912–1944
Lubbock	1969
Lynchburg	1930
Madison[10]	1889
Marietta	1930–1942
Memphis[11]	1950–1953
Memphis-Oxford[12]	1949–1950; 1953–1959
Middletown[13]	1921–1943
Midwestern Ontario	1978–1988
Milwaukee	1925–1931; 1968
Minnesota (Minneapolis)	1910–1916; [?]–1920; 1949
Mississippi-Memphis[14]	1950–1953; 1959
Missouri[15]	1901–1906
Montreal	1908–1923; 1967
Narragansett[16]	1982
Nashville	1913–1922; 1930–1936; 1965
New Haven (Connecticut)[17]	1898
New Jersey[18]	1908–1923
New Orleans	1964
New York	1884
Niagara Peninsula	1968
North Carolina	1949
North Coast	1983
North Shore[19]	1968–1988
Northeastern Massachusetts	1962–1969
Northern New Jersey	1970

Oberlin-Ashland-Wooster[20]	1917–1918; [?]–1920; 1924
Ohio Valley	1990
Orange County	1991
Ottawa	1908–1918
Ottawa-Hull	1977
Oxford	1913
Philadelphia (Pennsylvania)[21]	1889
Pittsburgh	1891–1898; 1903
Portland, Oregon	1909–1936
Princeton[22]	1923
Providence[23]	1936–1982
Pueblo, Colorado	1913–1920
Quebec	1909–1918
Regina	1913–1915
Rhode Island	1908–1931
Richmond	1913
Roanoke	1930–1943
Rochester	1906
Rockford	1968
Saint John	1909–1918
Saint Louis	1906
Saint Paul	1913–1931
Salem	1995
Salt Lake City	1927–1931
San Diego	1913–1936; 1962
San Francisco	1906
San Joaquin Valley	1994
Santa Barbara	1964
Santa Fe	1916
Seattle	1913–1932; 1957
Southern California	1944
Southern Florida	1959–1969
Southern Pennsylvania	1971
Southwest[24]	1904–1912
Southwest Texas	1968
Spokane	1926–1936; 1949
Springfield	1921

Appendix 3

Stanford	1961
Staten Island	1965
Syracuse	1911–1936
Tallahassee	1956
Tampa Bay	1988
Toledo	1917–1941; 1953
Toronto	1908
Tucson	1976
Utah	1906–1911
Valparaiso	1985
Vancouver	1911–1918; 1966
Victoria	1912–1915
Walla Walla	1913
Washington, D.C.	1895–1899; 1902–1936; 1949
Washington State[25]	1906–1913
Westchester	1976
Western Illinois	1985
Western Massachusetts	1949
Western New York	1967
Williamsburg	1995
Winnipeg	1909–1923; 1978
Winona-Hiawatha	1967–1980
Worcester	1954

NOTES

[1] Discrepancies in dates with those given in part 1 are a result of conflicting information presented in the minutes; therefore, the listing is based upon the "Analysis of Membership" table printed in each *Bulletin of the Archaeological Institute of America*. Consequently, some societies in this listing may not have been formerly chartered by the Council, but it was felt that it might be useful to include all of the societies.

[2] Formerly the Central Texas society.

[3] Renamed the Austin society in 1977.

[4] Known as the Oxford society from 1913 to 1923.

[5] Formerly the Dallas society, renamed the Dallas-Fort Worth society in 1994.

[6] Sometimes listed as the Iowa society.

[7] Formerly the Kent society, renamed the Kent-Akron society in 1989.

[8] Formerly the North Shore society.

[9] Merged with the Southern California society in 1944.
[10] Formerly the Wisconsin society.
[11] Became the Memphis-Oxford society in 1953.
[12] Became the Mississippi society in 1959.
[13] Merged with the Hartford, Connecticut society in 1943.
[14] Formerly the Mississippi society, renamed Mississippi-Memphis society in 1983.
[15] Renamed the St. Louis society in 1906.
[16] Formerly the Providence society, renamed the Narragansett society in 1982.
[17] Listed as the Connecticut society from 1899 to 1924
[18] Renamed the Princeton society in 1923.
[19] Renamed the Long Island society in 1988.
[20] Formerly the Oberlin Society, renamed the Oberlin-Ashland society in 1968, and renamed the Oberlin-Ashland-Wooster society in 1982.
[21] Listed as the Pennsylvania society from 1899 to 1924.
[22] Formerly the New Jersey society, renamed the Princeton society in 1923.
[23] Renamed the Narragansett society in 1982.
[24] Renamed the Los Angeles society in 1904.
[25] Included Seattle, Walla Walla, and Spokane societies.

— APPENDIX 4 —

Charles Eliot Norton Lecturers

Priscilla Murray

1907/1908	David G. Hogarth
1908/1909	John L. Myres
1908/1909	Christian Huelsen
1909/1910	David G. Hogarth
1911/1912	Caspar Gregory
1911/1912	Franz Cumont
1913/1914	Eugenie Sellers Strong
1917/1918	Victor Horta
1918/1919	Ernest Arthur Gardner
1919/1920	Bertram Windle
1920/1921	Michael Rostovtzeff
1921/1922	Josef Strzygowski
1922/1923	Byron Cummings
1922/1923	Byron Khun de Prorok
1923/1924	Alan J.B. Wace
1924/1925	Esther Boise Van Deman
1924/1925	Bruno Roselli
1924/1925	David Robinson
1925/1926	Thomas Ashby
1926/1927	T. Leslie Shear
1927/1928	John Garstang

1928/1929	David Robinson
1929/1930	Charles Seltman
1930/1931	Robert Conway
1931/1932	Henry Sanders
1932/1933	Axel Boethius
1933/1934	Rhys Carpenter
1934/1935	Humfry G.G. Payne
1936/1937	Bert Hodge Hill
1937/1938	John Myres
1938/1939	Henri Seyrig
1939/1940	Martin Nilsson
1941/1942	Julio Tello replaced due to war by: Harold Ingholt; Olov R.T. Janse; and G.C. Vaillant
1942/1943	Harold Ingholt
1943/1944	Rhys Carpenter
1943/1944	Herbert Spinden
1944/1945	Clarence Ward; Mary Hamilton Swindler; and Henri Frankfort
1945/1946	Nelson Glueck
1946/1947	William B. Dinsmoor
1948/1949	Kenneth J. Conant
1949/1950	Claude Schaeffer
1950/1951	Jotham Johnson
1950/1951	Paolo Zancani-Montuoro
1951/1952	Mortimer Wheeler
1953/1954	George Mylonas
1954/1955	William B. Emery
1955/1956	William Beare
1956/1957	P.C. Sestied
1957/1958	Frank Brown
1958/1959	Kathleen Kenyon
1959/1960	Spyridon Marinatos
1960/1961	Oscar Broneer
1961/1962	John M. Cook
1962/1963	Louisa Bellinger
1963/1964	Bernard Ashmole

Appendix 4

1964/1965	Richard D. Barnett
1965/1966	Emilie Haspels
1966/1967	Edith Porada
1967/1968	John Caskey
1968/1969	Rodney Young
1969/1970	P.J. Riis
1971/1972	Ezat Negahban
1972/1973	Sinclair Hood
1973/1974	Paul Courbin
1975/1976	Charles McGimsey
1976/1977	Emeline Richardson
1977/1978	Saul Weinberg
1978/1979	Homer Thompson
1980/1981	David Stronach
1982/1983	Reynold Higgins
1984/1985	Lilly Kahil
1985/1986	Kenan Erim
1986/1987	Victor Daszewski
1987/1988	Thomas W. Jacobsen
1988/1989	Jan Bouzek
1989/1990	R. Ross Holloway
1990/1991	William Devar
1991/1992	Willem Willems
1992/1993	James R. Wiseman
1993/1994	Stephen L. Dyson
1994/1995	Anna Marguerite McCann
1995/1996	James Russell
1996/1997	Patricia R. Anawalt
1997/1998	Lanny Bell
1998/1999	Seymour Gitin
1999/2000	A. Trevor Hodge
2000/2001	Eugene Borza and A. Trevor Hodge
2001/2002	Eugene Borza and A. Trevor Hodge
2002/2003	Elizabeth Barber

INDEX

Academia Herculanensis, 31
Académie des inscriptions et belles lettres, 35, 43
Accademia Etrusca, 34
Aegean archaeology, xx, 21–2, 40–1, 115–21
Agazziz, Alexander, 172
AIA Annual Meeting, 1, 9, 16, 18, 19, 21, 130, 141, 149, 150, 169, 171, 179, 182, 190, 191, 199, 201
AIA archives, 1, 27
AIA awards and fellowships, 207–15
  Anna C. and Oliver C. Colburn Fellowship, 23, 214
  Archaeology of Portugal Fellowship, 215
  Centennial Award, 23, 208
  Conservation and Heritage Management Award, 23, 211
  Gold Medal Award, 19, 207–8
  Harriet and Leon Pomerance Fellowship, 23, 213–4
  Helen M. Woodruff Fellowship, 214
  Honorary Fellow for Life, 211
  James R. Wiseman Book Award, 20, 23, 209–10
  Kenan T. Erim Award, 23, 215
  Kershaw Outstanding Local Society Prize, 23, 210
  Martha and Artemis Joukowsky Distinguished Service Award, 23, 210
  Olivia James Traveling Fellowship, 23, 211–3
  Outstanding Public Service Award, 23, 211
  Pomerance Award for Scientific Contributions, 20, 23, 208–9
  Undergraduate Teaching Award, 23, 211
  Woodruff Traveling Fellowship, 215
AIA Code of Ethics, xxi, xxiv, 181–4
AIA Code of Professional Standards, 185, 193, 200
AIA committees
  Archives Committee, xiii
  Committee on American Archaeology, 130, 137
  Committee for Professional Responsibilities, 172, 181, 183–5
  Committee for the Preservation of Archaeological Resources, 180–1
  Committee on Computer Applications and Electronic Data, 190–1, 193, 201–2
  Committee on Near Eastern Archaeology, 120
  Committee on the Preservation of the Ruins of American Antiquity, 130, 174
  Subcommittee on the Protection of Archaeological Resources, 172, 180, 181, 182
  Subcommittee on Women in Archaeology, 18, 20
AIA Council, 16, 178
AIA Department of Canada, 4, 141–51
  Calgary, 143, 145
  Edmonton, 143, 149
  Halifax, 142
  Hamilton, 142, 144
  Kingston, 142
  Montreal, 141, 142, 146, 149–51
  Niagara Peninsula, 151
  Ottawa, 142–3, 146, 151
  Quebec City, 144
  Regina, 143
  St. John, 142
  Toronto, 141, 142, 144, 146, 150–1
  Vancouver, 141, 144, 146, 150–1
  Victoria, 144
  Winnipeg, 141–2, 144, 150–1
AIA Executive Committee, 6, 66, 68, 72, 176, 178, 180–2, 185
AIA Fellowships. *See* AIA awards and fellowships
AIA funding, 11–12, 76, 105, 106, 109–13, 117, 125, 129, 135, 147, 161, 164, 165, 167, 170, 171, 195
AIA lecture program, 17, 149, 157, 160, 165, 171
  Charles Eliot Norton lecturers, 19, 227–9
AIA List, 193–4
AIA local/affiliated societies, 53, 124–7, 136, 138, 147, 192, 217–26
  Baltimore, 12, 81
  Boston, 16
  Chicago, 163–4
  Colorado, 127, 133, 134, 135
  list of, current, 217–20

230

Index

list of, inclusive, 221–6
New York, 12, 107
Philadelphia, 107
Pennsylvania, 16
San Francisco, 127, 131
Southwest, 127–36
Utah, 127, 134, 135
Washington, 161, 162
AIA membership, 18, 25, 125–6, 129, 134, 136, 144, 149, 165, 166–7, 186, 191–2, 194
AIA outreach, 4, 13, 23–5, 53, 121, 124, 129, 163–7
AIA presidents, 205–6
AIA publications
   American Journal of Archaeology (AJA), 4, 22, 43, 49, 53, 86, 98, 162, 171, 178–9
   Editors-in-Chief, 19, 198, 206
   AJA Web Site, 198
   AIA Web Site, 195–8
   Archaeological Fieldwork Opportunities Bulletin, 196
   Archaeology, xix, xxi–xxiv, 4, 12, 23, 25, 49, 160, 167, 171, 194, 197
   Archaeology's Dig, 23, 198
   Art and Archaeology, 4, 160–5, 167
AIA resolution on the protection of cultural property (1899), 173
AIA seal, *frontispiece*, 16
AIA timeline, xv–xxv
AIA UNESCO Resolution (1970), 172, 175–80, 183
Allen, Susan Heuck, 12, 63, 205, 207, 217
American Academy in Rome, 43, 56, 94, 160
American Anthropological Association (AAA), 137, 195
American Antiquarian Society, 172
American archaeology, 9, 10, 12, 14, 21, 53, 116, 123–39, 169
American Association for the Advancement of Science (AAAS), 17
American Association of Dealers in Ancient, Oriental, and Primitive Art, 181
American Council of Learned Societies (ACLS) Committee on the Protection of Cultural Treasures in War Areas, 175
American Eurocentrism, 10
American Exploration Society, 16, 17, 118
American Institute of Architects, 72

American Institute of Iranian Studies, 120
American Journal of Philology, 98
American Oriental Society (AOS), 5, 17, 117, 118, 176
American Numismatic Society, 180
American Philological Association (APA), 141
American Philosophical Society, 17
American Research Center in Egypt (ARCE), 120
American Research Institute in Turkey (ARIT), 120
American School of Classical Studies at Athens (ASCSA), 3, 11, 13, 17, 19, 43, 53, 55, 56, 73, 74, 79, 85, 93–103, 105, 108, 109, 110, 111, 116–20, 158, 159, 160, 166, 173
   AIA Fellowship, 17
   Hoppin Fellowship, 17
American School of Classical Studies at Rome, 43, 56, 158, 173
American Schools of Oriental Research (ASOR), 119, 120, 121, 176
   Baghdad, 119
   Jerusalem, 118, 119, 173
American Southwest, 116, 123–38, 173
Anawalt, Patricia, 183
anthropological archaeology, 20–2
anthropology, 170
American Antiquity Act (1906), 133, 174
antiquities laws, 36, 67, 77, 78
Archaeological Data Archive Project (ADAP), 194–5, 200–1
Archaeological Society in Athens, 36, 66, 109
Archaeological Society of Berlin, 85
Archer, Archibald, 40
Architectural League of New York, 76
Aristarchi Bey, 77
Arizona Antiquarian Society, 126
Art, Historical and Scientific Association of Vancouver, 146
Armour, Allison, 12
Arnold, Matthew, 50, 53
art history, 95
Association of Literature, Science, and Art (Hamilton), 146
Ashfield Dinners, 54
Assyrian empire, 116

Babylonian empire, 116
Babylonian Exploration Fund, 117
Bacon, Alice Calvert, 79
Bacon, Francis Henry, 43, 63–87, 65, 85
Bacon, Henry, 86
Baltazzi Bey, Demetrios, 77
Bandelier, Adolph F., 10, 106–7, 123
Bandelier, Fannie, 16
Bass, George, 21
Bates, William N., 162
Baum, Henry Mason, 174
Bennett, Richard Bedford, 145
Biblical vs. classical archaeology, 6
Blaine, James, 111
Blegen, Carl W., 85
Blouet, Guillaume Abel, 36, 37
Böckh, August, 35
Bory de Saint-Vincent, Jean-Baptiste, 36
Boston Society of Architects (BSA), 64, 79, 81, 83, 86
Boston Society of Arts and Crafts, 52
Bowditch, Charles P., 130, 132
Bowditch Fellowship, 132
Boyd, Harriet (Hawes), 17, 21, 158
Bradley, Charles W., 68
Braidwood, Robert, 21
Brooks, Van Wyck, 55
Brown, Shelby, 18
Bunsen, Christian Karl Julius, 35
Bureau of American Ethnology (BAE), 9, 124, 131, 132, 134
Bureau of Indian Affairs (BIA), 131

^{14}C dating, 23
Cabot, Edward Clarke, 64, 79, 83, 85
Calder, W.M. III, 56
Calvert, Alice Mary, 79, 80
Calvert, Frank, 74, 79, 82
Canada, 4, 14, 141–51
Carlyle, Thomas, 50, 51, 52, 54
Carpenter, Rhys, 161
Carroll, Mitchell, 127, 148, 149, 161–2
Casa Tarpeia, 34
Center for the Study of Architecture, 193, 195, 201
Chandler, Richard, 30
Chase, George H., 163
Clarke, Joseph Thacher, 13, 15, 43, 63–87, 65
classical antiquity as cultural heritage, 5, 6, 7, 8, 96–9, 123

classical archaeology, 2, 8, 10, 21, 100
classical vs. American, 123–39, 159, 169–70
classical vs. anthropological archaeology, 3, 4, 7, 9, 10, 14, 20–2
classicism, 96–103
Clay, Albert T., 119
Cockerell, Charles Robert, 36
Coggins, Clemency, 4, 169
College Art Association (CAA), 159, 176
Colorado Cliff Dwellings Association, 126
Columbian Exposition, 17
computer technology, 189–202
Conkey, Margaret, 20
conservation, 23
Corpus Vasorum Antiquorum, 178, 184
Cullen, Tracey, 18
cultivated erudition, 93–4, 99–103
cultural patrimony, 8, 24, 38, 186
cultural property, 4, 23, 24, 169–86
Cultural Property law (1983), 172, 183
Cummings, Byron, 134, 135
cuneiform, decipherment, 5
Currelly, Charles Trick, 146
Curtis, George William, 51, 54, 55
Curtius, Ernst, 8

Dante, 52, 56
Dante Society of America, 51–2
Dardanelles, 74, 80, 85
Darwin, Charles, 5, 9, 50
Dawkins, James, 30, *31*
de Cou, Herbert Fletcher, 118, 158
de Grummond, Nancy, 2, 3, 29
de Luynes, Duc, 35
de Witt, N.W., 150
di Cesnola, Luigi Palma, 42, 68
Dickens, Charles, 50
Diller, J.S., 68, 74, 79
Dinsmoor, William Bell, 86, 161, 163, 164, 165, 166, 175
Donne, John, 52, 56
D'Ooge, Martin, 108, 126, 128
Dörpfeld, Wilhelm, 83
Dorian, 64, *65*
Dort, Anne V., 49
Dow, Sterling, 2, 167
Drisler, Henry, 94
Dyson, Stephen, 2, 3, 4, 21, 22, 103, 157

Eastern archaeology, 63–87

Index

Eastman, George, 81
Eaton, Adoniram Judson, 144, 147, 148, 149, 150
École française d'Athènes, 13, 35, 43, 99–100
École française de Rome, 35
Egbert, James, 161, 163
Egypt Exploration Fund, 146
Eiteljorg, Harrison II, 4, 189
Emerson, Alfred, 15
employment, 14–16
environmental studies, 21
essay contributors, xi
ethics, 24
Etruscan antiquities, 38
Etruscan tombs, 36
Euphronios Krater, 178
excavations, 7–11, 19
  Aigina, 36, 41, 63
    Temple of Aphaia, 41, 63, 66
  Argive Heraeum (Argos), 113
  Assos, 3, 10, 11, 12, 43, 44, 67–72, 101, 107, 116, 173
    exportation of antiquities, 76–79
    plans, *69, 70*
    publication, 81–3
    Temple of Athena, 66, 68, 72, 74, 76, 77, 78, 83, 85
  Athens, 36, 38, 66
    Agora, 12, 13, 38, 119, 166
    Akropolis, 36, 97, 102
    Library of Hadrian, 41
    Tower of the Winds, *30*, 38, 41
    Theater of Dionysos, 36
    Theseum, *41*
  Babylon, 82
  Bassai, 36
  Cañon de Chelly, 133
  Cannonball Ruins, 136
  Corinth, 13, 43, 119, 159
  Crete, 17, 66
  Croton, 11
  Cyprus, 42
  Cyrene, 11, 81, 118, 158, 159
  Delos, 8, 66, 112
  Delphi, 3, 11, 43, 66, 81, 105–13, 117, 126
  Epidaurus, 66
  Eretria, 113
  First Arizona Expedition, 131–2

Gortyn, 11, 107
Gournia, 17, 21
Gözlü Kule, 119
Guatemala, 136, 171
Herculaneum, 30
Idaean Cave, 68
Knossos, 11, 68, 69, 71, 107
Kavousi, 17
Libya, 118
Mesa Verde, 134
Mycenae, 42
Nineveh, 5, 116
Nippur (Nuffar), 107, 117
Olympia, 8, 42, 67, 74, 76, 116
Orchomenos, 65
Palmyra, *31*
Pecos, 159
Pergamon, 8, 67, 76, 77
Pompeii, 30
Puyé, 135, 136
Redondo Beach, 131
Rome, 5, 38
Samos, 65, 66, 67
Samothrace, 40, 66, 67
Sardis, 65, 67, 76
Sarepta, 120
Second Arizona Expedition, 132
Sikyon, 108
Sparta, 113
Tarquinia, 36
Tarsus, 119, 165
Thera, 8
Troy (Hisarlik), 8, 42, 66, 85
Volterra, *32, 34*
Wolfe Expedition, 117, 120
Yucatan, 172
Expédition scientifique de Morée, 36, *37*, 40

Fairclough, Henry Rushton, 144
Fea, Carlo, 35, 38, *39*
Fearn, Walker, 97, 108
Fewkes, Jesse W., 135
financial crises, 12
Fiorelli, Giuseppe, 38
foreign schools, 13
Fouqué, Ferdinand, 8
Fowler, Harold North, 101, 102, 158
Foy, Mary, 135
French expedition to the Morea, 36
Furness, Horace Howard, 108

Gardner, Isabella Stewart, 50, 52
gender in archaeology, 16, 18, 20–1
gender equity, 19
Gerhard, Eduard, *33*, 35
German Archaeological Institute (Deutsches Archäologisches Institut [DAI]), 6, 7, 13, 35, 43, 44, 80, 100, 166
G.I. Bill, 15
Gilded Age, 93–103, 117
Gildersleeve, Basil Lanneau, 94, 98, 99
Gilman, Daniel Coit, 99
Goldman, Hetty, 119, 158, 165
Goodwin, William Watson, 79, 96, 100, 110, 112
Gori, Francesco, 32, 34
Great Depression, 164
great divide, 20–2, 169–86
Gregory, Timothy, 196
Greece, 5
Greek Archaeological Service, 36
Greek War of Independence, 5

Hague Convention on the Protection of Cultural Property in the Event of Armed Conflict (1954), 176
Hall, Edith, 17, 18
Hamdi, Bey, 77–8
Hamilton, Gavin, 30
Hamilton, Sir William, 30, 40
Hawes, Harriet Boyd, 17–8, 21, 158
Haynes, John H., 68, 73, 74, 77, 79, 80, 81
Hebert, Kim M., 205, 207, 217
Hellenic studies, 115–21
Hellenism, 3, 5, 8, 14, 98, 172
Henzen, Gerhard, 35
Henzen, Wilhelm, 35
Hewett, Edgar Lee, 132–7
high culture, 98–103
Hill-Tout, Charles, 146
Hinsley, Curtis, 16
Hogarth, David, 145
Holmes, William H., 131
Hoppin, Agnes, 17
Howells, William Dean, 50, 55
Humann, Carl, 77
Hyperboreans, 34, 36

illustrations list, ix
Instituto di Corrispondenza Archeologica, *34*, 35

interdisciplinary approaches to archaeology, 21

Jahn, Otto, 35
James, Henry, 50, 52
Jebb, Richard, 79
Jefferson, Thomas, 97

Kantor, Helene, 119
Kelsey, Francis Willey, 3, 14, 98, 126–8, 130, 132, 133, 137, 141, 142, 144, 145, 146, 147, 148, 149, 150, 158–60, 163, 164
Kestner, August, 35
Koldewey, Robert, 74, 82, 84
Kroeber, Alfred, 131

Lawton, William C., 68, 79
Layard, Austen Henry, 5
lecturers, Charles Eliot Norton, 227
Lehmann-Hartleben, Karl, 166
Levy, Warren, 184
Libby, Willard F., 23
Lincoln Memorial, 86
Loeb, James, 12, 83
Longfellow, Henry Wadsworth, 50
Lord, Louis Eleazar, 84, 163, 164, 165
Low, Seth, 111–2, 118
Lowell Institute, 160
Lowell, James Russell, 50, 55, 97
Lucas, Stephen, 163
Lummis, Charles Fletcher, 127, 128, 129, 130, 131, 132, 133, 135, 136, 137
Lyell, Charles, 5

Magoffin, Ralph, 162, 163, 164, 165
Mahabali puram, 53
Marquand, Alan, 13, 95
Matson, Frederick, 180
Mausoleum of Halicarnassus, 40
McDonald, William, 21
McKay, Alexander, 4
McKim, Mead and Bigelow, 64
McLain Decision, 182
Merriam, Augustus Chapman, 109
Meritt, Benjamin, 166
Meritt, Lucy Shoe, 86
Mommsen, Theodor, 35
Morea, 36
Morey, Charles Rufus, 163, 166
Morgan, J.P., 116

Morgan, Lewis Henry, 123, 173
Moss-Bennett bill, 180
Moundbuilders in Ohio, 5
Muhly, James, 120
Murray, Priscilla, 227
Muscarella, Oscar W., 181
museums
   archaeological museums, 38–42, 106, 129, 130
   Art Gallery of New Haven, 8
   Ashmolean Museum, 145
   Berlin, 8, 35, 40, 42
   Boston Museum of Fine Arts, 8, 42, 43, 72, 76, 77, 80, 106, 107
   British Museum, 6, 40
   Elgin Room, *41*
   De Young Museum, 201
   Fitzwilliam Museum, 111
   Florence, 38
   Imperial Ottoman Museum, 77
   Louvre, 40, 68, 76
   Madrid, 41
   Metropolitan Museum of Art (New York), 42, 68, 106, 107, 116, 178, 180, 181
   Munich Altepinakothek, 41
   Munich Glyptothek, 41, 63
   Museo Nazionale, 38
   Museo Nazionale di Villa Giulia, 38
   Museo Nazionale Romano, 38
   Naples, 35
   National Archaeological Museum, 41
   Palmer-Campbell Collection of Southern California Antiquities, 130
   Peabody Museum, 16, 172
   Prado, 41
   Royal Ontario Museum, 146
   Smith College, 17
   Southwest Museum, 130, 131, 133, 135, 136, 137, 140
   University Museum, University of Pennsylvania, 16
Myres, John L., 145

Napoleon, 40
National Endowment of Humanities (NEH), 12
National Geographic Society, 12, 24
National Research Council, 12
National Science Foundation (NSF), 12
National Stolen Property Act, 182

nationalism in archaeology, 7–8, 13, 38, 63, 107–13, 124, 175–81
Native American cultures, 42
Nazism in Germany, 166
Near Eastern archaeology, 115–21
New archaeology, 21
Newall, Edward, 163
Niagara Falls, 3, 55
Nichols, May Louise, 17
Norton, Andrews, 54, 57
Norton, Charles Eliot, 3, 4, 5, 6, 9, 43, 49–61, *50*, *54*, 63, 71, 73, 83, 95, 105–13, 116, 118, 124, 157, 172
Norton, Eliot, 57, 61 n. 8, 68, 71, 118
Norton, Richard, 54, 57, 61 n. 8, 81, 83, 118
Norton, Susan R.S. (Mrs. C.E. Norton), 57
Novick, Peter, 1

O'Brien, Wendy, 196, 221
Olmsted, Frederick Law, 50, 55
Ottoman empire, 8, 67, 118, 175
Overbeck, Johannes, 36

Packard, Lewis R., 94
Palestine Exploration Fund, 116
Palmer, Frank, 131–3, 135, 136
Panofka, Theodor, 35
Parkman, Francis, 9, 172, 184
Pars, Revett, 30
Pars, William, 30
Parthenon marbles, 40
Patterson, Thomas, 13–14, 21
Peck, Annie Smith, 17
Peterson, Joseph, 131
Peterson, William, 147
Petrakis, Susan, 36
Petrie, W.M. Flinders, 146
philology, 13, 95, 97, 98, 99, 159, 170
Platner, Samuel B., 158
Pomerance, Harriet/Leon, 23
populism, 14, 157–67
postprocessual archaeology, 22
Powell, John Wesley, 9
prehistoric archaeology, 21, 22, 124
preservation, 23
Presidential Cultural Property Advisory Committee, 24, 182, 183
Pritchard, James, 120
processual archaeology, 21

professional ethics, 182
professional vs. nonprofessional, 14, 15, 53, 80, 93, 100, 101–3, 169–86
professionalization, 14–6, 80–2, 87
public museums, 38–41
Putnam, Frederic Ward, 16, 123, 172, 174

Rawlinson, Henry, 5
Read, General John Meredith, 66
Reagan, Ronald, 182
Registry of Professional Archaeologists, 181
religion of culture, 53
Renfrew, Colin, 21, 23, 169
Revett, Nicholas, 29–30
Reynolds, Sir Joshua, 30
Richter, Gisela, 163
Ridley, Ronald, 38
Robert, Carl, 35
Robert College, Constantinople, 74
Robinson, David M., 160–1
Robinson, Edward, 68, 73, 163
Robinson, Edwin Arlington, 50
Rockefeller, John D., 12
Romanticism, 5
Roosevelt, Theodore, 128
Ruskin, John, 50, 51, 52, 65
Ruspi, Carlo, 36
Russell, James, 3, 4, 141

Sachs, Paul, 166
Salisbury, Stephen, 172
Sanderson Academy, 54, 55
Santa Fe Archaeological Society, 126, 133
Sanusiyya, 118
Schliemann, Heinrich, 8, 42, 66, 76
School for American Research in Santa Fe, 159, 173
School of American Archaeology, Santa Fe, 133, 134, 136, 173
Semitic studies, 115–21
Semple, Louise Taft, 12
Semple, William, 12
Seymour, Thomas Day, 128, 174
Shear, Theodore L., 166
Sheftel, Phoebe, 2, 3, 23, 43, 49, 105
Simpson, William K., 180
Shipley, Frederick William, 144, 149
Shorey, Paul, 101, 102
Silberman, Neil, 3, 115

Sixth International Archaeological Congress (1939), 166
Slauson, J.S., 128
Sloane, William, 94
Slocum, John, 182, 183
Smith, Baldwin, 160
Smithsonian Institution, 124, 131, 174
Snead, James, 3, 123
Snow, C.P., 170
Society for American Archaeology (SAA), 18, 159, 180, 195
Society for Biblical Literature (SBL), 118
Society of Dilettanti, 29–30, 106
Society of Professional Archaeologists (SOPA), 181
Southwest Program, 133–6
Spanish-American War, 55, 56
Spector, Janet, 20
Spencer, Herbert, 5
Squier, Ephraim, 5
Stanford, Leland, 110
Sterrett, John Robert Sitlington, 11, 15, 74, 80, 101
Stevenson, Sarah Yorke, 16, 173, 184
Stillman, William James, 66, 68, 71, 72, 109, 112
Stuart, James, 29–30
Sturgis, Russell, 110
surveys in archaeology, 21
Swift, Emerson H., 163
Swindler, Mary H., 163

Taylor, Franklin H., 102
Thompson, Homer, 2, 86, 161, 179–81
Thorvaldsen, Bertel, 35
Ticknor, George, 50
Tozzer, Alfred, 130, 132
traditionalists, 21–2, 157–67
Tricoupis, Harilaos, 110, 112
Turner, James, 5, 59 n. 1

underwater archaeology, 21
UNESCO (United Nations Educational, Scientific and Cultural Organization), 175
UNESCO Convention on the Means of Prohibiting and Preventing the Illicit Import, Export and Transfer of Ownership of Cultural Property (1970), 9, 171–2, 176, 177–9, 181, 185

Index

UNESCO Draft Convention, 176–7
UNESCO National Commission, 176
UNESCO World Heritage Convention, 180
Unidroit, 185
United Nations, 175
Universities and colleges, 93–103
  Boston University, 170
  Bryn Mawr College, 163, 193, 195–8
  Cambridge University, 111
  Carnegie Mellon University, 200
  Columbia University, 24, 86, 94, 101, 158, 161
  Cornell University, 101
  Dartmouth College, 98
  Harvard University, 5, 8, 16, 51, 52, 53, 54, 66, 67, 74, 80, 86, 96, 100, 101, 107, 108, 126, 127, 128, 130, 132, 134, 135, 157, 158, 163, 167, 172
    Fine Arts Department, 54, 95, 172
    Peabody Museum, 123, 172, 174
  Hofstra University, 196
  Johns Hopkins University, 81, 94, 98, 99, 142, 144, 159, 160–2
  Massachusetts Institute of Technology, 64, 79
  McGill University, 144, 147
  Munich Polytechnic, 63
  New Mexico State Normal School, 132
  New York University, 162
  Oberlin College, 163
  Ohio State University, 196
  Princeton University, 13, 94, 158, 163
  Smith College, 17–8
  Stanford University, 144
  University of Chicago, 101
  University of Michigan, 14, 28, 108, 126, 158
  University of Pennsylvania, 16, 17, 107, 117
  University of Southern California, 128
  University of Toronto, 141
  University of Utah, 134

Washington University, St. Louis, 144
Western Reserve College, 158
Yale University, 94, 119, 158

Vanderbilt, Cornelius, 111
Virchow, Rudolf, 76, 79
Virtual Pompeii, 200–1
von Bothmer, Dietrich, 178
von Brunn, Heinrich, 35
von Hallerstein, Carl Christoph Haller, 36
von Reber, Franz, 63, 66
von Stackelberg, Otto Magnus, 35, 36

Waldstein, Charles, 102, 105, 109, 110, 111, 112
Walker, Charles Howard, 68
Wallace, Lewis, 78
Ward, William H., 16, 80, 117
Ware, William Robert, 64, 68, 72, 109
Weber, Karl, 31
western idea, 125, 129, 135, 137, 138
Wheeler, Blanche, 17
Wheeler, James Rignall, 101
White, John Williams, 94, 100, 108, 126
Whitman, Sarah Wyman, 16
Wiener, Malcolm, 178
Will, Elizabeth Lyding, 3, 49–61
Wilson, Harry Langford, 142, 144, 149
Winckelmann, Johann Joachim, 5, 31
Winterer, Caroline, 3, 93
Wiseman, James, 170, 180
Wolf, Friedrich Augustus, 98
Wolfe, Catherine Lorillard, 12, 16, 117
Wolfe Expedition to Mesopotamia, 16, 80, 107, 117, 120
women in archaeology, 16–20
Wood, Robert, 30, *31*
Wright, John H., 98
Wrigley, Maxwell, 68

Young, Rodney S., 176, 177–8
Young Turks Revolt, 118